C000127349

THE EUROPEAN UNION SEI

General Editors: Neill Nugent, William E. Pat

The European Union series provides an authoritative library on the European Union, ranging from general introductory texts to definitive assessments of key institutions and actors, issues, policies and policy processes, and the role of member states.

Books in the series are written by leading scholars in their fields and reflect the most up-to-date research and debate. Particular attention is paid to accessibility and clear presentation for a wide audience of students, practitioners and interested general readers.

The series editors are **Neill Nugent**, Visiting Professor, College of Europe, Bruges and Honorary Professor, University of Salford, UK, and **William E. Paterson**, Honorary Professor in German and European Studies, University of Aston. Their co-editor until his death in July 1999, **Vincent Wright**, was a Fellow of Nuffield College, Oxford University.

Feedback on the series and book proposals are always welcome and should be sent to Stephen Wenham, Palgrave – Macmillan Education, 4 Crinan Street, London, N1 9XW, or by e-mail to s.wenham@palgrave.com

---

General textbooks

Published

Laurie Buonanno and Neill Nugent **Policies and Policy Processes of the European Union**
Desmond Dinan **Encyclopedia of the European Union** [Rights: Europe only]
Desmond Dinan **Europe Recast: A History of the European Union (2nd edn)** [Rights: Europe only]
Desmond Dinan **Ever Closer Union: An Introduction to European Integration (4th edn)** [Rights: Europe only]
Mette Eilstrup Sangiovanni (ed.) **Debates on European Integration: A Reader**
Simon Hix and Bjørn Høyland **The Political System of the European Union (3rd edn)**
Dirk Leuffen, Berthold Rittberger and Frank Schimmelfennig **Differentiated Integration**
Paul Magnette **What is the European Union? Nature and Prospects**
John McCormick **Understanding the European Union: A Concise Introduction (6th edn)**
Brent F. Nelsen and Alexander Stubb **The European Union: Readings on the Theory and Practice of European Integration (4th edn)** [Rights: Europe only]

Neill Nugent (ed.) **European Union Enlargement**
Neill Nugent **The Government and Politics of the European Union (7th edn)**
John Peterson and Elizabeth Bomberg **Decision-Making in the European Union**
Ben Rosamond **Theories of European Integration**
Sabine Saurugger **Theoretical Approaches to European Integration**
Ingeborg Tömmel **The European Union: What it is and how it works**
Esther Versluis, Mendeltje van Keulen and Paul Stephenson **Analyzing the European Union Policy Process**
Hubert Zimmermann and Andreas Dür (eds) **Key Controversies in European Integration**

Forthcoming

Magnus Ryner and Alan Cafruny **A Critical Introduction to the European Union**

Also planned

The European Union and Global Politics
The Political Economy of European Integration

Series Standing Order (outside North America only)
ISBN 978–0–333–71695–3 hardback
ISBN 978–0–333–69352–0 paperback
Full details from www.palgrave.com

Visit Palgrave Macmillan's EU Resource area at www.palgrave.com/politics/eu/

The major institutions and actors

Published

Renaud Dehousse **The European Court of Justice**
Justin Greenwood **Interest Representation in the European Union (3rd edn)**
Fiona Hayes-Renshaw and Helen Wallace **The Council of Ministers (2nd edn)**
Simon Hix and Christopher Lord **Political Parties in the European Union**
David Judge and David Earnshaw **The European Parliament (2nd edn)**
Neill Nugent **The European Commission**
Anne Stevens with Handley Stevens **Brussels Bureaucrats? The Administration of the European Union**

Forthcoming

Ariadna Ripoll Servent **The European Parliament**
Sabine Saurugger and Fabien Terpan **The European Court of Justice and the Politics of Law**
Wolfgang Wessels **The European Council**

The main areas of policy

Published

Karen Anderson **Social Policy in the European Union**
Michael Baun and Dan Marek **Cohesion Policy in the European Union**
Michele Chang **Monetary Integration in the European Union**
Michelle Cini and Lee McGowan **Competition Policy in the European Union (2nd edn)**
Wyn Grant **The Common Agricultural Policy**
Martin Holland and Mathew Doidge **Development Policy of the European Union**
Jolyon Howorth **Security and Defence Policy in the European Union (2nd edn)**
Johanna Kantola **Gender and the European Union**
Stephan Keukeleire and Tom Delreux **The Foreign Policy of the European Union (2nd edn)**
Brigid Laffan **The Finances of the European Union**
Malcolm Levitt and Christopher Lord **The Political Economy of Monetary Union**
Janne Haaland Matláry **Energy Policy in the European Union**
John McCormick **Environmental Policy in the European Union**
John Peterson and Margaret Sharp **Technology Policy in the European Union**
Handley Stevens **Transport Policy in the European Union**

Forthcoming

Hans Bruyninckx and Tom Delreux **Environmental Policy and Politics in the European Union**

Sieglinde Gstöhl and Dirk de Bievre **The Trade Policy of the European Union**
Christian Kaunert and Sarah Leonard **Justice and Home Affairs in the European Union**
Maren Kreutler, Johannes Pollak and Samuel Schubert **Energy Policy in the European Union**
Paul Stephenson, Esther Versluis and Mendeltje van Keulen **Implementing and Evaluating Policy in the European Union**

Also planned

Political Union

The member states and the Union

Published

Carlos Closa and Paul Heywood **Spain and the European Union**
Andrew Geddes **Britain and the European Union**
Alain Guyomarch, Howard Machin and Ella Ritchie **France in the European Union**
Brigid Laffan and Jane O'Mahoney **Ireland and the European Union**

Forthcoming

Simon Bulmer and William E. Paterson **Germany and the European Union**
Brigid Laffan **The European Union and its Member States**

Issues

Published

Derek Beach **The Dynamics of European Integration: Why and When EU Institutions Matter**
Christina Boswell and Andrew Geddes **Migration and Mobility in the European Union**
Thomas Christiansen and Christine Reh **Constitutionalizing the European Union**
Robert Ladrech **Europeanization and National Politics**
Cécile Leconte **Understanding Euroscepticism**
Steven McGuire and Michael Smith **The European Union and the United States**
Wyn Rees **The US–EU Security Relationship: The Tensions between a European and a Global Agenda**

Forthcoming

Graham Avery **Enlarging the European Union**
Senem Aydin-Düzgit and Nathalie Tocci **Turkey and the European Union**
Thomas Christiansen, Emil Kirchner and Uwe Wissenbach **The European Union and China**
Tuomas Forsberg and Hiski Haukkala **The European Union and Russia**

Social Policy in the European Union

Karen M. Anderson

 palgrave

© Karen M. Anderson 2015

All rights reserved. No reproduction, copy or transmission of this publication may be made without written permission.

No portion of this publication may be reproduced, copied or transmitted save with written permission or in accordance with the provisions of the Copyright, Designs and Patents Act 1988, or under the terms of any licence permitting limited copying issued by the Copyright Licensing Agency, Saffron House, 6–10 Kirby Street, London EC1N 8TS.

Any person who does any unauthorized act in relation to this publication may be liable to criminal prosecution and civil claims for damages.

The author has asserted her right to be identified as the author of this work in accordance with the Copyright, Designs and Patents Act 1988.

First published 2015 by
PALGRAVE

Palgrave in the UK is an imprint of Macmillan Publishers Limited, registered in England, company number 785998, of 4 Crinan Street, London N1 9XW.

Palgrave Macmillan in the US is a division of St Martin's Press LLC, 175 Fifth Avenue, New York, NY 10010.

Palgrave is the global imprint of the above companies and is represented throughout the world.

Palgrave® and Macmillan® are registered trademarks in the United States, the United Kingdom, Europe and other countries.

ISBN: 978–0–230–22349–3   hardback
ISBN: 978–0–230–22350–9   paperback

This book is printed on paper suitable for recycling and made from fully managed and sustained forest sources. Logging, pulping and manufacturing processes are expected to conform to the environmental regulations of the country of origin.

A catalogue record for this book is available from the British Library.

A catalog record for this book is available from the Library of Congress.

Typeset by Aardvark Editorial Limited, Metfield, Suffolk.

Printed in China

In memory of Marie Gallagher Anderson (1934–2014)

Contents

List of Figures and Tables

Figures

Tables

Acknowledgements

One of the best things about finishing a book is being able to thank friends and colleagues who helped along the way. Ruud van Druenen and Nienke Bos provided excellent research assistance. Traute Meyer and Ellen Mastenbroek read and commented on draft chapters, and Mieke Verloo gave me the chance to present parts of the book to her students. Paulette Kurzer deserves special mention for reading every chapter (sometimes more than once) and providing indispensable feedback. Katja Stamm commented on several chapters, helped me sharpen my understanding of vocational education and training, and kept me sane. Steven Kennedy, my publisher at Palgrave Macmillan, has been patient, encouraging and enormously helpful.

Abbreviations

Cedefop	Centre for the Development of Vocational Training
CEEP	European Centre of Employers and Enterprises providing Public Services
Coreper	Committee of Permanent Representatives
DG	Directorate-General
EAPN	European Anti-Poverty Network
ECJ	European Court of Justice
ECOFIN	Economic and Financial Affairs Council
ECSC	European Coal and Steel Community
ECVET	European Credit System for Vocational Education and Training
EEC	European Economic Community
EES	European Employment Strategy
EFSF	European Financial Stability Facility
EFSM	European Financial Stabilisation Mechanism
EIOPS	European Insurance and Occupational Pensions Authority
EMCO	Employment Committee
EMU	Economic and Monetary Union
EPC	Economic Policy Committee
EQF	European Qualifications Framework
ERDF	European Regional Development Fund
ESF	European Social Fund
ESM	European social model
ETUC	European Trade Union Confederation
EU	European Union
GDP	gross domestic product
IGC	Intergovernmental Conference
ILO	International Labour Organization
IMF	International Monetary Fund
IORP	institutions for occupational retirement provision
ITF	International Transport Workers' Federation
LMP	labour market participation
NAP	National Action Plan

NGO	nongovernmental organization
NHS	National Health Service
NMS	new member states
NRP	National Reform Programme
NSR	National Social Report
OECD	Organisation for Economic Co-operation and Development
OMC	open method of coordination
PAYG	pay as you go
PES	Party of European Socialists
PWD	Posted Workers Directive
QMV	qualified majority voting
SAP	Social Action Programme
SEA	Single European Act
SGP	Stability and Growth Pact
SPA	Social Policy Agenda
SPC	Social Protection Committee
TEU	Treaty on European Union
TFEU	Treaty on the Functioning of the European Union
UNICE	Union of Industrial and Employers' Confederations of Europe
VET	vocational education and training
WTD	Working Time Directive

Chapter 1

Introduction

The men who negotiated the Treaty of Rome in the 1950s viewed social policy as the exclusive province of the member states; European Union (EU) intervention would only be necessary in order to facilitate labour mobility within the common market and channel resources (administered by the member states) to regions experiencing high unemployment. These limited social policy competences bore little resemblance to the social policy regimes in the member states. Indeed, the principle underlying EU social policy in the 1950s held that the member states would retain control over nearly all aspects of social policy. EU social policy would merely complement, rather than challenge or constrain, national social policy. Intergovernmental decision-making based on unanimity would ensure that the member states retained social policy sovereignty.

For all six original EU members (I will use the terms EU and EC (European Communities) synonymously throughout the book), the preservation of national social policy autonomy was a prerequisite for ratifying the Treaty of Rome; economic integration was predicated on the idea that social policy would be kept strictly separate from the process of market-building. At the time, Western European welfare states were in the initial phase of what would become a long expansion period, in which state policies guaranteed full employment and protection against a wide range of social risks (Esping-Andersen, 1990; Huber and Stephens, 2001). National social policies were to be essential elements of this process of state-building and rebuilding after the Second World War. Thus, the Treaty of Rome was signed against a backdrop of economic expansion and the extension of the *national* welfare state. In the new EC, European and national levels of social policy-making seemed to be safely separate. As Ferrera (2005) puts it, 'national closure' was a chief characteristic of welfare states in the decades immediately following the Second World War, and in signing the treaty, the six original member states wanted to keep things this way.

1

After nearly six decades of European integration, it is clear that things did not turn out as the EU's founders expected. Today, EU law and policy touch almost every aspect of social policy:

- A highly developed body of law regulates equal treatment in statutory and occupational social security, as well as access to employment, and extensive regulation guarantees the coordination of national social security schemes, enabling workers to aggregate and export benefits earned in any member state.
- EU law intrudes into social services once considered immune to supranational influence. National health care systems have been opened up to allow patient mobility and service providers from other member states, and an extensive set of rules governs the translation of vocational and educational certificates across all member states.
- The EU has extended its reach to the areas of employment promotion, fighting social exclusion, and promoting the reform of national pension systems by using 'soft' governance tools.

The scope and content of EU social policy is in many ways different from conventional definitions of social policy. 'Social policy' refers to the set of public policies that influence the well-being and life chances of individuals (Titmuss, 1974). Conventional definitions of social policy emphasize the collective organization and financing of policies that protect individuals against market and social risks like sickness, unemployment, old age and parenthood. These policies are typically distributive, in the sense that they redistribute financial resources across social groups and involve the provision of collective social services. Elected governments – at local and national level – are usually viewed as the most important actors in the social field, although non-state actors like firms and mutual societies may also be involved in social policy. Core social policies include income maintenance programmes such as pensions and unemployment insurance, as well as social services like education and health care. These social policy programmes require the mobilization of considerable financial resources via taxes and social contributions, as well as extensive state administration in the case of publicly organized schemes.

The role of the EU in social policy differs dramatically from the conventional definition of social policy. The EU has extremely limited financial and administrative resources at its disposal, so its role in the social field is mainly *regulatory* (Leibfried and Pierson, 1995; Majone, 1996; Mabbett, 2009). In other words, the member states continue to dominate the taxing and spending aspects of distributive social policy, but they do so in an environment in which the EU sets regulatory boundaries to these distributive policies.

A large literature explores the expansion of EU social policy competence despite the weakness of the social policy provisions in the founding treaties, stressing the unintended, uneven and incremental expansion of European initiatives (Collins, 1975; Leibfried and Pierson, 1995; Hantrais, 2007; Leibfried, 2010). If scholars largely agree on the drivers of these remarkable policy developments, they disagree mightily about the consequences of EU social policy integration. One school of thought stresses the largely negative impact of social policy-making that is 'left to judges and markets' (Höpner and Schäfer, 2010; Leibfried, 2010; Scharpf, 2010), arguing that the supranational activism of the European Commission and the European Court of Justice (ECJ) has given the European integration process a strong neoliberal dimension that undermines core features of the welfare states of Continental Europe and Scandinavia. A second group of scholars highlights the progressive dimensions of EU social policy integration. A growing literature argues that social policy integration has created an expanding catalogue of social rights that individuals may seek to enforce via national courts (Cichowski, 2007; Caporaso and Tarrow, 2009; Keleman, 2011). Similarly, accounts of EU soft governance in the social field stress the positive contribution of experimental and deliberative governance in highly sensitive policy areas like pensions and employment (de la Porte and Pochet, 2002a; Heidenreich and Zeitlin, 2009; Hemerijck, 2013). Analysts also point to the tangible successes of activist social policy, most prominently the increasingly strong status of social policy in the treaties and Commission initiatives like Social Action Programmes (Palier and Pochet, 2005), as well as the strengthening of social policy in the EU's current growth agenda, Europe 2020 (Ferrera, 2008; Marlier and Natali, 2008).

This book enters these debates by emphasizing the variable effects of EU social policy in the context of multilevel governance. The impact of EU social policy on national welfare states differs across policy sectors and member states, because European integration reconfigures political opportunity structures, giving individual and collective actors new avenues to influence policy development.

The reconfiguration of political authority in the EU reflects the emergence of a novel form of multilevel governance (Scharpf, 1994; Leibfried and Pierson, 1995; Streeck, 1995; Hooghe and Marks, 2001). Member states pursue national policy objectives within the constraints of European law; national welfare states are embedded in a multilevel system of social policy governance. Member states participate in supranational policy-making, so European legislation largely reflects a compromise concerning member states' interests. But the EU's market-building efforts also affect the viability and desirability of national social policies, so national social policies face not only the constraints of European law, but also the pressures of the single European market. As Scharpf (1996) argues, European integration unleashes 'positive' and 'negative' integration. Positive integration refers to EU efforts to formulate common policies that apply to all member states, such as minimum rules governing occupational health and safety. Negative integration refers to EU policies that aim to remove barriers to competition and free movement, such as EU legislation and legal rulings concerning the right of EU nationals to live and work in other member states. The period since about 2000 has been a particularly interesting one in terms of positive integration, since social policy is increasingly subject to soft coordination via the open method of coordination (OMC). Despite this innovation, Pochet (2011) shows that the production of binding social policy directives at European level has not declined (see also Falkner et al., 2005). Nonetheless, the OMC is a core element of the new politics of European social policy integration, especially in areas where the member states jealously guard their social policy-making autonomy, such as pensions and health care.

As noted, the expansion of the EU's social policy role was neither intended nor foreseen by the framers of the Treaty of Rome (Leibfried and Pierson, 1995; Pierson, 1996). Indeed, the preservation of national social policy autonomy has been an important goal underlying the intergovernmental bargains driving the European integration process. Even when the member states could agree on the importance of 'Social Europe', there has been very little consensus on what Social Europe should look like. The member states, each with their own national social traditions, have been reluctant to relinquish their policy-making autonomy in a politically sensitive area. Unlike many other policies in which the EU is actively involved, social policy is characterized by institutional stickiness and member states' attempts to safeguard their policy-making autonomy. Social policies like pensions, unemployment insurance and health care are the largest spending items in national governments' budgets; they often decide national elections, and have been central elements in the nation-building efforts of the 19th and early 20th centuries. These are sources of considerable institutional resilience. Thus, the transfer of social policy competences to the EU level is a particularly contested area because the benefits of integration are not easily visible for many member states. One need only think of the UK's opt-out of the Social Charter and the French and Dutch rejection of the Constitutional Treaty in 2005 to understand the controversy surrounding social policy-making in the EU.

This book analyses the development of social policy in the EU in the context of formidable barriers to social policy integration. Its approach is to analyse EU social policy-making in light of the welfare state and European integration literatures. The central arguments informing the chapter analyses of distinct policy areas draw on important contributions from both these literatures. The book argues that the status quo bias of EU decision-making institutions, the diversity of welfare provision in the EU, and the importance of social policies in member states' electoral politics shape patterns of EU social policy integration, as well as the ways in which the members states respond to EU social policy initiatives. Even if attempts at *positive* integration in the social policy field have been modest, the ECJ and the European Commission have done much to propel *negative* social policy integration forward (cf. Leibfried, 2010). The ECJ often promotes negative integration via its interpretations of the legal meaning of the treaties, and the Commission contributes to it because of its role as legislative agenda-setter and 'guardian of the treaties'. By drawing on the analytical concepts of historical institutionalism in the EU and welfare state literatures, this book intends not only to describe the development of social policy in the EU and its impact on national welfare states, but also to provide an analytical framework for understanding these developments.

The literature on EU social policy

Any account of the role of the EU in social policy must address two puzzles. The first concerns the expansion of EU social policy despite a weak treaty basis. The EU's social policy competences have steadily increased since the Treaty of Rome took effect in 1958. In

2014, the EU shares authority with the member states in many fields of social policy, including workplace health and safety, pensions, employment and health care. The extent of shared decision-making varies across social policy areas, but EU social policy has now developed far beyond the original six's resolution to shield national social policies from the European integration process. The second puzzle concerns the variable impact of EU social policy initiatives in the member states. The comparative political economy literature shows that national welfare regimes differ in their vulnerability to pressures for liberalization (Scharpf and Schmidt, 2000a, 2000b; Scharpf, 2010). In other words, positive and negative social policy integration affect member state social policies in different ways. These two puzzles frame the analysis in the chapters on specific policy areas that follow.

The first wave of research concerning the role of the EU in social policy emphasized the minimal nature of EU policy initiatives, attributing this mainly to the weakness of the relevant EU institutions. It was argued that EU influence on social welfare policy was likely to result in 'fragmented, partial, and piecemeal' policies (Lange, 1992) and the EU's role in social policy-making would be limited to a neoliberal, regulatory approach in which symbolic politics play a large role (Majone, 1996). In the 1990s, scholars began to question the minimalist interpretation of the EU's impact in the field of social policy. For example, Leibfried and Pierson (1995) conceptualized the EU as the central level of a multi-tiered system of social policy governance (see also Hooghe and Marks, 2001). Other important studies during this period investigated the expanded role of policy-making at EU level, especially corporatist policy-making institutions (Falkner, 1998), the influence of the Commission on EU social policy-making (Cram, 1993), the expansion of EU social policy in several fields (Hantrais, 2007), the EU's role in promoting women's rights (Hoskyns, 1996) and the social dimension of the internal market (Springer, 1992).

By the 2000s, European integration scholarship began to investigate more carefully the effects of EU policy-making on politics and policies in the member states. The centre of gravity of research concerning social policy and the EU thus shifted from efforts to explain the development of social policy at the EU level (EU policies as dependent variable) to the investigation of the 'domestic impact' of the EU (Falkner et al., 2005). This period saw the emergence of a large literature on the Europeanization of public policy, including social policy. Research in this tradition traces the impact of European integration on politics and policies in member states. The purview of this literature is wide, encompassing every nook and cranny of public policy, from Economic and Monetary Union to environmental policy to agricultural and fisheries policy. Despite the often fragmented nature of this literature, there is widespread agreement that domestic institutions 'filter' the impact of European policies, even if researchers disagree about which domestic institutions matter most in mediating the effects of European integration (see most prominently Cowles et al., 2001). The central argument in much of this literature is that the European and national levels of policy-making interact largely in the way the multilevel governance literature argues (Leibfried and Pierson, 1995; Hooghe and Marks, 2001). Moreover, the impact of European initiatives on national social policy has not been as marginal as many early analyses argued (Falkner et al., 2005). Chapter 2 explores these theoretical perspectives in more detail. The next section summarizes the arguments that inform the policy chapters that follow.

Central arguments

The status quo bias of EU institutions

One of the central arguments of this book concerns the well-known constraints on large-scale, binding social policy decision-making in the EU (Leibfried and Pierson, 1995; Streeck, 1995; Scharpf, 2002). Despite the extension of qualified majority voting (QMV) to internal market issues in the Treaty of Maastricht (1993) (including several social policy areas) and the inclusion of employment as a matter of common concern in the Treaty of Amsterdam (1997), the EU has relatively few robust social policy competences. The member states remain masters of their own welfare states, at least on paper, and they want to keep it this way because of the importance of the welfare state in national politics. The most sensitive social policy areas remain subject to unanimity in the Council of Ministers. Even where QVM is possible, there must be a clear rationale for EU action because of the principle of subsidiarity.

The Treaty of Amsterdam broke with established practice by introducing 'soft coordination' to overcome the obstacles to supranational policy agreement. Thus, the OMC has been introduced for employment policy, public pensions, social inclusion and health care. The rapid extension of the OMC stems from its non-binding nature; soft coordination occurs via target-setting, benchmarking and mutual surveillance. As such, it is emblematic of what Streeck (1995) calls 'neo-voluntarism'. The OMC and other forms of soft law have expanded largely because the European legislative decision-making channel is often blocked, making soft coordination (non-binding agreements) preferable to no agreement at all (Scharpf, 2002).

Social policy diversity in the member states

The second argument advanced in this book is that the wide diversity in social policy institutions in the member states renders positive integration difficult. Scharpf (2002) is the foremost proponent of this perspective, arguing that national social policies not only express normative and partisan commitments, but are also legitimate because they are the result of democratic decision-making. These normative and partisan commitments differ across the member states, as do the institutional arrangements adopted to realize them. This institutional diversity – and the high political salience of social policy (discussed below) – means that the member states are reluctant to relinquish their control over social policy. Chapter 2 discusses this institutional diversity at more length.

Why social policy is different from other European policies

The third argument underpinning the analysis is that social policy-making in the EU can only be understood when we recognize the role of social policy in national politics. Modern European democracies are, first and foremost, welfare states. Social programmes make up the lion's share of public budgets; indeed, the primary task of government seems to be to tax and spend. In 2012, the 27 member states spent 27.2% of GDP on social protection and health. Denmark was the highest spender at 33.8% of GDP and Latvia was the lowest at 15.1% of GDP (Eurostat, 2014a). To use another measure, social protection and health accounted for more than half of government spending in the EU 27 in 2012 (Eurostat, 2014a). These statistics demonstrate the centrality of social policy in the domestic political processes of the member states. Simply put, social policy is the single largest area of government activity. It is fair to say that the welfare state touches the lives of all EU citizens in the form of public education, income protection during unemployment, sickness, disability and old age, and social services such as health care. Social policies supplement and/or replace the incomes of large groups of voters, and social programmes provide essential services to large swathes of the electorate. As Chapter 2 discusses, the organization of social policy is an area of high political salience; elections are won and lost on issues of social policy, and social policy provides much of the legitimation for modern democratic governments.

Supranational activism and the expansion of negative integration

Despite the obstacles to social policy integration, the EU has expanded its reach into many areas of social policy, especially concerning the expansion of the internal market. Both the ECJ and the European Commission have, over time, loosed themselves from (some of) the shackles imposed on them by the Treaty of Rome. The ECJ succeeded in 'constitutionalizing' the treaties (Burley and Mattli, 1993; Alter, 1998), effectively asserting its sole right to interpret the legal meaning of the treaties. As many scholars have documented, 'legal integration' driven by the ECJ has benefited the market-making process and liberalization more than it has attempts to build Social Europe (Scharpf, 2002). Similarly, the Commission has exploited the modest powers allocated to it under the treaties to expand its role in policy-making. The Commission has agenda-setting powers (shared with the European Parliament) via its right to propose legislation, and it is the designated 'guardian of the treaties', which allows it to monitor the application of EU law. Both the ECJ and the Commission have used their powers to push the integration process in directions never intended by the Treaty of Rome.

To summarize, despite the considerable obstacles to social policy integration, the history of European integration is marked by considerable expansion of social policy competences. The introduction and expansion of the OMC represents an innovative approach to social policy integration in the face of strong institutional constraints, and it arguably marks a new phase in the development of social policy in the EU. The recent period of soft law innovation in social policy comes on the heels of several decades of legally driven expansion of treaty-based employment rights and the modest extension of EU social policy legislation concerning internal market issues like workplace health and safety, parental leave and free movement. There are now 28 member states, and EU policies reach into the core areas of the welfare state. That the EU would be involved in influencing member states' pension, health care and social inclusion policies was certainly not on the minds of the men who negotiated the Treaty of Rome in 1957. The judicial activism of the ECJ, the entrepreneurial role of the Commission, and the unforeseen consequences of treaty commitments have been the central drivers of European social policy (Leibfried, 2010).

Plan of the book

Chapter 2 discusses the two relevant theoretical literatures concerning social policy in the EU: the comparative social policy literature and the literature that focuses on the dynamics of European integration, especially the 'Europeanization' of social policy. It provides the conceptual foundations for the chapters that follow by discussing the most important dimensions of social policies, including rules governing benefit access, financing and administration/provision. The chapter also discusses Esping-Andersen's well-known typology of 'welfare regimes' and other classifications that argue that there is a 'fourth' or Southern European model of welfare, as well as a poorly understood 'fifth' model after the accession of 13 Central and Eastern Europe nations since 2005. This section of the chapter provides the reader with the conceptual tools for understanding the ways in which member state social policies differ in terms of the role of the state, market and family in the provision and regulation of welfare. The chapter then moves to the EU level, discussing the central features of the multilevel governance perspective, as well as arguments focusing more specifically on social policy (Leibfried and Pierson, 1995; Majone, 1996; Scharpf, 1999, 2010). The chapter provides a synthesis of both sets of arguments in order to explain why agreement on common European social policies is difficult, but not impossible. It also considers the recent literature on the impact of European initiatives on member state policies (Falkner et al., 2005).

Chapter 3 discusses the social policy-making process at the EU level in historical perspective, tracing the ambiguous origins of social policy since the 1957 Treaty of Rome. Social policy was not an important component of the Treaty of Rome except for provisions covering the rights of migrant workers. Until the late 1970s, social policy-making at the EU level was modest, but the plans for the internal market pushed social policy onto the EU's decision-making agenda. The Social Charter was adopted in 1989 (without the UK), and the Single European Act also expanded EU competences in social policy. The Treaties of Maastricht, Amsterdam and Nice all extended EU competences further, so that by the time the heads of government met in Lisbon in December 2007 to sign the EU's newest treaty, the extent of supranational control over important aspects of social policy in the EU was indeed impressive. Against this historical backdrop, Chapter 3 discusses the treaty bases for different types of social policy legislation, emphasizing the competences and activities of the Commission, the Council of Ministers and the ECJ. One important characteristic of EU social policy is the important role of the ECJ in interpreting the meaning of EU legislation as well as the market compatibility requirements of member states' social policies. The chapter emphasizes the dilemmas of multilevel or shared policy-making when the national policy space is already occupied by strongly institutionalized social policies.

Chapters 4–8 analyse the role of EU social policy in five areas: pensions and social insurance, employment policy, vocational training and higher education, health policy, and social inclusion. The choice for these policy fields has two advantages. First, they represent the most important types of social policy in the member states in terms of function and scope, which permits investigation of how the institutionalization of social policy in the member states shapes EU social policy-making and the implementation of EU social initiatives at the national level. Second, the dynamics of positive and negative integration operate differently in each of these five policy areas. In terms of negative integration, EU law concerning labour mobility has long shaped cash benefit programmes like pensions and social insurance, whereas the EU's competition regime has only recently begun to intrude into nationally organized services like health care. In contrast, the success of positive integration, at least in terms of binding legislation, is more limited. EU initiatives have been particularly important in the field of public health, occupational health and safety, and the reconciliation of work and family. In addition, EU policies based on soft governance tools (social inclusion, employment, pension reform) are important recent examples of positive integration.

Chapter 4 considers EU policies that affect statutory social security as well as collectively organized occupational schemes, such as pensions. EU legislation and ECJ judgements concerning the rights of mobile workers and the internal market have sometimes had far-reaching impacts on national social policies (gender equality provisions are discussed in Chapter 5). The chapter traces the policy-making dynamics at EU level as well as the influence of these two broad influences on national policies. Although the bulk of the chapter analyses the impact of 'hard law' on statutory and collective social security, it also includes a discussion of the recent introduction of the OMC process for reforming public pensions.

Chapter 5 focuses on the set of policies aimed at promoting a high level of employment in the member states, as well as the reconciliation of work and family. The inclusion of a separate employment title in the Treaty of Amsterdam was important in two respects: first, it marked the extension of EU-level efforts to promote higher levels of employment as well as 'better' employment conditions; and second, it marked the substantial expansion of the use of the OMC for social policy-making at the EU level. The chapter assesses the extent to which the European Employment Strategy (EES) has been successful in terms of concrete policy impact (more and better jobs) and 'output-oriented legitimacy' (Scharpf, 1999). The chapter's second thematic focus is the EU's recent activity in promoting the reconciliation of work and family in member states. EU policies in this area rely on hard and soft law, including the Parental Leave Directive as well as aspects of the EES. The chapter discusses and analyses this bundle of policies as well as their impact on the member states.

Chapter 6 charts and analyses EU policy concerning vocational training and higher education. The chapter discusses the role of the EU concerning the mutual recognition of educational and vocational qualifications, the Bologna Process and member state responses to it, as well as EU-level initiatives related to the establishment of a European Credit System for Vocational Education and Training and the European Qualification Framework. These two areas of policy innovation are analysed in the context of EU law concerning free movement, the Lisbon Strategy and the EES.

Chapter 7 addresses health care. European integration has never had much impact on national systems of social service provision and regulation, but the introduction and deepening of the internal market has changed this. This chapter discusses and analyses the ways in which the legal ramifications of the internal market, as well as other dimensions of European law, impinge on the autonomy of member states to organize their social services on a purely national basis. It discusses the impact of EU law on patient mobility, as well as the impact of EU competition law. The chapter also describes and analyses EU-level initiatives in the area of occupational health and safety, in which the EU has long been active. Beginning in the 1970s and 80s, the EU expanded its competences in this area, and several directives and regulations have introduced European-wide health and safety standards in the workplace. The chapter considers the origins and impact of these policies.

Chapter 8 discusses and analyses the origins and impact of EU policy concerning poverty and social inclusion. It discusses the emergence of the EU's first initiatives concerning poverty in the 1970s, and the development of a fully fledged strategy for fighting social exclusion as part of the Lisbon Strategy and the Europe 2020 strategy. The chapter compares the use of the OMC in social inclusion to other policy fields that rely on the OMC: pensions and employment policy.

Chapter 9 provides a discussion of the direction and impact of EU social policy-making in the context of enlargement. It discusses the differential impact of EU social policy initiatives, such as the substantial progress concerning gender equality but limited results in employment and social inclusion. The chapter then discusses the likely future direction of social policy in a 28-member EU deeply affected by the global financial crisis and the euro crisis. The accession of 13 member states with radically different social policy traditions compared to the 'old' 15 member states is likely to slow down 'positive' social policy integration for the foreseeable future and increase the incentives for lowest common denominator regulatory policies.

Chapter 2

Explaining Social Policy-making in the EU

This chapter provides the conceptual and theoretical tools for understanding the development of social policy in the EU. First, it supplies the conceptual foundations for the chapters that follow by discussing the most important dimensions of social policies, including rules governing benefit access, financing and administration/provision. Second, it discusses the dominant approaches to explaining the development of EU social policy within the overall framework of multilevel governance, including the Europeanization literature (Majone, 1996; Scharpf, 1999, 2002; Hooghe and Marks, 2001). The chapter provides a synthesis of arguments drawn from the welfare state and multilevel governance literatures in order to explain the paradox of social policy integration despite institutional constraints.

The argument developed in this chapter is that the distinctive features of national social policies interact with EU governance structures to shape patterns of social policy-making at the EU level and member state responses to them. This argument is based on a long-term view of institutional development that emphasizes increasing returns, path dependence and unintended effects. The high salience of social policy in domestic politics owes much to the specific manner in which it has been institutionalized in different member states over several decades. Similarly, the long-term development of EU governance structures is marked by decreasing member state control as supranational institutions have expanded their influence, and policy networks and civil society groups have emerged as important actors in specific policy sectors. These networks, operating at all levels of EU and member state governance, shape the development of EU social policy, along with the member states and supranational institutions.

14

The distinctiveness of social policy stems from its political and social salience. The postwar European welfare state is rooted in a series of political compromises originating in the second half of the 1800s. These social policy choices were politically contested and have been subject to continual renegotiation. Moreover, social policies are crucial sources of national political legitimacy and fundamental components of electoral politics. As noted in Chapter 1, social policies comprise by far the largest proportion of public budgets: national welfare states distribute and redistribute vast financial resources, provide employment to large swathes of the electorate, shape individual life chances, and fundamentally alter the operation of market and family relations. Where the state itself does not provide welfare, it often mandates private actors (usually employers) to provide 'private social policy' (Hacker, 2002). Thus, the defining features of European states are their welfare-providing and welfare-regulating functions.

Over the past century, political actors – especially governments – devised, advocated and enacted social policies that were consistent with their programmatic goals and attracted support. These policies had the following effects:

- individuals responded by adapting their own 'welfare-maximizing' strategies to existing public social policies
- interest groups formed around specific social policies – pensioners' groups and so on
- organized business and labour adapted their membership and bargaining strategies to the constraints and opportunities offered by public social policies.

Employers also incorporated the existence of public social policies into their production strategies (Martin and Swank, 2001; Swenson, 2002; Mares, 2003). To borrow from Pierson (1994), the welfare state has become a permanent part of the political landscape, and political actors and individual voters have organized their vote-getting, organizing and welfare-seeking strategies around these policies. This means that the structure of social policies is politically consequential, because the details of policy design encourage certain behaviours and discourage others. Over time, these individual and group choices add up to substantial investments in the status quo and produce 'increasing returns' or self-reinforcing dynamics (Pierson, 2000). If EU policies collide with the incentive structure built into national social policies, the welfare state is thrown out of equilibrium or, as Ferrera (2005) describes it, 'de-structured'. But how are we to conceptualize and explain this de-structuring process? The first step is to understand the salient dimensions of welfare state structure.

Why social policy is different from other policies

Dimensions of welfare statism

Modern democratic welfare states are based on the idea of social citizenship, introduced by T.H. Marshall in 1950. Marshall ([1950] 1992, p. 8) argued that all citizens not only enjoy civil and political rights, but also *social* rights, that is, a range of rights, from:

> a modicum of economic welfare and security to the right to share to the full in the social heritage and to live the life of a civilized being according to the standards prevailing in the society.

Social citizenship naturally entails measures to modify the workings of competitive markets in capitalist societies. The goal of social policy is thus to modify market processes in order to guarantee a minimum standard of living, ensure access to essential social services like health care and education, and promote public goods like workplace health and safety. Because they modify the effects of markets, social policies have the potential to be redistributive across individuals and/or within generations, household types and social classes. Moreover, social citizenship signifies full membership in a national community, because the same set of social rights is guaranteed to all citizens. As Ferrera (2005) puts it, welfare states are institutionalized systems of 'social sharing' and their specific form is heavily influenced by political processes.

Social science scholarship on welfare state variations typically focuses on the ways in which the structure of social protection differs along three dimensions: benefits, financing and administration. This means asking:

- What is the basis for benefit entitlement – citizenship, residence, employment, or family status?
- How are cash benefits calculated – flat rate, previous earnings, need?

- How will benefits and services be financed – general tax revenues, employer/employee contributions, VAT?
- Which group or agency will administer the scheme – unions, employers, mutual societies, private actors, or the state?

These questions are loaded with political significance. Since the first modern social policy reforms under Bismarck in the 1880s, social policy questions have exposed fundamental cleavages and interests in every European society. The division of labour between the state, market and family has often been one of the most conflictual issues in democratic politics (Esping-Andersen, 1990). The specific structure of national welfare states – the division of labour between the state, family and market in the provision of welfare – is often rooted in political contestation, and modern welfare states reflect established political compromises, social contracts and institutional arrangements. The Second World War cemented these social contracts in most Western European countries. After the devastation of two world wars in the space of 30 years, many accepted the need to take responsibility for social security and smoothing out the business cycle.

Esping-Andersen's (1990) contribution to the study of welfare states was to identify and explain the emergence and development of distinct patterns of welfare provision, and his regime approach is now the standard point of departure for analysing cross-national variations in social policy mixes. Esping-Andersen argues that welfare states cluster into three distinct regimes: liberal, conservative (sometimes known as Christian democratic or corporatist) and social democratic. The regime concept is based on the idea that specific welfare mixes assign different functions to the state, family and market. This typology is thus based on three dimensions of social policy:

- the quality of social rights – whether social benefits are awarded as a matter of right, rather than on the basis of labour market performance or status
- social stratification – whether programmes are universal, means-tested, or occupationally based
- the relationship between state, market and family – the extent of state-produced and financed welfare as opposed to family or market-produced welfare.

The notion of social rights also captures the extent to which welfare states promote 'decommodification', or the ability of citizens to secure basic needs outside the market:

1. A *liberal* welfare regime privileges the market and, to a lesser extent, the family. It relies on means-tested benefits, modest social insurance, and private and occupational alternatives to state welfare. The UK and Ireland come closest to this ideal type.
2. The *conservative* regime privileges the state and the family, and the market is marginalized. Publicly provided social insurance programmes reinforce status and income differentials, and the family is still largely responsible for caring functions. As a result, state-provided or sponsored social services are relatively underdeveloped, and married women's labour market participation is lower than in the other two regimes.
3. The *social democratic* welfare regime privileges the state and is characterized by the dominance of universal, state-financed benefits and services and a minimal role for private or market alternatives to state welfare. Caring functions are largely socialized, so the state spends considerable resources on social services, and women's labour market participation is high (see Orloff, 1993 for an important critique).

Esping-Andersen's typology has not escaped criticism. Ferrera (1996) argues that the threefold typology does not adequately capture the central features of Southern European welfare states: a weak role for the state and the uneasy coupling of universal access to health services with extreme occupational fragmentation and dualism in social insurance. Thus, the Southern (also called the Mediterranean) European welfare regimes combine important elements of all three welfare regimes: social democratic universalism, conservative occupational fragmentation, and a weak role for the state. Ferrera explains Southern Europe's developmental trajectory as the result of divisions on the left, the role of patronage in union and party strategy, and the historical weakness of the state.

The accession of 13 member states from Eastern and Central Europe muddies the analytical waters even more, and suggests a fifth world of welfare. The new member states do not fit easily into Esping-Andersen's three categories, or Ferrera's fourth world of welfare. Perhaps the most salient feature of social protection in the new member states is the coexistence of extensive social insurance commitments inherited from the pre-transition period, modest social insurance, and publically mandated but privately provided welfare (Cerami, 2006). The Polish welfare state is a good example: citizens who accrued social rights before the transition to democracy and capitalism in the early 1990s are protected by modest state welfare, especially pensions. Younger workers and citizens are covered by basic social insurance and increasingly private income protection such as pensions. Universal social services survived the transition. In sum, the new member states spend less on social protection, and combine elements of the conservative and liberal regimes (Orenstein, 2008a).

A brief look at several cross-national indicators of the structure of social protection illustrates the utility of the regime approach. Table 2.1 shows the classification of EU member states according to the worlds of welfare discussed above. This classification is used in the charts containing cross-national indicators of social protection.

Figure 2.1 shows expenditure on social protection for the EU 28 as a percentage of GDP in 2007 and 2012. Consistent with the Esping-Andersen typology, social democratic and conservative

Table 2.1 *Welfare regimes and EU member states*

Social democratic	Conservative	Liberal	Mediterranean	New member states
Denmark	Germany	United	Italy	Czech
Sweden	Belgium	Kingdom	Greece	Republic
Finland	France	Ireland	Spain	Estonia
	Netherlands		Portugal	Cyprus
	Luxembourg			Malta
	Austria			Latvia
				Lithuania
				Hungary
				Poland
				Slovenia
				Slovakia
				Bulgaria
				Romania
				Croatia

Figure 2.1 *Government expenditure on social protection as a percentage of GDP, 2007 and 2011*

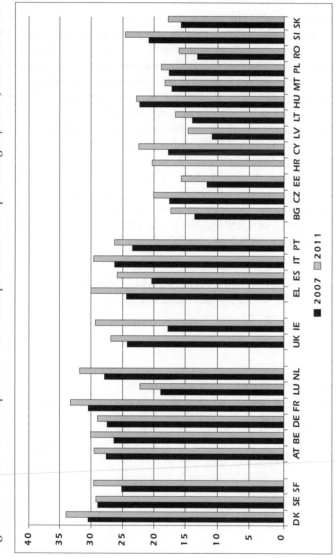

Source: Data compiled from www.epp.eurostat.ec.europa.eu (2007, 2011)
Note: 2011 data for DE, IE, ES, FR, IT, LV, LT, NL, PT, SI, SK and SE is provisional

regimes are characterized by the highest levels of social expenditure. However, the Mediterranean cluster, especially Italy, also shows high spending levels. Liberal regimes and new member states all show lower levels of spending. Figure 2.2 shows general government employment, in order to tease out one of the key differences between social democratic and conservative regimes: the role of public social services (data is not available for all 28 member states). Social democratic regimes rely heavily on publicly financed and provided health care, childcare, education and care for the elderly. Conservative regimes rely on a mix of public, private and third sector. The liberal cluster is marked by moderate levels of government employment, largely because of the role of the NHS in the UK and public education. New member states do not indicate a stable pattern: some, like Hungary, maintain some of the imprint of state socialism in terms of public employment, whereas others, especially Poland, have a level of public employment more in line with conservative regimes.

Figure 2.2 *Employment in general government and public corporations as a percentage of the labour force, 2011*

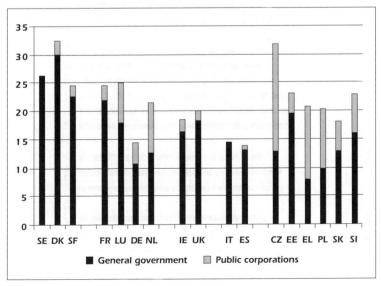

Source: Data compiled from OECD (2011, 2013)
Note: Data for Italy is from 2008

Figure 2.3 *Labour force participation rates of men and women, 2012 (as a percentage of the labour force aged 20–64)*

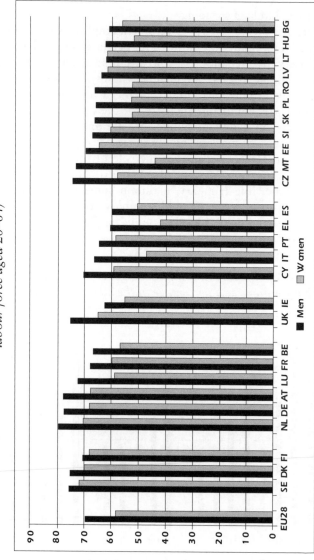

Source: Data compiled from www.epp.eurostat.ec.europa.eu (2012)

Another key distinction between social democratic and conservative welfare states concerns general employment rates and the employment rate of women. Figure 2.3 shows the employment rates of males and females in all 28 member states in 2012. Employment rates for men are high in the three social democratic regimes and in several of the conservative regimes and new member states. The UK level is also high. In contrast, women's employment rates are uniformly high in social democratic regimes, but vary substantially in conservative regimes.

Figure 2.4 shows the proportion of national spending on public and private social protection. In general, the old member states, no matter what their regime type, spend the highest proportion on private social policy. The robustness of collective bargaining institutions in, for example, the Netherlands, Denmark and Sweden, means that collective social benefits top up public ones. Relatively high levels of private social policy spending in the UK are a consequence of employer voluntarism in, especially, pensions (Bridgen and Meyer, 2011).

Figure 2.4 *Spending on public and private forms of social protection in 2009, as a percentage of GDP*

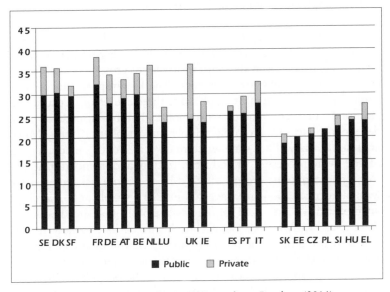

Source: Data compiled from OECD Social Expenditure Database (2014)
Note: Private expenditure includes mandatory and voluntary spending

To summarize, consistent with Esping-Andersen's analysis:

• Overall spending on social protection is highest in conservative and social democratic regimes.
• Expenditure on social services is higher in social democratic regimes than in liberal and conservative regimes.
• Conservative regimes channel most of their welfare spending to social insurance schemes segregated by occupational status.
• Liberal regimes spend the most on 'private' social policy, such as private pensions, although this pattern is also present in the social democratic and conservative regimes.
• Social democratic regimes not only channel large resources into social insurance, but also have the highest levels of public sector employment, consistent with the socialization of caring functions.
• Mediterranean countries show comparatively low levels of female employment and government employment, reflecting the underdevelopment of public social services.
• New member states spend less than the other regime types on social expenditure (including private social spending), and there is considerable variation within the cluster concerning government employment and female employment.

The previous discussion demonstrates the political importance and institutional diversity of welfare provision across EU member states. What have been the central drivers of cross-national differences in social policy arrangements? The literature in this area is extensive, but in general it emphasizes three causes of institutional variation: socioeconomic pressure, political mobilization, and path dependence (see, for example, Huber and Stephens, 2001). Most analyses of the welfare state agree that social policies emerged out of the twin processes of industrialization and democratization: social and economic groups affected by the social risks associated with industrialization and wage labour (sickness, old age, disability, unemployment) mobilized for the passage of the first social policies. Even conservatives, like Chancellor Bismarck in Germany in the 1880s, realized the value of social policies (in this case social insurance) in quelling the emerging radicalism of the working class. Similarly, organized religion used social policies (public and non-public) as an outgrowth of Christian workers' relationship to the church (Manow and van Kersbergen, 2009). The essential point here is that social policies, because they protect workers and their families from the risks associated with capitalist society, have social, economic and often political functions and have therefore been historically politically contested.

The stability of the welfare state

One of the central insights of historical institutionalist scholarship concerning welfare state development is that social policies are often very stable, even in the face of strong pressures for change (Pierson, 1994). Historical institutionalism conceives of institutions as humanly created rules and norms that set constraints on subsequent human behaviour. The temporal development of institutions is central to this perspective: institutions emerge and develop within specific periods and are based on political support coalitions that may change over time (Thelen, 1999; Immergut and Anderson, 2008). The concept of 'policy feedback' helps us understand the stability of social policy: social policies provide important resources to political and economic actors and thereby create the conditions for institutional stability. Thus, historical institutionalism highlights the difficulty of significantly changing social policies once they have been in place for a long period of time. Social policies shape political processes and behaviour in two ways: by creating incentives for interest group activity and by shaping actor preferences and strategy. As Pierson (2007) argues, public policies define (or at least influence) who the relevant political actors are in a given policy area, what these actors want, and how they organize. This argument has important implications for the study of the EU's impact on domestic policy and politics because domestic actors' preferences, strategies and resources shape member state preferences concerning social policy integration, as well as domestic responses to European policy initiatives.

Another source of social policy stability stems from the long-term commitments that often characterize social policies. Many social policies involve long-term commitments (pensions, for example) and affect other sectors of society and the economy, so individuals and families plan their life course around the existence of these institutions, and economic actors adjust to them by offering products and services that complement publicly provided social policies; that is, social policies generate 'coordination effects'. A well-known example is public pensions: where generous public pension provision exists, the market for private pension insurance is usually small and private pensions are marketed as supplements to public provision. Similarly, if employers provide workplace pensions, public pension provision is likely to be modest, and vice versa. In sum, social policies are enormously consequential in social, economic and political terms, and there are often considerable political costs associated with attempts to change them.

Public policies as institutions generate 'increasing returns' in terms of actors' adaptation to and investment in that set of policies (Pierson, 2007). To the extent that social policies are firmly established, they are likely to generate the types of 'increasing returns' processes that lead to path dependence because actors adapt to the existence and operation of an institution by incorporating the institution into their behaviour and planning in that area. Actors join or create organized interest groups that protect and defend the essential structure and substance of that policy regime.

Based on these arguments about increasing returns, coordination effects and networks of support, historical institutionalist analyses of social policy development emphasize the frequent 'stickiness' of social policies once they are enacted. Where social policies generate increasing returns, path dependence is likely to occur, and policy change is difficult because of the electoral risks associated with attempts to change the status quo (Pierson, 1994, 2001). In other words, social policies are politically popular because they confer extensive benefits to important groups of voters and often take on the character of quasi-property rights. This means that it is often difficult to scale back or reorganize social policies when increasing returns processes are present. And, given the importance of social policy in domestic politics, it is clear that member states should be reluctant to relinquish control over highly institutionalized social policies by transferring competences to the European level.

Another important source of social policy stability concerns the relationship between social policy development and nation-building processes. For Ferrera (2005), welfare states are territorial entities characterized by the 'nationalization of redistribution'. Social policies played a key role during nation-building processes, creating and consolidating national 'membership spaces'. The essential point for Ferrera is that welfare states are national states and they relied on boundary control for their legitimacy and effectiveness. National governments controlled the design of social policy, including the pool of beneficiaries, conditions of access and consumption, and the distribution of financial burdens. In other words, nationally distinct systems of social sharing emerged as central components of nation-building and democratization, thus creating an important source of national legitimacy. Although the precise division of labour between the state, market and family varied across countries, European states were welfare states, and the state derived much of its legitimacy from this fact. To borrow from Scharpf (1999), the welfare state provided both 'input' and 'output' legitimacy, because democratic political processes shaped the 'nationalization of redistribution' (the input side) and social policies provided tangible benefits to most if not all citizens (the output side).

One of Ferrera's (2005) key claims is that internal structuring – nation- and state-building – depended on stable boundaries. Social policies not only provided protection against social risks, they also bound citizens to the nation-state. The process of European integration has reduced the salience of national boundaries, often with destabilizing effects for the welfare state.

What should emerge from this discussion of welfare regimes and historical institutionalism is the substantial variation in national approaches to social protection and the institutional durability of social policies over time. Esping-Andersen (1990) stresses the structure of welfare regimes – their mix of state, market and family – rather than absolute spending levels, because it is the details of social policy design that are politically contested. Social policies in the member states have high political salience in domestic politics because of their importance in electoral politics and as a source of democratic legitimacy. These features make many social policies (depending on their structure) difficult to fundamentally change, even by majority governments. The political stakes associated with major reform are often high, because of the sources of stability discussed above. In other words, shifting the parameters of social policy is difficult for member state governments, and this shapes their preferences concerning the direction of EU social policy initiatives.

European integration and the welfare state

Negative versus positive integration

As the previous section shows, national governments have good reasons to try to keep social policies under their control. What happens when firmly institutionalized national social policies are subject to the forces of European integration? EU social policies emerge from legislative initiatives at EU level and the requirements of market compatibility in the single market. Most analyses of EU social policy point to what Scharpf (2002) calls the 'constitutional asymmetry' of market-enhancing policies and social protection policies: EU primary and secondary law promote market-building, but offer few legal resources for policies promoting social protection. How do the 'four freedoms' (labour, capital, services and goods) and EU social policy initiatives intersect with national social policies? EC law concerning the free movement of labour renders national borders irrelevant for many labour market issues, and the opening of national welfare markets to competition from other member states undermines national control over the consumption of welfare services. Recent Swedish and German reactions to ECJ cases concerning industrial relations and the freedom to provide services (*Laval*, *Viking* and *Rüffert*) demonstrate how sensitive these issues are (see Chapter 5).

As noted in Chapter 1, the distinction between positive and negative integration is crucial to understanding the role of the EU in the field of social policy. Positive integration refers to EU initiatives aimed at establishing common standards or policies, whereas negative integration refers to the process of removing barriers to economic activity in order to create a common market. We can think of positive social policy integration as initiatives that would create common European standards and policies for pensions, health care, unemployment and other types of social policy. Similarly, negative social policy integration would encompass initiatives such as regulations facilitating the free movement of labour, for example coordinating social security schemes for migrant workers.

Negative integration was a key element of the Treaty of Rome and has been a core principle driving subsequent treaties (Majone, 1996; Scharpf, 1996). The European integration project has been much more concerned with breaking down barriers to economic exchange than with polity-building. The bulk of the Treaty of Rome concerns the steps required to implement a customs union, and its core provisions established the primacy of economic integration over the harmonization of social policy. Moreover, the doctrines of direct effect and supremacy of European law (discussed below) confer to the Commission and the ECJ important roles in enforcing the treaty. These two institutions thus function to propel negative integration forward. Even if the member states do nothing, the

Commission and the ECJ are required to enforce treaty provisions agreed to by the member states in the past. Moreover, the expansion of the ECJ's influence naturally favours negative integration, because most binding legislation and treaty provisions concern breaking down barriers in pursuit of a common market, rather than the kinds of market-correcting policies aimed at correcting the negative effects of markets on social conditions. Thus, the economic nature of treaty obligations inherently favours negative integration. In contrast, the rules governing EU decision-making constrain positive integration; EU decision-making is characterized by a distinct status quo bias, rendering interventionist social policy-making elusive. The expansion of co-decision (discussed below) and QMV in many fields of social policy in the 1990s appeared to signal a shift towards more social policy initiatives. However, social security legislation is still subject to unanimity. Moreover, Eastern enlargement exacerbates the dilemmas of shared social policy decision-making; social policy diversity among the member states is now so great that agreement on substantial policies is difficult even under co-decision.

The EU as a regulatory state

Chapter 1 introduced the distinction between social policy goals pursued via (re-)distributive policies based on fiscal policy instruments and those achieved by means of regulatory policy instruments. Most areas of traditional social policy – public pensions, public health care provision, social insurance – rely on fiscal policy: governments raise taxes or levy social insurance contributions on employers and/or employees to finance cash benefits and social services administered by public authorities or publically authorized actors. Regulatory social policy pursues social policy goals by mandating or encouraging private actors to provide social protection to specific groups, for example employer-provided occupational pensions, requiring or encouraging private actors to buy social protection on the market, for example private health insurance, and specifying the conditions under which public and private actors carry out social policy functions, for example fee schedules for private medical providers, rules concerning private pension scheme membership, and employment protection. In contrast to (re-)distributive social policy, regulatory social policy is inexpensive, because the costs of compliance fall on individuals, firms and other non-state actors.

The EU's emphasis on market-building naturally implies a large role for the EU in setting the rules and standards that govern the process of liberalization, and these rules and standards may interfere with social policy institutions in the member states. For example, the principle of mutual recognition is a key element of the EU regulatory regime. The free movement of goods requires some mechanism for determining which goods should be allowed to be sold in the member states. The principle of mutual recognition provides a regulatory solution to this by stating that any product marketed and sold in one member state must be permitted to be marketed and sold in all other member states. Similarly, promoting the free movement of labour requires rules and standards that facilitate and govern the employment of EU nationals in other member states. For example, how will educational and vocational qualifications from one member state be recognized in other member states? How will pension rights earned in one member state be aggregated and transferred to other member states? These questions require detailed answers in the form of legislation, and for the EU this means regulations and directives.

The limited size of the EU budget, especially for social policy, also points to the central role of regulation rather than (re-)distribution. Despite public perceptions of profligate EU spending, the EU budget is relatively small at about €144 billion (figure for 2013) (about 1% of the GDP of the EU). The bulk of the budget is allocated to the Common Agricultural Policy (30%) and Cohesion Policy (35%), which includes the European Social Fund (ESF). The ESF is the largest single expenditure item related to social policy in the EU budget (10% of the total budget). However, the goals of the ESF differ fundamentally from national social policy as commonly understood: the ESF provides funding to member states and regions for purposes such as worker retraining and relocation (see Chapter 6), rather than to individuals and families. Only a small share of the EU budget funds the social policy initiatives of Commission departments, known as Directorates-General (such as DG for Employment, Social Affairs and Inclusion and DG for Health and Consumers), most concerned with social policy.

To sum up, one of the keys to understanding the development of EU social policy is the notion of the EU as a regulatory state. The EU is in the business of market-making rather than using redistributive social policy in a process of polity-building. Moreover, the small size of the EU budget only increases the importance of regulatory policy-making. Regulation does not cost anything for the entity doing the regulating; the costs of implementing rules falls on the actors subject to the regulation. This means that the development of social policy in the EU is a story of regulatory politics mainly in the service of negative integration.

Regulatory law-making in action

The distinction between *hard* and *soft* law is important for understanding the dynamics of negative and positive integration and the EU's role as regulator. Hard law originates in principles set out in the treaties, as well as requirements detailed in EU legislation. Soft law refers to non-binding policy instruments used to pursue goals set out in the treaties, social policy action programmes, as well as the use of benchmarking and target-setting in the open method of coordination (OMC). For analysts of social policy-making at the national level, this distinction is relatively unimportant because of the centrality of binding legal provisions (hard law). At the international and supranational level, however, soft law plays a much more significant role because it allows the member states to accept the general principles enshrined in treaties without backing up these goals with binding legal force. Many observers of international law and European integration view soft law as a compromise between 'doing nothing' (because of the difficulty of coming to agreement) and accepting undesirable binding provisions.

There are three sources of binding legal provisions in the EU: the EU treaties (primary legislation), directives and regulations (secondary legislation), and ECJ rulings concerning the interpretation of EU law. The treaties set out the areas in which the EU has the competence to act, as well as the rules governing these competences. The European Commission acts as agenda-setter in the process of translating these treaty obligations into secondary legislation, within the constraints of subsidiarity. According to Article 5 of the Lisbon Treaty, the Commission may not propose legislation beyond the exclusive EU competences set out in the treaties, unless EU legislation is deemed to be more effective than national, regional or local legislation. The Commission proposes regulations and directives, and the Council of Ministers, often in conjunction with the European Parliament, decides on the pace and content of legislation. The ECJ is a key actor in determining the meaning of treaty obligations. A large literature charts the ECJ's successful efforts to expand its influence (Alter, 2000; Conant, 2002; Cichowski, 2007). The doctrines of direct effect and supremacy established the ECJ as a central arbiter of the integration process less than 10 years after the entry into force of the Treaty of Rome. As many analysts have noted, the doctrines of the direct effect and supremacy of European law were not foreseen by the framers of the Treaty of Rome (see, for example, Scharpf, 1996; Alter, 2000). Direct effect, established in the ECJ's 1963 *Van Gend en Loos* ruling (Case 26/62), means that EU law is directly enforceable in national courts. The supremacy of EU law over national law was established in 1964 in the ECJ's *Flaminio Costa* v. *ENEL* ruling (Case 6/64). Once direct effect and supremacy were established, however, the ECJ emerged as an independent player. The role of these institutions is discussed in more depth below.

Theoretical perspectives on European integration

Even if most scholars agree on the importance of regulatory policy-making for EU social policy, there is still considerable disagreement about the causes and consequences of EU social policy. Until recently, theoretical debates about the development of European integration were dominated by two schools of thought: intergovernmentalism and neofunctionalism. Intergovernmentalism and its variants, for example liberal intergovernmentalism, emphasize the central role of the member states in creating and sustaining European integration (Moravcsik, 1998). The member states are argued to control the integration process, deciding on the basis of self-interest and the distribution of power among them whether and how to transfer competences to the European level. Supranational institutions, like the Commission and the ECJ, are argued to be agents of the member states. Neofunctionalism explains the dynamics of integration with reference to functional and political spillovers. Initial steps on the path to European integration generate pressures for more cooperation in other policy areas. At the same time, the member states lose control over the integration process as supranational actors such as the European Commission and the ECJ become more autonomous and pursue their own integration agenda. The neofunctionalists point to the role of the Commission as agenda-setter and political entrepreneur, the autonomous role of the ECJ in defining what EC law actually means and expanding the scope of EC law, and the European Parliament as a co-negotiator of European legislation.

The multilevel governance perspective rejects the state-centrism of intergovernmentalism and the centrality of spillover in neofunctionalism, arguing instead that the EU represents a multi-tiered system of governance. Hooghe and Marks (2001), the foremost proponents of this view, would not deny the existence of spillover or that member states are important actors in the integration process. However, they conceive of European integration as a 'polity-creating process' (Hooghe and Marks, 2001, p. 2), in which multiple layers of government share political authority. This multilevel system is the result of intentional decisions by the member states as well as the unintended consequences of the integration process.

The multilevel governance perspective has inspired a vast literature on 'Europeanization'. Although there is much disagreement about the conceptual meaning of Europeanization (Olsen, 2002), most analyses in this research tradition focus on the impact of European integration on politics, policy and polity in the member states (Cowles et al., 2001; Jachtenfuchs, 2001; Raedelli, 2003; Graziano and Vink, 2007; Sedelmeier, 2012). One dominant strand of the literature focuses on the domestic transformation of policies and institutions as a result of adaptational pressures emanating from European integration (Cowles et al., 2001). Thus, the process of market-building and polity-building driven by the member states and European institutions generates policies that must be implemented in the member states, treaty commitments that must be honoured, and spillover effects that demand responses. In other words, Europeanization is a top-down process, from EU level to member state level. Other scholars argue that the top-down approach ignores a key aspect of the Europeanization process: the bottom-up process whereby member states participate in the bargaining that produces EU policies. The member states themselves are key actors driving integration, and they attempt to 'upload' their policies during EU-level bargaining in order to avoid adjustment costs later. According to Börzel (2002), the bottom-up and top-down phases are two sides of the same coin: the 'uploading' and 'downloading' of EU policies are driven by member state preferences and resources.

Despite the often fragmented nature of this literature, there is widespread agreement that domestic institutions 'filter' the impact of European policies. Pinning down the precise ways in which specific domestic institutions mediate the impact of Europe is, however, quite another issue, and the literature is disappointingly vague on this point. Broadly speaking, existing scholarship emphasizes the mediating impact of three types of domestic institutions: constitutional rules, norms and cognitive understandings, and political resources. For example, Haverland (2000) focuses on the mediating impact of veto points, Martinsen (2007) emphasizes domestic political actors and legal rules, and Falkner et al. (2005) highlight the role of national compliance cultures.

This book takes its inspiration from the multilevel governance literature and the Europeanization literature, but embeds these approaches in a more temporal perspective. This is not new; indeed, some of the most influential analyses of EU social policy rest on a long-term perspective (Leibfried and Pierson, 1995; Hoskyns, 1996). Moreover, EU research increasingly draws on core assumptions of historical institutionalism (Meunier and McNamara, 2007a). As discussed above, historical institutionalism argues that public policies should be analysed as institutions because they have important *political* effects (Pierson, 2000). If we want to understand the processes that shape social policy-making at the EU level as well as member state responses to EU social policy initiatives, the obvious place to start is to ask: What is the policy status quo and relevant actor constellation? Do European policies challenge or reinforce existing member state policies, and with them actor preferences, strategies and resources? Posing these questions will tell us quite a bit about why it is difficult for many member states to agree to a considerable transfer of social policy competences to the EU level.

Historical institutionalism also provides answers to another aspect of EU social policy development: the expansion of EU social policy competences despite a weak treaty basis and member state reluctance to relinquish social policy sovereignty. One of the central claims of historical institutionalism is that institutions, once designed and put in place, develop in ways that depart from their creators' original intentions. The original design of the EU and its subsequent development have been fertile ground for the kinds of processes that historical institutionalism emphasizes:

- independent behaviour by supranational organizations
- policy-makers' tendency to discount the future
- unintended consequences
- changes in member state preferences over time.

These processes create what Pierson (1996) calls 'gaps' between the intentions of the actors who created the institutions and the long-term development of those institutions. Once these gaps emerge, they are difficult to close, and they reconfigure the political opportunity structure within the multilevel EU governance system (Marks and McAdam, 1996).

What do these arguments mean for the study of EU social policy?

1. By emphasizing how organizational power and self-interest drive long-term institutional development, historical institutionalism provides a convincing explanation for the accretion of power by supranational institutions like the ECJ, the Commission and the European Parliament. The activism of these actors is less the result of functional and political spillovers, as neofunctionalism would argue, and much more the product of these institutions' self-interested attempts to exploit ambiguous treaty provisions and other legal openings (in the case of the Commission) to extend their power.

2. Electoral politics means that member state bargaining in the Council is often dominated by short-term policy preferences and pays little attention to potential long-term consequences (to the extent that these can even be known). In contrast, the Commission and the ECJ are, by their very nature, likely to discount the future much less than the member states.

3. Because of the enormous complexity of the EU itself and EU policy-making processes in specific areas, unintended consequences are widespread.

4. Even if the member states remain the most important actors in the EU, their policy preferences are variable over time, simply because of the nature of electoral politics. Member state governments come and go, so the composition of the Council and European Parliament changes regularly. The variability in member state preferences over time increases the likelihood of unintended effects and creates opportunities for supranational activism.

In summary, a historical institutionalist analysis of the development of EU social policy highlights the sources of member state resistance to large-scale transfers of social policy sovereignty to the EU level. As a result, the development of EU social policy competences has been slow, incremental, uneven and partial. The surprising thing, however, is that despite these constraints on EU social policy development, a hard core of EU competences – albeit limited – has emerged over the past 55 years. How do we reconcile the creeping

Europeanization of many aspects of social policy with the sources of social policy stickiness at member state level? What are the political and economic processes that trumped member state resistance to a larger role for EU institutions in the regulation of social policy? The next section explores these questions in light of the historical institutionalist arguments presented above.

Social policy-making in a multilevel system

The development of social policy in the EU owes much to the dynamics of shared decision-making inherent in the EU policy-making process. How should we conceptualize this system of shared decision-making and its impact on the development of EU social policy? The policy-making process in the EU is complex. The EU shares many features with federal systems, and is best understood as a system of multilevel governance. The literature on comparative federalism emphasizes the ways that EU institutions mirror those of federal systems:

- political authority is shared between territorial units and a central government
- there is a division of labour between the centre and the territorial units in terms of decision-making authority
- a constitutional court settles legal conflicts concerning the division of powers within the system (Leibfried and Pierson, 1995; Keleman, 2003).

In contrast to most federal systems, however, the EU lacks the financial resources that federal systems typically enjoy. Rather than using the instruments of fiscal federalism (revenue-sharing policies) typical of federal polities like Germany and the US, the EU must rely on regulatory policy-making that requires little or no expenditure.

The multilevel governance approach focuses on the interdependence of different levels of government and the emergence of issue-specific policy networks. Interactions among governmental and nongovernmental actors extend horizontally and vertically. The key claim is that political authority is no longer the monopoly of national governments, but, instead, authority is shared across levels of governance and between public and private actors (Hooghe and Marks, 2001).

The structure of EU institutions

The institutional structure of the EU and the mechanics of decision-making are clear examples of multilevel governance rather than the hierarchical institutions of government found in most Western democracies. The treaties specify the areas in which the EU has legislative competence, the structure and authority of EU institutions, legislative procedures, and the relationship between the EU and the member states. The major institutions are:

1. The *European Commission* is the EU's executive, but it has no counterpart in national systems of government. The Commission has a relatively small staff (about 25,000 civil servants) and is run by 28 commissioners, one from each member state, who head the issue-specific Directorates-General (DGs) and commission services. The Council appoints the Commission for five-year terms by QMV with the consent of the European Parliament. The Commission is responsible for upholding the treaties, proposing legislation and managing the work of the EU. The treaties provide the Commission with varying powers depending on the issue area. The Commission's power in the field of social policy is limited, but it has been able to expand its influence in social policy over time (Cram, 2009). The DG for Employment, Social Affairs and Inclusion is responsible for most aspects of social policy, while the DG for Health and Consumers is responsible for public health.

2. The *Council of the EU* (also referred to as the Council of Ministers, and shortened to the Council hereafter) is composed of representatives from the member states and provides a framework for legislative negotiation between the member states, the Commission and, if relevant, the European Parliament. Council decision-making is complex, especially under QVM, because each member state is assigned a specific number of votes based on population (see Buonanno and Nugent, 2101, p. 53 for details). In keeping with standard practice, the Council meets in policy-specific configurations. The Committee of Permanent Representatives (Coreper), composed of representatives of member states' permanent representations in Brussels, prepares the work of the Council. The Employment, Social Policy, Health and Consumer Affairs Council is responsible for most social policy legislation. Although the Council remains the EU's key

decision-making actor, it may not initiate legislation, and its power has diminished over time as treaty revisions have recalibrated the institutional balance between the Council and Parliament (discussed below).

3. The *European Council* comprises the heads of state or government of the member states and sets the EU's broad policy agenda. It meets twice yearly in Brussels (these meetings are usually called summits), and special meetings may be called if necessary.

4. The *European Parliament* has been directly elected since 1979, and each treaty revision has strengthened its legislative powers. The European Parliament's role as co-legislator now means that the Council formulates a common position, which must be reconciled with the Parliament's position in the conciliation procedure. Like national parliaments, the European Parliament relies on specialized committees to prepare legislation. There are currently three modes of decision-making in which the European Parliament is involved: co-decision, cooperation and consultation.

5. The *European Court of Justice* (ECJ) is a major player in EU social policy-making. It is composed of 28 judges (one from each member state) and 9 advocates-general who are authorized to formulate preliminary decisions on cases. Judges and advocates-general serve for six-year renewable terms. The Single European Act introduced the Court of First Instance in 1986 to help deal with the workload of the court. Known as the General Court since the Treaty of Lisbon (2009), it has the power to determine the meaning of treaty provisions and other aspects of secondary legislation.

The Treaty of Rome allowed for both hard and soft law. Each subsequent treaty revision has modified the mechanics of making both types of legislation, as well as the division of competences among the main institutional actors. More important for present purposes is the institutional development of the central actors in EU legislative decision-making: the Commission, Parliament, European Council, Council of Ministers and ECJ. One of the core insights of historical institutionalism is that institutional development over time is not efficient, in the sense that institutions remain in line with the intentions of the actors who created them (Pierson, 1996). EU institutions display this tendency quite clearly: the four central EU institutions involved in social policy-making have evolved over the past 55 years in ways that depart substantially from the purposes set out in the Treaty of Rome. This long-term process of institutional evolution has resulted in declining member state control over key aspects of the integration process as supranational institutions have increased their influence over EU decision-making. Certainly, the member states have intentionally ceded some influence to EU institutions with each treaty revision. However, the supranational institutions themselves – especially the Commission and ECJ – have played important roles in increasing their own influence.

There is a large literature concerning the supranational activism of the European Commission and the ECJ (Alter, 2000; Cram, 2009). Once created, organizations try to increase their autonomy and resources, and they have every incentive to try to exploit these gaps and increase their resources and autonomy. The member states also have an incentive to reassert their control over European institutions. However, the European integration project cannot function without stable and authoritative institutions like the ECJ and the Commission. The short-term time horizon of member state preferences and the periodic changes in government among democratically elected member state governments generate an environment in which supranational institutions can often expand their influence without fear of member state control (Pierson, 1996).

The Commission has a well-known record of creatively exploiting opportunities presented by the treaties and gaps in member state control to expand its influence on social policy-making. As discussed in Chapter 1, the chief impediment to EU social policy-making is the weak treaty basis for EU action. The treaties simply do not confer many social policy competences to the EU; even social security for migrant workers – the area in which the EU has a fairly robust mandate – remains subject to unanimity. Cram (2009, p. 97) analyses the Commission's long-term efforts to increase its influence in social policy, arguing that the Commission acts as a 'purposeful opportunist'. The Commission uses several strategies to do this:

1. The Commission has a long history of encouraging the involvement of civil society in policy-making. This may include providing the financial support necessary for establishing pan-European stakeholder groups, such as the European Platform against Poverty and Social Exclusion. In addition, the Commission has always tried to include a diverse group of actors in the policy-making process partly to legitimize its own involvement.
2. The Commission has used action programmes and other soft law instruments like guidelines since the early 1960s. Despite the

weaknesses inherent in soft law, the Commission has strategically introduced action programmes in 'sensitive policy areas ... as a means for claiming that the Commission now had some competence in that particular field' (Cram, 2009, p. 89). By creating action programmes, like the poverty programmes or the action programme for health and safety in the 1970s, the Commission establishes itself in a policy area and then tries to chip away at resistance to EU action and thereby prepare the ground for EU action (Cram, 2009).

3. The Commission strategically selects policy instruments that match legal and political opportunities, often framing policies so that the member states are more likely to accept them. The Commission does this by framing policy proposals with reference to Presidency Conclusions or other Council proclamations, or by flexibly interpreting its legal powers to gain access to policy areas where it normally would be excluded.

The ECJ has also been able to expand its influence beyond the original intentions of the framers of the Treaty of Rome. In the first half of the 1960s, ECJ jurisprudence established the doctrines of direct effect and supremacy, setting the stage for a prominent role for the ECJ in shaping the integration process. Like the Commission, the ECJ has been able to escape the complete control of the member states and establish itself as an independent actor in EU decision-making. A series of rulings in the 1970s concerning equal pay between men and women established its central importance in social policy and prepared the ground for more far-reaching rulings in the 1980s and 90s (see Chapter 4). Building on the doctrine of direct effect, the ECJ ruled in *Defrenne II* (Case 43/75) that Article 119 of the Treaty of Rome (now Article 157 TFEU) had horizontal direct effect – it was enforceable between private parties – thereby giving individuals the opportunity to claim their right to equal pay under the treaties in national courts (see Chapter 4). In the decades since *Defrenne II*, the ECJ has expanded its reach into more and more aspects of EU policies that impinge on social policy.

The literature concerning the role of 'judicial policy-making' in the European integration process is divided on the question of whether the ECJ has been a force for social progress. One group of scholars highlights the role of the ECJ in helping European citizens to mobilize in pursuit of 'rights claims' in areas such as gender equality, non-discrimination, consumer protection and patient mobility (Cichowski, 2007; Caporaso and Tarrow, 2019; Keleman, 2011), while another group highlights the role of the ECJ (and Commission) in pursuing a liberalization agenda that undermines key elements of social democratic and conservative welfare regimes (Höpner and Schäfer, 2010; Scharpf, 2010). These different evaluations of ECJ involvement in social affairs demonstrate the very real impact of judicial activism on the development of EU social policy.

A growing literature analyses interest group formation and lobbying at the EU level (Beyers and Kerremans, 2004; Coen and Richardson, 2009; Berkhout and Lowery, 2010). Successive treaty revisions have increased the power of the European Parliament relative to other EU institutions, especially the Commission, making the Parliament an important target for lobbying. The introduction of co-decision with the Maastricht Treaty in 1992 and its expansion with the Amsterdam (1999) and Lisbon Treaties (2007) reconfigured the structure of political opportunity in the EU. Co-decision is important for social policy because it applies to most aspects of the internal market, freedom of movement for workers and education. Moreover, the Lisbon Treaty extended co-decision to new areas, including regional policy and the Structural Funds.

The essence of co-decision is that Parliament may effectively veto Council decisions. Although the Commission retains the sole right of legislative initiative, the European Parliament is a co-legislator in many important areas. The Parliament also has limited agenda-setting powers; it may formulate its political priorities every year, and a majority of Parliament may request the Commission to formulate legislative proposals in specific areas.

Lobbying in Brussels has become an increasingly important strategy for groups seeking to influence EU policies. The early years of the EU were marked by interest group mobilization via national channels of representation. Today, interest groups lobby directly, approaching the Commission, Parliament and Council with specific appeals and expertise. Thus, lobbying is now a multilevel process with multiple entry points rather than a bottom-up, nationally managed process. The Commission plays an important role in encouraging and financing the activities of stakeholder groups at the European level and is known for its openness to the European lobbying efforts of nationally organized interests. The increasing influence of the European Parliament and its openness to organized interests mean that it, like the Commission, is a magnet for stakeholder groups seeking to influence EU policy. Indeed, there is now an 'inter-institutional triangle' comprising the Commission, the Council and the Parliament; all three corners of this triangle are the target of intensive lobbying activities. Interest organizations engage in 'venue shopping' – targeting their lobbying activities at the institution that will be most responsive (Lehmann, 2009). Thus, EU institutions themselves have helped create interest organizations and a specific kind of EU model of lobbying (Coen and Richardson, 2009). The judicial activism of the ECJ has also encouraged the mobilization of organized interests at the national and European level. As Cichowski (2007, p. 1) argues, the EU is a 'quasi-constitutional polity granting individual rights and public inclusion'. Thus, opportunities for litigation reconfigure political opportunity structures because they give individuals and groups the opportunity to pursue their rights at the EU level after their attempts to secure their rights at the domestic level have failed (Cichowski, 2007). This would not be possible in the absence of the ECJ's judicial activism.

Regulation through litigation has always been more important in the US than in Europe. Until recently, most Western European countries relied on informal regulatory networks based on stakeholder cooperation encouraged or regulated by the state. These networks were often opaque and did not require much legal enforcement because they were sanctioned by the state. Relevant stakeholders cooperated with bureaucrats in the formulation of policy, and they could rely on guaranteed acceptance in the absence of legal challenges (Keleman, 2011). The completion of the internal market changed this. Liberalization challenged existing forms of socioeconomic governance 'by introducing new actors, both foreign and domestic, into previously sheltered domestic markets' (Keleman, 2011, p. 22). Moreover, the internal market required a set of clear and binding rules concerning economic activity that were enforceable throughout the EU. In order to guarantee the four freedoms, the conditions of access to national markets had to be made transparent, and litigation became an important strategy for actors claiming their right to non-discrimination under EU law.

In summary, the institutional development of the EU has been characterized by the loss of member state control over the integration process. Certainly, member states remain central actors in EU decision-making, but they are embedded in a system of multilevel governance in which supranational institutions autonomously shape policy development. Moreover, the EU's multilevel institutional structure has reconfigured political opportunities at the national and European level. The European Commission actively promotes the activities of social policy stakeholders, the European Parliament is now the locus of intensive lobbying efforts by social policy stakeholders, and the European legal order provides private actors with opportunities to claim their rights in national courts by invoking EU law.

Social policy and EU legitimacy

As discussed above, social policy and legitimacy are intrinsically linked. The emergence and development of national welfare states has been an important element in state-building, and states have derived much legitimacy from this process. Returning to Ferrera's (2005) arguments about the 'de-structuring' of European welfare states, an important implication is that de-structuring has not been accompanied by measures to compensate for the loss of domestic political legitimacy. In other words, EU member states find themselves in the unfortunate position of powerlessly witnessing the destabilization of social policy institutions. Of course, the member states willingly transferred some social policy competences to the EU level, but some effects of European integration were clearly not foreseen.

The French and Dutch electorates' rejection of the Constitutional Treaty in referendums held in spring 2005 provided additional evidence of the public's ambivalence about de-structuring. The French 'no' was motivated partly by widespread fears about the viability of the French welfare state under the provisions of the Constitutional Treaty. The Dutch 'no' had less to do with perceived threats to the welfare state and more to do with the weak legitimacy of EU governance (Taggart, 2006).

Ferrera's (2005) arguments have important implications for the analysis of social policy in the EU. As the boundaries of the welfare state weaken as a result of European integration, the member states lose control over access to social benefits and services and are no longer the sole arbiters concerning who may or may not provide welfare functions inside their national borders. This weakens the ties between citizens and the state, robbing governments of important sources of national political legitimacy. Moreover, the de-structuring of national social policies has the potential to reconfigure political processes associated with the welfare state: domestic actors may change their social policy preferences and strategies in the context of more open welfare markets.

EU public opinion shows high levels of support for the goals of social policy – social solidarity and social equality. Figure 2.5 shows the results of a 2009 Eurobarometer survey that asked respondents to choose two items that society should emphasize in order to face global challenges: 45% of respondents chose 'social equality and solidarity' as one of their two answers; in contrast, 31% mentioned 'free trade/ market economy'. Despite these high levels of support for social solidarity, there are considerable cross-national differences, shown in Figure 2.6. The UK and Ireland stand out for their relatively lower levels of support for the values of social solidarity and social equality.

Recent economic and political developments continue to reinforce the tension between high levels of public support for social policy and public ambivalence about the role of the EU in regulating and promoting social protection. The onset of the global economic and financial crisis in 2008 severely tested the capacity of social policy at national and EU level to alleviate the negative effects of the crisis on employment and individual wellbeing. Moreover, the sovereign debt crisis led to painful austerity measures in those member states receiving EU assistance – Greece, Cyprus, Ireland and Portugal – and in those with serious economic imbalances, especially Spain (see Chapter 3 for details). For many Europeans, the sovereign debt crisis demonstrates the subordination of social policy goals to the imperatives of Economic and Monetary Union. Indeed, support for European integration has decreased in the countries hardest hit by the crises, and this is especially true among younger people (Gomez, 2014).

It is probably impossible to determine the precise contribution of EU policies and institutions to the sovereign debt crisis. However, it is clear that Europeans' perceptions of the impact of the crisis on their own wellbeing, as well as the EU's inability to orchestrate an effective and coordinated response to the crisis, played an important role in the May 2014 elections to the European Parliament. Far right parties experienced significant increases in support, although the results vary significantly by country. Although the election was not an earthquake for the far right, the results expose the fault lines running through the EU electorate in the wake of the crisis. Far right party success was greatest in EU member states least affected by the crisis – Denmark, the Netherlands, Austria, France and Sweden – where EU membership and financial support to the EU's weaker members were framed as threats to national identity. In contrast, support for left parties increased in member states hardest hit by the crisis (Mudde, 2014).

Figure 2.5 *EU-wide support for social equality and solidarity*

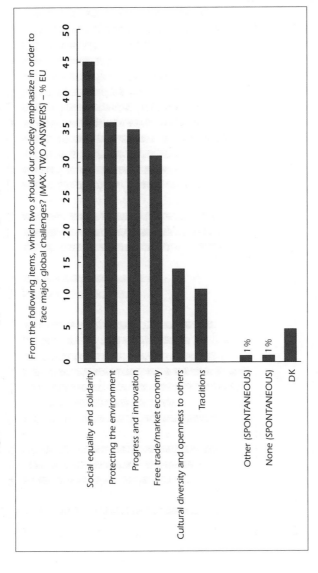

From the following items, which two should our society emphasize in order to face major global challenges? (MAX. TWO ANSWERS) – % EU

- Social equality and solidarity
- Protecting the environment
- Progress and innovation
- Free trade/market economy
- Cultural diversity and openness to others
- Traditions
- Other (SPONTANEOUS) 1%
- None (SPONTANEOUS) 1%
- DK

Source: Eurobarometer (2010, p. 6), © European Union, 1995–2014

Figure 2.6 *Share (percentage) of respondents who say that 'society should emphasize social equality and solidarity in order to face global challenges'*

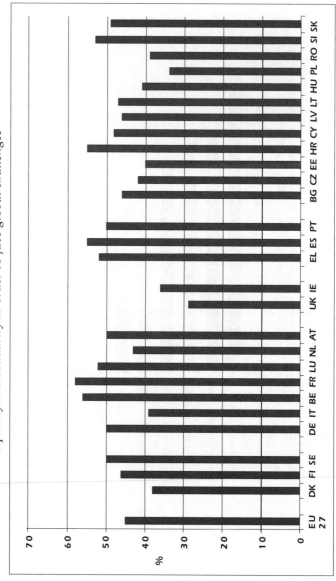

Source: Data compiled from Eurobarometer (2010, p. 7)

Towards a synthesis

One of the central messages of this chapter is that social policies are core elements of domestic politics, and the member states are understandably wary of delegating social policy competences to the EU, except at the margins. Thus, the structure of social protection should tell us quite a bit about member state policy preferences concerning social policy integration. The enormous institutional diversity in social policy in the member states is an important barrier to integration and explains the relatively narrow treaty bases for EU social policy-making. The problem of institutional diversity was clear from day one when the French wanted equal pay to be included in the Treaty of Rome; the historical record shows that the other five founding member states never anticipated the implications of this for domestic pay practices.

Thus, the history of social policy development at EU level (to be discussed in Chapter 3) is one of slow and uneven progress. The member states generally only agree to expand the social policy competences of the EU when they are confident they can 'upload' their own policy designs to the EU level. To borrow Börzel's terminology (2002), there are too many member states competing for the position of 'pace-setters' at the same time that there are vocal 'foot-draggers' who want to block social policy integration. And the recent accession of 13 new member states with vastly different welfare state institutions and levels of economic development has added to social policy diversity. In short, social policy is highly politicized, much more so than in areas like environmental or monetary policy where the EU has a robust policy mandate. This creates obstacles to far-reaching initiatives, but it does not prevent integration altogether.

Indeed, the EU has expanded its reach into areas of social policy that would have been unthinkable even 20 years ago. The Commission, the ECJ and, more recently, the European Parliament have been key actors in this process. The Commission has slowly and incrementally expanded its social policy powers by exploiting openings provided by creative use of its modest powers (Cram, 1993, 2007). Similarly, the ECJ gradually increased its judicial authority via the doctrines of direct effect and supremacy. Indeed, the ECJ has succeeded in 'constitutionalizing' the treaties. Finally, the European Parliament has emerged as an important actor in legislative procedures requiring co-decision, and is now a co-legislator with the Council in important policy areas. The increase in influence of these supranational actors is best understood in terms of historical institutionalism: organizational actors exploiting gaps in control over them to take advantage of opportunities to expand their influence.

Chapter 3 takes up these issues in more detail, tracing the origins and development of social policy since the Treaty of Rome.

Social Policy and Multilevel Governance

This chapter focuses on the development of EU social policy in historical perspective, emphasizing the ambiguous status of social policy in the 1957 Treaty of Rome and subsequent efforts to enlarge the EU's social policy remit despite weak treaty provisions. As Chapters 1 and 2 discussed, the European integration project has been dominated by negative integration, or the liberalization of markets for goods, labour, services and capital. This process of removing barriers to economic exchange has encroached on national welfare states, affecting core areas like pensions and health care. Despite growing support for positive social policy initiatives at EU level since the 1970s, positive social policy integration has lagged significantly behind the market-building process, largely because of the difficulty of transferring social policy competences from the national to the EU level. The wide diversity of social policy institutions in the member states makes compromise in the Council difficult, and the high level of agreement required in EU decision-making institutions for positive measures exacerbates this.

The account of EU social policy development that follows emphasizes the very real progress achieved in terms of negative integration in the field of social policy, for example the rights of migrant workers, patient mobility, and the freedom to provide social services, and the limited advancement of positive integration concerning social policy. Treaty revisions have progressively increased the EU's social policy competences, but these are fairly weak in comparison to the progress in areas of social policy affected by negative integration. Partly in response to the limited success of positive integration, the EU relies increasingly on new modes of governance based on soft law for much of its social policy agenda. Table 3.1 lists the major events in EU social policy development. The chapter then proceeds chronologically through the treaties, discussing the gradual increase in the

Table 3.1 *Chronology of important events*

1951	Foundation of the European Coal and Steel Community (ECSC). Treaty signed by Belgium, France, Germany, Italy, Luxembourg and the Netherlands
1956	Spaak Report
1957	Negotiation of the Treaties of Rome establishing the European Economic Community (EEC)
1958	Treaties of Rome entered into force
1961	First legislation on the free movement of labour Social Charter of the Council of Europe and ILO conventions
1962	European Social Fund (ESF) operational
1973	Accession of Denmark, Ireland and the UK
1974	Adoption of first Social Action Programme (SAP)
1979	European Monetary System in force
1981	Accession of Greece
1985	Publication of White Paper by European Commission on the completion of the internal market European Council agrees on Single European Act (SEA), including qualified majority voting (QMV) for health and safety issues
1986	Accession of Spain and Portugal
1987	SEA entered into force
1988	European Commission introduces a social dimension for the internal market
1989	Delors Report published (three-step progression to EMU) Social Charter is adopted
1989–90	SAP of 1989 is implemented
1991	Agreement on the Treaty of the European Union by European Council Expansion of QMV for social policy and creation of Social Policy Protocol in order to overcome UK veto
1993	Maastricht Treaty/Treaty on European Union (TEU) entered into force White Paper, *Growth, Competitiveness, Employment*

$\rightarrow$

1994	Social Protocol used for the first time to pass Works Council Directive
1995	Accession of Austria, Finland and Sweden
1995	Launch of 1995–97 Medium-term SAP
1997	Change of UK government: Conservative government is defeated and new Labour government accepts Social Protocol
1997	Agreement on the Treaty of Amsterdam by the European Council: integration of the Social Policy Protocol into the text of the treaties
1998	Launch of 1998–2000 SAP
1999	Special meeting of European Council (Berlin), agreement on Agenda 2000 on conditions for the accession of candidate states Treaty of Amsterdam entered into force
2000	Lisbon Strategy adopted
2003	Treaty of Nice entered into force Open method of coordination (OMC) adopted as working method for social exclusion and other issues
2004	Accession of Czech Republic, Estonia, Cyprus, Latvia, Lithuania, Hungary, Malta, Poland, Slovenia and Slovakia
2004–06	Failure of ratification of Constitutional Treaty for Europe
2007	Accession of Bulgaria and Romania
2008	Beginning of global economic crisis
2009	Treaty of Lisbon entered into force Tripartite Social Summit for Growth and Employment
2010	European Council adopts Europe 2020 strategy Financial assistance for Greece and Ireland Establishment of European Financial Stabilisation Mechanism (EFSM)
2011	Financial assistance for Portugal Establishment of European Financial Stability Facility (EFSF) Stability and Growth Pact (SGP) reformed by six pack of legislation
2013	Accession of Croatia Two pack of legislation to improve economic monitoring

EU's powers to regulate social policy. The final section considers recent reforms of the EU's economic governance regime and their implications for social policy.

The development of social policy in the EU

Four founding treaties, the 1951 Treaty of Paris establishing the European Coal and Steel Community (in force on 23 July 1952), the 1957 Rome Treaties (in force 1 January 1958) establishing the European Economic Community (EEC) and the European Atomic Energy Community (Euratom), and the Treaty on European Union (the Maastricht Treaty, in force in 1993) form the basis for the EU's legal order. Several major treaty revisions have amended and expanded the provisions of the founding treaties (see Table 3.2 for the main provisions and abbreviations of each treaty).

The (re-)negotiation of the EU treaties on seven occasions means that treaty numbering has changed over time (the Amsterdam and Lisbon Treaties included extensive renumbering of treaty articles). The approach taken here is to provide the Rome or Amsterdam Treaty number when discussing legal developments in historical context and to include the equivalent Lisbon Treaty article in parentheses. The abbreviation 'EEC' refers to the European Economic Community Treaty (the 1958 Treaty of Rome, amended by the 1987 SEA and 1993 Treaty on European Union), and 'EC' refers to the European Community Treaty (the Treaty of Amsterdam, amended by the 2003 Treaty of Nice). The Lisbon Treaty, in effect since 2009, has two parts: the Treaty on European Union (TEU) and the Treaty on the Functioning of the European Union (TFEU), which replaces the EC treaty (see Barnard (2013) on treaty amendments and (re-)numbering).

The Treaty of Rome

The Treaty of Rome contains few provisions concerning social policy. Economic integration was the primary objective of the EEC and its predecessor, the ECSC, and the founding treaties reflected this. Certainly, the Treaty of Rome paid 'lip service' to social goals (Shanks, 1977, p. 1), and it gave the EU the authority to issue legislation concerning labour mobility and other aspects of market creation, but the bulk of the treaty was concerned with establishing supranational institutions and regulations that would

Table 3.2 *European Union treaties*

Name of treaty	Entry into force	Main provisions
Treaty of Paris: Treaty establishing the European Coal and Steel Community (ECSC)	1952	• Established the common administration of coal and steel
Treaty of Rome: Treaty establishing the European Economic Community (EEC)	1958	• Introduced plans for a common market and a common agricultural policy
Treaty establishing the European Atomic Energy Community (EAEC/ Euratom)	1958	• Common administration of nuclear energy
Single European Act (SEA)	1987	• Introduced provisions for the completion of the internal market • Extension of QVM

Maastricht Treaty: Treaty on European Union (TEU)	1993	• Established the European Union with a three pillar structure:
		  1. Justice and home affairs
		  2. Common foreign and security policy
		  3. European Community (EC)
		• EEC is renamed the EC
		• Plans for Economic and Monetary Union
		• Introduction of co-decision

Treaty of Amsterdam	1999	• Reform of EU institutions • Extension of co-decision • First major renumbering of treaty articles
Treaty of Nice	2003	• Reform of EU institutions in anticipation of Eastern enlargement
Treaty of Lisbon	2009	• Reform of EU institutions to enhance democracy and efficiency • Second major renumbering of treaty articles

Note: The EEC and EAEC treaties are known as the 'Treaties of Rome', and the EEC, ECSC and EAEC were known as the 'European Communities' until the Treaty of Maastricht enable the construction of a common market. Thus, the early development of EU social policy was marked by the primacy of economic integration over social policy. The early focus on the construction of a European labour market established the framework for the subsequent development of European social policy. Attempts at more activist social policy on the part of the Commission faltered in the 1970s, and it was only in the 1980s, with the adoption of the Single European Act (SEA) in 1986, that social policy has taken on a more prominent role. Many areas of social policy are now covered by co-decision and qualified majority voting (QMV). This applies especially to occupational health and safety, gender equality and other aspects of employment conditions. Soft governance has become more prominent in employment policy, pensions and social inclusion.

Hantrais (2007) notes that the treaties establishing the ECSC in 1952 and the European Atomic Energy Community (EAEC) in 1957 emphasized social policy more than the Treaty of Rome did. Because they were concerned with specific industries (coal, steel, nuclear energy), the ECSC and EAEC had fairly strong social policy mandates in order to deal with the employment and health effects of these rapidly changing industries. The ECSC had funds to deal with redundant workers, and the EAEC was empowered to set health and safety standards.

The success of the ECSC encouraged the six member states to go forward with plans for more far-reaching economic cooperation. The 1956 Spaak Report that formed the basis for the Treaty of Rome negotiations left redistributive social policy to the member states (Hoskyns, 1996; Barnard, 2012). The report advocated the introduction of a customs union, but rejected any movement towards the harmonization of economic conditions in the member states, including social policy, arguing that harmonization would follow naturally from the development of a common market. In other words, harmonization was not a precondition to, but would be a result of, the development of a common market. The Spaak Report drew on the conclusions of the 1956 Ohlin Report, prepared by International Labour Organization (ILO) experts, which advocated a minimal role for the EC in social policy, except in specific areas that might distort competition, such as equal pay and paid holidays (ILO, 1956). Crucially, the Ohlin Report argued that in most areas of economic exchange, market competition would eliminate the need for any sort of harmonization. The principle of comparative advantage would ensure that cross-national differences in wages and social costs would not lead to distortions of competition. Thus, the general emphasis of the Ohlin Report was the salutary effect of markets: there was no need to harmonize redistributive social policy, because markets would produce the correct level of harmonization on their own.

Despite the seeming clarity of these messages, there was considerable disagreement among the member states during the Treaty of Rome negotiations. In particular, the French position was especially at odds with the preferences of Germany and the Netherlands. One of the core concerns of the French was the competitiveness of French industry, and the common market would make many existing protective measures illegal. Moreover, the French were concerned about the higher levels of social contributions paid by employers, fearing that their comparatively pro-labour legislation concerning vacations, overtime pay and equal pay for men and women might put French industry at a competitive disadvantage in the common market. The French thus advocated the harmonization of relevant social policies, but this position clashed with the German preference for non-interference in the social policy field. Based on the findings of the Ohlin Report, the German negotiators argued that economic integration would lead to social progress, obviating the need for the harmonization of social policy. The French insisted on the inclusion of equal pay provisions, accepting lower tariffs in exchange (Collins, 1975; Hoskyns, 1996). The compromise reached by the negotiators was that equal pay and provisions concerning paid vacations would be included in the treaty.

The Treaty of Rome reflected the compromises concerning these issues. The preamble refers to the signatories' goal of ensuring 'the economic and social progress of their countries by common action in eliminating the barriers which divide Europe' and the 'essential purpose of constantly improving the living and working conditions' of Europeans. Despite these lofty social aspirations, the core of the treaty was the creation of the common market. Indeed, only 12 of the 248 articles in the Treaty of Rome dealt with social policy (these original articles are now Articles 151–164 TFEU). Social policy was relevant in two ways: it could distort competition and was intimately connected to one of the treaty's core goals: worker mobility (Hantrais, 2007). Articles 117–128 EEC of the Treaty of Rome covered the following areas:

- Article 117 EEC (now Article 151 TFEU) provided for the establishment of a social fund to aid displaced workers, called for social policy cooperation among the member states, and included the general goal of promoting improvements in the 'living and working conditions of labour' so that equalization upward would occur
- Article 118 EEC (Article 156 TFEU) tasked the Commission with promoting 'close collaboration' in social policy, particularly in employment, labour legislation, vocational training, social security, occupational safety and health, and industrial relations. However, the means to achieve these goals were vague: the Commission could conduct studies, opinions and consultations
- Article 119 EEC (Article 157 TFEU) required equal pay for men and women
- Article 120 EEC (Article 158 TFEU) addressed holiday regulations
- Article 121 EEC (Article 48 TFEU) empowered the Council to delegate to the Commission tasks related to the social security of migrant workers
- Article 122 EEC (Article 161 TFEU) charged the Commission with issuing an annual assessment on 'the social situation' in the EC
- Articles 123–128 EEC (Articles 162–164 TFEU) established the European Social Fund (ESF) to promote employment and worker mobility. The Commission was authorized to administer the ESF.

What is striking about Articles 117–128 EEC (Articles 151–164 TFEU) is the tension between ambitious but rather vague goals and the relative absence of potent instruments for pursuing them (Hantrais, 2007; Barnard, 2012). The preamble and the social policy articles refer several times to the goals of raising living standards, improving working conditions and promoting social progress. However, Articles 117–128 EEC (Articles 151–164 TFEU) provided little in the way of forceful, binding instruments. The two exceptions to this are Article 119 EEC (Article 157 TFEU) on equal pay and Articles 123–128 EEC (Articles 151–164 TFEU) concerning the ESF. Even these exceptions are somewhat deceiving:

- Article 119 EEC (Article 157 TFEU) defined equal pay and specified a deadline for achieving it (the end of the 'first stage' of integration, or four years after the entry into force of the treaty), but it did little else; the member states were simply exhorted to apply the treaty's equal pay provisions. As Chapter 4 shows, this did not happen. It was only after the ECJ took up the issue in its jurisprudence more than 10 years later that equal pay was enforced.

- Similarly, Articles 123–128 EEC (Articles 151–164 TFEU) concerning the ESF seem to establish a specific and significant role for the EU in worker retraining and mobility. The design of the ESF, however, preserved member state autonomy and assigned the EU the role of co-financer of existing member state policies rather than an important independent role in shaping policies for redundant workers.

Debates about the relationship between social and economic policy in the Treaty of Rome negotiations presage the debates that would shape EU social policy for the next 55 years. Indeed, the treaty left a partial vacuum in terms of social policy because goals were not matched with effective instruments. As Collins (1975) argued, the weak status of social policy in the treaty was a compromise, in the sense that it ended up in the treaty at all, if only in weak form.

Despite the weakness of its social policy provisions, the treaty provided legal openings for the Commission to take a positive social policy stance. Early analyses of EU social policy demonstrate that the Commission did not view social policy integration as something subordinate to economic integration (Collins, 1975). Indeed, the Commission saw in Articles 117 EEC (Article 151 TFEU) and 118 EEC (Article 156 TFEU) the rationale for an active Commission role in EU social policy, arguing that 'the sphere of action of the institutions and social matters has no strict limits, the problems listed in Article 118 EEC being in no way exclusive' (Commission, 1958, para. 103). In 1958, the Commission stated that:

> It is clear that the objectives of a social character are placed on the same footing as those of economic character; it is from this standpoint that the future of the community in the social field will have to be conceived and judged. (Commission, 1958, para. 102)

The Treaty of Rome's provisions concerning social policy were thus an invitation to institutional innovation and expansion. In

Collins' words (1975, p. 39): 'the treaty was given a limited view of social policy, did not always express it without ambiguity and left uncertainties for future resolution'. In the following decades, the Commission would exploit these openings to expand its social policy competence (Cram, 2009).

In the two decades after the Treaty of Rome entered into force, the Commission proposed, and the Council adopted, several directives and regulations concerning the status of migrant workers, including social security, and the principle of equal treatment. In addition, the ESF was up and running by 1962. The first regulation on the free movement of labour was adopted in 1961. Regulation 1612/68, adopted in 1968, abolished discrimination in employment for EC nationals.

The 1970s marked a shift towards a more active orientation concerning social policy. The Commission began to play a more activist role, and the climate concerning social policy was more favourable than in the EC's first decade. Thus, the 1970s changed the equilibrium implied by the Treaty of Rome and saw the first attempts at legislative activity in the field of social policy. One of the first signs of this change in orientation was the Council's adoption of the first Social Action Programme (SAP) in January 1974 (Commission, 1974a). The SAP was the result of a decision by the heads of state meeting in Paris in 1972 to step up EC efforts in the social field. The background to the initiative was the onset of economic stagnation in Western Europe in the early 1970s resulting from the oil shocks and rising unemployment, as well as the social unrest that swept Western Europe in the late 1960s and early 1970s. The postwar period of sustained economic progress appeared to be over, or at least stalled, and the EC seemed poised to take on a greater role in social affairs. With three new members set to join the EC in 1973 (the UK, Ireland and Denmark), the heads of state thought that more vigorous action in the social field was necessary (Barnard, 2013). What is striking about the conclusions of the Paris Summit is that the participants declared that the member states 'attached as much importance to vigorous action in the social field as to the achievement of Economic and Monetary union' (Barnard, 2013, p. 9).

The Council based its resolution authorizing the SAP on Article 2 of the Treaty of Rome concerning improvements in the standard of living. The SAP included the first EC poverty initiatives (see Chapter 8) and special provisions to improve the status of migrants;

by 1974, the number of migrants (including family members) had reached 10 million, in an EC of nine countries. This resulted in concentration in already industrialized areas and depopulation in peripheral areas. The SAP also emphasized the need to improve the status of the growing numbers of third country nationals. Thus, the SAP emphasized improving their status by improving access to vocational education, providing better housing, and enhancing rights for community migrants. For EC migrants, this would include the extension of non-employment-related social benefits to non-nationals, the right to take family members with them, and accelerating the mutual recognition of diplomas. The 1974 SAP included a battery of measures to be carried out over three or four years, aimed at three core goals:

1. full and better employment
2. improved living and working conditions
3. increased participation of workers and employers in EC decision-making concerning economic and social affairs, and of labour in companies.

As Barnard (20013, p. 9) put it: the 'Action Programme precipitated a phase of remarkable legislative activity'. Treaty provisions concerning market-building were the basis for many of the directives that followed from this first SAP, particularly a series of directives concerning worker health and safety. In addition, under the header of employment policy, the SAP established the beginnings of a common vocational training policy, including the establishment of a European Vocational Training Centre (see Chapter 6). The EU also adopted the first directives concerning the equal treatment of men and women in employment in the wake of *Defrenne II* and other ECJ rulings (see Chapter 4). However, as economic stagnation continued, the member states turned more and more to national strategies for fighting the employment crisis, and the SAP 'disintegrated into a series of piecemeal actions' (Wise and Gibb, 1973, p. 134).

The Single European Act and social policy

Despite the burst of legislative activity in the social field in the 1970s, the 1980s were largely a decade of stagnation for EC social policy. The accession of five new member states in the 1970s and

80s (Greece, Spain, Portugal, the UK, Ireland and Denmark) increased social policy diversity among the member states. Moreover, the election of the Conservative government in the UK meant that at least one member state would vigorously and consistently oppose any EU intrusion into the field of social policy. Indeed, the UK blocked two important directives on employee representation and consultation (Barnard, 2012).

The Single European Act (SEA), signed in February 1986 and entered into force in July 1987, was the first major revision of the Treaty of Rome. The SEA was intended to jump-start the process of completing the internal market by reforming EC decision-making and striking a new balance between economic integration and the EC's 'social dimension'. The most important procedural change introduced by the SEA was the extension of QMV to all legislation concerning the internal market. There were important exceptions, however: taxation, the free movement of persons and employee rights. The movement away from a single-minded focus on economic integration meant that the SEA reinvigorated discussion about the role of the EC in social policy. Given the ambitious nature of the internal market project, there was strong support in some quarters for creating a 'social dimension' to the proposed internal market. Headed by François Mitterrand who took office as president in 1981, the socialist government in France publicized its preference for a more 'social' and employment-oriented Europe, and the 1985 appointment of Jacques Delors as president of the European Commission strengthened the position of the coalition in favour of a social dimension. More importantly, the June 1984 Fontainebleau European Council settled lingering disagreements about the size of the UK budget rebate and the remaining obstacles to the accession of Spain and Portugal, clearing the way for a possible compromise. In addition, the Fontainebleau European Council resulted in a new Social Action Plan, with the aim of introducing a balance between the social and economic goals of the EU (Council, 1984; Wise and Gibb, 1993). National trade unions and the European Trade Union Confederation (ETUC) also lobbied for a strong social dimension to the SEA, particularly after the publication of the Commission's 1985 White Paper titled *Completing the Internal Market* (Commission, 1985; Silvia, 1991).

The ratification of the SEA was thus based on renewed attempts to strengthen the social aspects of the next phase of European integration. These efforts were only partially successful, because the SEA contained only limited innovations in the field of social policy:

1. The SEA introduced QMV in occupational health and safety (the new Article 118a, now Article 153 TFEU). The SEA also increased the power of the European Parliament, creating more opportunities for mobilization on the part of citizens and other private actors, thus amplifying the impact of Article 118a, because it was subject to the new 'cooperation procedure'. Article 118a was a significant shift in primary law because it gave the EU competence to pursue harmonization of occupational health and safety. By creating minimum standards, Article 118a would help to deter social dumping in the single market. The member states were free to adopt and/or maintain higher standards. This meant that the status quo bias of EU social policy decision-making became somewhat less pronounced, while the lines of conflict concerning social policy became more pronounced because of enlargement (Leibfried, 2010). In the past, the unanimity rule meant that even if one member state opposed, legislation would fail. Under the new QVM rules, veto players became more visible and the basis of disagreement clearer. Leibfried (2010) observes that the expanded treaty base for occupational health and safety has not resulted in lowest common denominator policies, but rather an overall raising of standards.

2. The SEA strengthened the EU's commitment in the social field by adding a new Title V on 'Economic and social cohesion' to Part 3 of the Treaty of Rome. The new Article 130a strengthened the ESF (and the European Regional Development Fund) with the aim of reducing regional disparities and assisting less developed regions in the EC. This move was not innovative, however; it simply promised more resources to existing ESF programmes that co-financed member state schemes for worker retraining and relocation.

3. The SEA resurrected the social dialogue process. The new Article 118b (Article 156 TFEU) states that:

> the Commission shall endeavour to develop the dialogue between management and labour at European level which could, if the two sides consider it desirable, lead to relations based on agreement.

The Treaty of Rome included labour and management via the Economic and Social Committee, but its function was merely consultative. The 1974 SAP also had the goal of increasing the involvement of labour and management in workplace decision-making, but little had come of this. Tripartite conferences had been held since 1974 and were public-private forums for social policy issues (Falkner, 1998, p. 83). The European Trade Union Confederation (ETUC) was established in 1973, and the Council contributed to the establishment of the European Trade Union Institute shortly thereafter. Tripartite conferences were held six times between 1974 and 1978, but little came of them because of the inexperience of the ETUC and a lack of commitment on the part of the Union of Industrial and Employers' Confederations of Europe (UNICE; now known as BusinessEurope). The Delors Commission revived tripartite discussions in 1985, and Delors pressed for the inclusion of the social dialogue article in the SEA. It was hoped that European-level collective agreements could be the basis for EC legislation as the completion of the single market progressed (Falkner, 1998).

The relative paucity of new social policy provisions in the SEA led to calls for a more developed social dimension to the internal market, particularly from organized labour (Silvia, 1991). The Commission continued to press for a more active EC social policy, publishing several White Papers in 1988. In particular, Commission President Jacques Delors used the resources of his office to publically advocate for a social dimension to the internal market (Barnard, 2012). After the ratification of the SEA and the 1985 publication of the White Paper *Completing the Internal Market* (Commission, 1985), Delors announced the Commission's call for a social dimension to the single market.

The ETUC responded by drawing up a draft Community Charter on Social Rights in December 1988 in an attempt to influence EC actors, especially the Commission (Silvia, 1991). Employers were lukewarm about the proposal, preferring a non-binding charter. The Commission responded with a proposal for a non-binding 'solemn declaration'. The UK, however, refused to accept even a non-binding charter, even after a weaker version was proposed in an ad hoc meeting of the Council of Ministers. In December 1989, the Community Charter of the Fundamental Social Rights for Workers was adopted by a declaration of all the member states, with the exception of the UK.

The charter was inspired by the 1961 Social Charter of the Council of Europe and ILO conventions. In a show of its increasing willingness to advocate for more far-reaching social provisions than the Council would accept, the European Parliament pushed for the charter to have binding legal effect. However, not only was the charter non-binding, it also attracted criticism from trade unions and other socially minded actors for its unambitious content. National unions and the ETUC nonetheless lobbied vigorously for the charter (Silvia, 1991). Barnard (2012) notes that early drafts of the charter referred to European *citizens* rather than workers, and its content adhered in many ways to the laissez-faire view set out in the Treaty of Rome concerning the relationship between economic integration and social affairs. As Barnard (2012, p. 13) puts it, the charter's content 'suggests that the concept of a European social area had been abandoned for the present; and that the social aspect of the internal market had been substituted in its place'.

Despite these setbacks, the Commission (1989) proposed the Social Charter action programme to implement it. Legislation following from this programme would be based on the EEC Treaty and thus binding on the UK. The action programme included 47 separate initiatives, but most of these were implemented via soft law, consultation and social dialogue. There were only 17 proposals for binding legislation (directives), and most of these dealt with fairly narrow aspects of occupational health and safety.

The Maastricht Treaty

The Maastricht Treaty (the Treaty on European Union, TEU), signed in February 1992 and entered into force in November 1993, was intended to advance the European integration project by expanding the EU's competences and introducing the pillar structure to accommodate the EU's new tasks. The centrepiece of the Maastricht Treaty was the commitment to Economic and Monetary Union (EMU). Plans for monetary union reignited debates about the necessity of expanding EU competence in social policy as a counterpart to deeper economic and monetary integration. After the member states failed to reach agreement on the social policy provisions of the treaty, they settled on a Protocol on Social Policy. The protocol stated that 11 member states (the UK was excluded) agreed to the provisions of the revised Social Chapter of the EEC Treaty. The new Social Chapter was based on the Agreement on

Social Policy negotiated by European-level employers and unions in October 1991. The protocol authorized the 11 member states to move forward in the social areas covered by the Agreement on Social Policy annexed to the protocol.

Negotiations on the social aspects of the treaty were difficult and took place in the context of limited progress concerning the implementation of the Social Charter action programme (Lange, 1993). The Commission's original proposals for the treaty's social provisions had to be toned down because of the opposition of several member states, especially the UK. The Social Policy Protocol was so controversial that the Netherlands, holding the presidency at the time, formulated a weaker version in order to gain British acceptance. This failed, and the final version of the Social Policy Protocol bears more resemblance to the Commission's original proposal. At the same time, Spain (a member of the EU since 1986) campaigned for a greater role for the EU in terms of redistribution from richer to poorer member states. Thus, the issue of social policy was linked to discussions about territorial redistribution in the EU.

The Agreement on Social Policy originated in negotiations among European-level union and employer organizations (ETUC, CEEP and UNICE) during the intergovernmental conference in December 1991. Prior to this, European-level employer organizations had been unenthusiastic about concluding European-level collective agreements, but their negotiating position changed, given the near certainty that new social policy provisions would be added to the treaty (Falkner, 1996). The Commission encouraged the European social partners (ETUC, CEEP and UNICE) to formulate an agreement concerning the role of the social partners in European social policy-making. This was a major step forward for euro-corporatism, because the existing institution for social partner involvement in policy-making, the Economic and Social Committee, was weak and only played a consultative role.

The Maastricht Treaty thus expanded the EU's competences and involvement in social policy in two ways: it expanded the EU's social policy remit, and included the Social Policy Protocol and Agreement on Social Policy – together referred to as the Social Chapter. The treaty's text was modified to include the goal of ensuring a high level of social protection, in addition to the existing goal of working to raise living standards. The ESF gained new competences, and a section on education and vocational training was added to the treaty. The protocol went beyond the charter adopted as a solemn declaration in 1989 by identifying a larger role for management and labour and extending QMV to several areas – working conditions, equal opportunities for men and women, worker consultation and right to information, and the labour market integration of groups excluded from the labour market. Wages, the right to strike, and the right of association were not addressed by the protocol. The protocol thus creates opportunities for harmonizing minimum standards of employment.

The protocol expands the policy-making influence of labour and employers at EU level. Article 3 requires the Commission to 'consult management and labour on the possible direction of community action'. The social partners must also be consulted on legislative proposals. Most important, employers and unions may jointly formulate a proposal for EU action. The member states are also permitted to allow employers and unions to implement union directives if they jointly request this. These provisions go a long way towards establishing corporatist policy practices at EU level (Lange, 1993; Falkner, 1998). The Val Duchesse talks on these issues began in 1985, and were the precursor to social dialogue in the Social Policy Protocol. On 31 October 1991, the social partners agreed on what became Articles 3 and 4 of the Social Policy Agreement (now Articles 154 and 155 TFEU).

The Social Policy Protocol was the basis for four directives in the following areas:

1. the introduction of a European Works Council (Directive 94/45)
2. a framework agreement on parental leave (Directive 96/34)
3. gender discrimination (Directive 97/80)
4. the framework agreement on part-time work (Directive 97/81).

Lange (1993) argued that the Social Policy Protocol does not necessarily reflect a commitment to the expansion of EU competence in social policy, but is the result of member state priorities in other areas. Indeed, the agreement of 11 of the 12 member states to the protocol is surprising, given that any member state could have vetoed it, or joined with the UK in opposing it. Although not radical, the Social Policy Protocol does increase the cost of doing business for some firms in some member states. In particular, it was not clear that the less developed member states (Portugal, Greece, Ireland and Spain) would benefit from the protocol. Lange (1993, p. 27) called the protocol negotiations a 'sideshow to the EMU negotiation'.

In the years immediately following the entry into force of the Maastricht Treaty, the Commission tried to capitalize on its limited social policy successes in the context of plans for EMU. The 1993 White Paper *Growth, Competitiveness, Employment* (Commission, 1993) adopted an integrated perspective, emphasizing the need for the EU to pursue policies that not only promoted economic growth, but also employment. The White Paper marked the first time there was any sort of concerted attempt at EU level to think about the EU's role in promoting employment. Indeed, the White Paper proposed a new sustainable developmental model for the EU – one that fostered economic growth and employment. In particular, the White Paper emphasized the need for more training, more flexible labour markets, and selective reductions in non-wage labour costs. The 1994 White Paper *European Social Policy* (Commission, 1994a) set out the main principles of EU social policy for the period 1995–99 and was intended to complement the *Growth, Competitiveness, Employment* White Paper. Both documents stressed the interdependence of economic and social progress and called for a more 'active' EU policy stance concerning social policy and efforts to reduce unemployment. This reorientation in EU social policy continues to shape EU policies concerning social protection, employment and social inclusion (Barnard, 2012).

The Treaty of Amsterdam

The Treaty of Amsterdam, signed in October 1997, entered into force in May 1999. The Maastricht Treaty had left several issues unresolved, and an Intergovernmental Conference (IGC) was held in 1996 to start the treaty revision process. The election of a Labour government in the UK in May 1997 removed an important obstacle to progress on the EU's social policy remit, and the UK quickly ratified the Social Charter. The agenda for treaty revision emphasized bringing the EU closer to European citizens, improving the transparency and democracy of EU decision-making, and preparing for Eastern enlargement.

With the UK no longer blocking new social policy initiatives, the Treaty of Amsterdam incorporated the Agreement on Social Policy into the text of the treaty in a new section, 'The Union and the Citizen'. The revised treaty articles modified the Maastricht Agreement on Social Policy in several ways:

- The European Parliament's role in legislative decision-making was strengthened. The new Article 137 EC (Article 153 TFEU) replaced the cooperation procedure with the co-decision procedure under QMV. It also introduced co-decision and QVM for the exchange of information and best practices in the field of social inclusion.
- The new Article 141 EC (ex Article 119, Article 153 TFEU) expanded EU competence in the field of equal opportunities.
- The new Article 6A EC (Article 19 TFEU) incorporated non-discrimination (based on sex, ethnicity, religion, disability, age and sexual orientation) into the treaty, allowing the Council to adopt measures (by unanimity, after consulting the Parliament) against discrimination.
- Article 117 EC (Article 151 TFEU) strengthened the status of fundamental rights by referring to the European Social Charter of Turin and the Community Charter of the Fundamental Social Rights of Workers.
- The treaty also introduced co-decision to decisions taken under unanimity for the ESF, the free movement of citizens, and social security for migrant workers.

Besides these modest advances, the Treaty of Amsterdam promoted the EU's role in other areas of social policy. Article 2 EC (Article 9 TFEU) now includes the promotion of 'a high level of employment and of social protection' as a task of the EU, and a separate title on employment was included in the treaty (see Chapter 5). Employment policy was not originally on the agenda of the IGC that negotiated the treaty, but took on more importance as a transnational coalition called more attention to the need for the EU to do more to balance the effects of EMU (Johansson, 1999). The confluence of two factors was decisive for elevating the status of employment in the IGC negotiations: unemployment remained stubbornly high in most member states, and social democratic governments were in power in 13 of the 15 member states. Thus, the heads of government negotiating the treaty had every reason to respond to calls for EU policies to balance the effects of EMU. As Goetschy and Pochet (1997, p. 608) put it: 'the inclusion of employment in the objectives of the Treaty of Amsterdam was intended to bring about a new equilibrium between monetary union and employment'.

The employment title was a compromise, in the sense that the EU would now promote, as the Treaty of Amsterdam states: the 'coordination between employment policies of the member states with a view to enhancing their effectiveness by developing a coordinated strategy for employment' (Article 3 EC). Moreover, the goal of a 'high degree of competitiveness' was inserted into the treaty to balance the emphasis on employment (Goetschy and Pochet, 1997). The new employment policy would not require new financial resources, and as the treaty states: 'the competences of the member states shall be respected' (Article 127 EC). This social policy innovation is thus a compromise between member state autonomy and union competence. While the EU began to play a more important role in supporting the coordination of national employment policies, the member states appeared to remain more or less in control.

The Treaty of Nice

Despite the advances of the Amsterdam Treaty, it left open important issues related to the balance between EU institutions that previous treaty revisions had not settled (Sbragia, 2002). The planned enlargement of the EU by at least 10 states, scheduled for 2004, was the backdrop to the negotiations for the Treaty of Nice in late 2000 (it was officially signed in February 2001, and entered into force in February 2003). Because it was largely concerned with reforming EU decision-making institutions, the Nice Treaty largely maintained the social policy status quo, except in two areas:

1. It established the Social Protection Committee (Article 144 EC, Article 160 TFEU), which had been informally established at the Lisbon European Council in 2000.
2. The Council could now decide by unanimity to use co-decision in social fields governed by unanimity (Article 42 EC, Article 48 TFEU). This did not apply to social security.

The Constitutional Treaty

The Nice Treaty provided only a partial institutional solution to the governance challenges facing the EU. Indeed, there was considerable support for a more ambitious reform agenda: the adoption of a constitution to replace the treaties. The European Council, meeting in Laeken, adopted a Declaration on the Future of the

European Union, or Laeken Declaration, on 15 December 2001, committing the EU to becoming more democratic, transparent and effective. Since the 1985 SEA, there had been three treaty reforms (Maastricht, Amsterdam and Nice), and EU actors wanted to use the Constitutional Treaty to do several things:

- consolidate the treaties
- clarify the fundamental rights and duties of EU citizens
- delineate the legal relationship between the member states and the EU
- reform the institutional architecture of the EU to meet the challenges of enlargement.

The Convention on the Future of Europe, led by Valéry Giscard d'Éstaing, departed from previous treaty negotiations by including representatives of the European Parliament, national governments and other stakeholders and civil society groups. The Treaty establishing a Constitution for Europe (known as the Constitutional Treaty) was signed in October 2004, and later ratified by 18 member states. However, the French and Dutch rejection of the treaty in referendums in May/June 2005 brought the ratification process to an end, dealing a fatal blow to the treaty (see Craig, 2010).

The Treaty of Lisbon

The European Council regrouped and converged around a less ambitious treaty in 2006 and 2007. The Lisbon Treaty was signed in December 2007 and entered into force in December 2009. It amends the existing treaties, rather than replacing them as the Constitutional Treaty would have done. The Lisbon Treaty pursued the goal of simplification: the EC Treaty was reconstituted as the Treaty on the Functioning of the European Union (TFEU), while the TEU remained. The EU also acquired a single legal personality. The European Parliament gained more power, and co-decision became the ordinary legislative procedure.

There were few explicit social policy innovations in the Lisbon Treaty, as it simply amends the TEU and EC Treaty. However, the status of the Community Charter of the Fundamental Social Rights of Workers remains ambiguous. The Lisbon Treaty refers to the charter, but it is not included in the treaty, even as an annex or protocol. In addition, several member states secured opt-outs: the UK, Poland and the Czech Republic. The UK feared the legal extension of rights, Poland wanted to retain control over family and morality issues (abortion), and the Czech Republic wanted to avoid German property claims resulting from the Second World War.

The Lisbon and Europe 2020 growth strategies

The Amsterdam Treaty negotiations demonstrated the tensions concerning the appropriate balance between growth, competitiveness and employment. Despite the completion of the internal market, the beginning of the new millennium was marked by the widespread perception among many member states and EU officials that the EU was lagging behind other parts of the world, especially the US, economically and technologically. This perception was the backdrop to the decision taken at the Lisbon European Council meeting in March 2000 to adopt a strategy to meet the challenges posed by globalization and create a new knowledge-driven economy. The new growth strategy – the Lisbon Strategy – was aimed at making the EU the most competitive economy in the world by 2010. The centrepiece of the Lisbon Strategy was the use of soft law – embodied by the OMC – rather than hard law, to pursue a modernization agenda.

As Annesley (2007) argues, Lisbon reopened debates about the role and status of a European social model (ESM). The Lisbon Strategy envisaged the modernization of the ESM by shifting emphasis from protecting and expanding the rights of those already employed, to an activation agenda focused on creating employment. According to Annesley, the 'emerging' ESM is an adult worker model approach to social provision that focuses on EU citizens as workers. In contrast to previous EU policy promoting paid employment, the Lisbon Strategy explicitly supports the activation of groups that were often inactive in many member states, especially older workers, women and the disabled. Thus, the Lisbon Strategy actively pushes all adults to enter paid employment, with reformed social protection schemes supporting this goal.

The launch of the Lisbon Strategy marks the first time that the EU formulated an integrated, long-term policy for social and economic (as well as environmental) modernization. Social Action Programmes (SAPs) and Social Policy Agendas (SPAs) have been a mainstay of EU social policy since the first SAP in 1974. With

Lisbon, however, the EU now had an overarching growth and modernization strategy to guide policy-making, and the SAPs/SPAs would now be formulated to serve the Lisbon Strategy. The mid-term evaluation of the Lisbon Strategy in 2005, however, quickly revealed the weaknesses of the new growth strategy and the soft law instruments for pursuing it (see Chapter 5). Not only were the Lisbon goals too ambitious, but the absence of sanctions and binding instruments meant that soft coordination was slow to show results. Despite slow progress in achieving the Lisbon goals, the strategy was revised and relaunched in 2005 and replaced by a new growth strategy, Europe 2020, in March 2010.

Europe 2020, the new growth strategy, is designed to overcome Lisbon's weaknesses by creating stronger governance structures that support simpler goals ('smart' growth, 'sustainable' growth and 'inclusive' growth). The governance architecture of Europe 2020 is complex, although it is based on soft governance instruments similar to those of the Lisbon Strategy. Like Lisbon, Europe 2020 integrates social, economic and employment goals into one strategy; the member states then formulate National Reform Programmes annually that lay out national strategies for achieving Europe 2020 goals and targets (see Figure 3.1). As the next section discusses, the economic crisis and sovereign debt crisis have overwhelmed the new strategy and prompted changes in its governance structure.

Economic crisis and the EU's social dimension

The global economic crisis that began in October 2008 caused a rapid deterioration of labour markets and economic conditions in most member states, threw the EU into a protracted sovereign debt crisis, and prompted a radical shift in EU policies concerning economic governance. This section considers these events in some detail, because the debt crisis has led to radical austerity measures in the EU's weaker economies and triggered the reform of the EU's economic governance architecture. Thus, the weaker economies have drastically curtailed social policies, and the EU now has unprecedented influence over the fiscal policies of eurozone members via the Fiscal Compact, which entered into force on 1 January 2013.

Between 2007 and 2012, unemployment rose dramatically in many member states, especially Greece and Ireland (see Figure 3.2). Economic growth slowed or turned negative in many member states, causing a dramatic deterioration in government budget

Figure 3.1 *The Europe 2020 strategy*

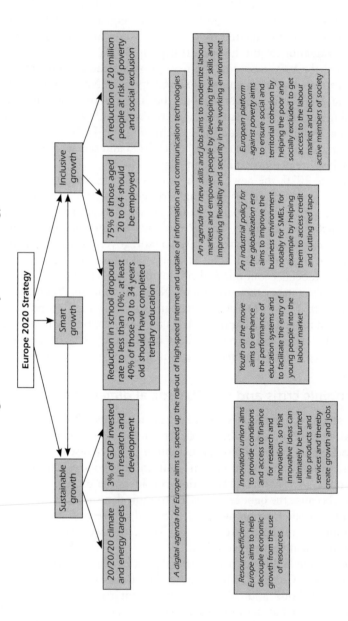

Source: Adapted from Commission (2013) *Europe 2020: Europe's Growth Strategy* (Luxembourg: Publications Office of the European Union)

balance (see Figure 3.4 below). The natural response for most, if not all, member states was to rely on the automatic stabilizers built into their own welfare states. These responses, however, unfolded within the constraints of monetary union, and the member states with the weakest eurozone economies had a vastly reduced set of policy tools to help them overcome the crisis. EMU ruled out interest rate cuts and devaluation, and the weaker economies soon faced rapidly growing borrowing costs.

Thus, the economic crisis had turned into a sovereign debt crisis in the eurozone by 2010. Greece, Ireland, Portugal and Spain were particularly hard hit. The EU response has been analysed well by others (see, for example, Armingeon and Baccaro, 2011), so the present discussion focuses on the EU's policies for assisting weak economies and moves towards fiscal union. Both have important implications for the EU's involvement in the social field.

Four eurozone countries have received EU assistance since 2010: Greece (€110 in May 2010 and €130 billion in February 2012), Ireland (November 2010), Portugal (€78 billion in May 2011) and Cyprus. The Greek bailout was cobbled together between the EU and the International Monetary Fund (IMF) and became the basis for a more formal cooperative arrangement between the European Commission, the European Central Bank and the IMF – the so-called 'troika'. The first Greek bailout prompted German Chancellor Merkel and French President Sarkozy to take the lead in establishing more formal EU institutions to respond to growing turbulence in financial markets and threats to the stability of the euro. The principal function of these new arrangements was to provide loans to the member states experiencing difficulty meeting their borrowing costs.

The first Greek assistance package in spring 2010 was the basis for the first joint rescue efforts, which the Council based on the emergency clauses in the Lisbon Treaty (Article 122(2) TFEU). These collective efforts required the establishment of financial arrangements to manage assistance to the member states. The process of setting up these institutions has been laborious and conflictual because of the vast sums involved and the growing differences between the more fiscally stable northern member states, exemplified by Germany, Finland and the Netherlands, and the financially weaker member states about how the costs of financial assistance would be distributed among the member states. The Council established the first of the new cluster of financial institutions, the European Financial Stabilisation Mechanism (EFSM) (Council Regulation 407/2010),

Figure 3.2 *Unemployment rates, 2007 and 2012*

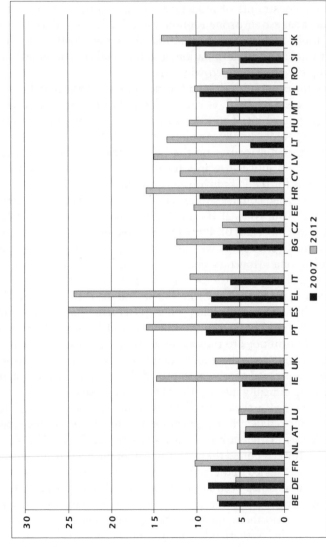

Source: Adapted from Commission (2013) *Europe 2020: Europe's Growth Strategy* (Luxembourg: Publications Office of the European Union)

with €60 billion in capital in 2010. The Council followed this in 2011 with the establishment of the European Financial Stability Facility (EFSF). The EFSF is a Special Purpose Facility covered by Luxembourg law, with €440 billion in capital. A more permanent financial assistance facility, the ESM (European Stability Mechanism) was established in late September 2012 via an intergovernmental treaty signed by the 17 members of the eurozone in February 2012. The ESM replaces the EFSF: the EFSF will be phased out after its existing loan programmes are completed. The EFSM continues to provide financial assistance to all EU members. The EU budget is collateral for ESFM borrowing on financial markets (up to €60 billion) for the purpose of providing financial assistance.

The EU's financial assistance to the member states, managed by the troika, has been accompanied by demands for tough economic reforms as a condition for assistance. Indeed, the reforms implemented by Greece, Ireland, Portugal and Cyprus have included austerity measures that cut to the heart of national welfare states (Spain required financial assistance to bail out its banks, so it was not subject to the same kinds of austerity requirements as the other governments receiving assistance). For example, the first Greek bailout included public sector wage freezes, cancellation of wage supplements, a three-year pension freeze, an increase in the retirement age, partial liberalization of dismissal regulations, and increases in indirect taxes (Armingeon and Baccaro, 2011).

The sovereign debt crisis exposed the weaknesses of monetary union and prompted negotiations about closer coordination and monitoring of national fiscal policies. Early 2011 saw the kick-off of the new European Semester, which gives the EU stronger oversight concerning national budgets and National Reform Programmes (Figure 3.3). The European Semester was adopted by the Council in 2010 to streamline and improve the coordination of fiscal and employment policy as part of the governance architecture of Europe 2020. The semester process aims to strengthen fiscal policy coordination by empowering the Commission to evaluate fiscal policy and reform agendas before national budget cycles begin. The first recommendations, released in January 2011, emphasized austerity: reduced spending, higher retirement ages and increased taxes. The recommendations were announced as part of the Annual Growth Survey, the first step in the European Semester (Figure 3.3).

The economic and financial crisis created the momentum for the member states to take concrete steps towards fiscal union. In

Figure 3.3 *The European semester*

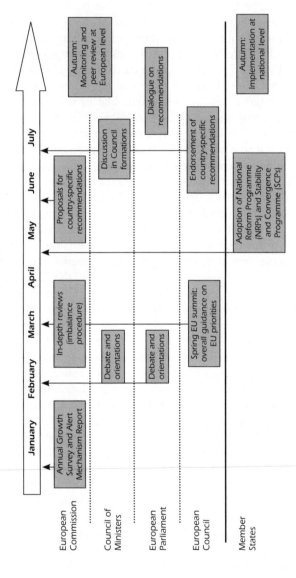

	January	February	March	April	May	June	July	
European Commission	Annual Growth Survey and Alert Mechanism Report		In-depth reviews (imbalance procedure)		Proposals for country-specific recommendations			Autumn: Monitoring and peer review at European level
Council of Ministers		Debate and orientations				Discussion in Council formations		
European Parliament		Debate and orientations					Dialogue on recommendations	
European Council			Spring EU summit: overall guidance on EU priorities			Endorsement of country-specific recommendations		
Member States					Adoption of National Reform Programme (NRPs) and Stability and Convergence Programme (SCPs)			Autumn: Implementation at national level

Source: Data compiled from www.epp.eurostat.ec.europa.eu (2007, 2012)
Note: Unemployment is defined as the share of the labour force aged 15–74 seeking work

December 2011, the member states decided that the economic governance procedures in Europe 2020 were insufficient for dealing with the ongoing crisis, and they called for even stronger fiscal coordination and control to stabilize the eurozone. The 1997 Stability and Growth Pact (SGP) has been reformed via the six pack of legislation (five regulations and one directive), proposed in September 2010, and in force since December 2011. The six pack includes a new procedure for macroeconomic monitoring – the macroeconomic imbalance procedure. This resulted in the Fiscal Compact (formally the Treaty on Stability, Coordination and Governance in the Economic and Monetary Union), which entered into force on 1 January 2013. The new rules require budgets to be balanced or in surplus (the structural deficit may not be greater than 0.5% of GDP). Deficits must also conform to country-specific benchmarks established as part of the preventive arm of the SGP.

The European Semester is a key element of fiscal coordination and surveillance: government progress towards specified goals is evaluated in the European Semester process. The new rules also include an 'automatic correction mechanism' that is triggered if a member state does not meet the balanced budget requirement. The member states are required to incorporate these new rules into their national legal frameworks. The excessive deficit procedure has also been made more stringent. Finally, the two pack (two regulations; in force since May 2013) refers to regulations to improve economic monitoring and coordination in the eurozone. These require eurozone countries to submit their draft budgets to the Commission in mid-October, prior to the national budget process. The Commission evaluates the draft budgets to see whether they are in line with budget commitments.

The EU's vastly strengthened tools for economic governance are likely to seriously constrain social policy initiatives in the member states for the immediate future. The SGP's reference values for public finances (budget deficit not more than 3% of GDP, accumulated public debt not more than 60% of GDP) will be enforced much more strictly than in the past, in a period in which many member state economies are still feeling the devastating negative effects of the crisis. Figure 3.4 shows member state budget deficits in 2007 and 2012. The effects of the crisis are very visible: a minority of member states recorded a smaller budget deficit in 2012 compared to 2007, and many countries went from surplus to deficit. Stronger economic governance means that social policy goals are now clearly subordinate to the principles of the SGP.

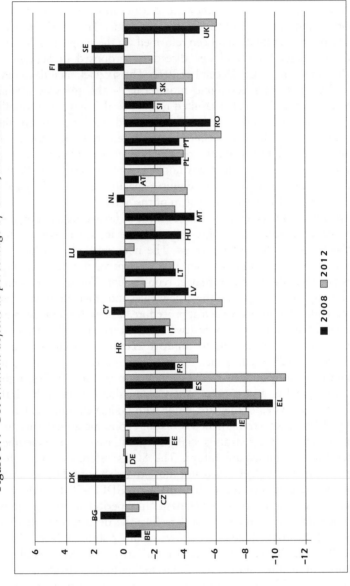

Figure 3.4 Government deficits as percentage of GDP, 2007 and 2012

Source: Data compiled from www.epp.eurostat.ec.europa.eu (2007, 2012)

Conclusion

The goal of this chapter has been to chart the development of EU involvement in the social field. As Chapter 1 stresses, a common interventionist social policy has never been a goal of the European integration process, largely because the member states have not been willing to surrender their social policy-making autonomy. Instead, the tension between the EU's economic and social goals has been a key dimension of the development of the EU's social role. The EU was conceived as an economic union, and it is this market-making function that continues to shape social policy-making in the EU. Certainly, the founding treaties acknowledged that economic change causes social dislocation, and they provided for limited EU involvement in the social field (via the ESF, for example). Over time, the EU has acquired considerable social policy competences. Indeed, the EU has social policy competences that the founding statesmen probably never dreamed possible. However, the sovereign debt crisis and the economic crisis more generally have led to an even stronger emphasis on the subordination of social policy to the goals of economic integration. The EU's reform of the governance structure of the SGP mean a substantial downgrading of social policy goals in the member states and at EU level. The Fiscal Compact requires the costs of social protection to be compatible with strict budget discipline as set out in the SGP. Thus, many member states will face strong pressure, backed by strong EU sanctions, to undertake reforms that reduce the costs of social protection.

The heterogeneity of social policy institutions is an important driver of EU social policy-making. Scharpf (2002) argues that the early years of the EU were the most hospitable to social policy harmonization because the original six member states all had conservative welfare states. This institutional similarity of welfare regimes would have made it easier to harmonize core social policies like pensions, unemployment insurance and health care. The central idea here is that it is easier to harmonize similar institutions than it is to harmonize heterogeneous institutions. As discussed in Chapters 1 and 2, social harmonization was a road not taken, largely because of German and Dutch resistance, and the formative period of EU social policy development was marked by efforts to implement the provisions of the Rome Treaty that dealt with labour mobility and equal pay. Successive enlargements have increased social policy heterogeneity among the member states; even in the context of QMV and expanded EU social policy competences, this heterogeneity hampers large-scale social policy initiatives based on hard law.

Barnard (2012) argues that the Amsterdam Treaty and the Lisbon and Europe 2020 strategies mark a 'sea change' in EU social policy because they shift the centre of gravity of EU social policy from protecting worker rights to fighting unemployment. This shift in policy priorities also means more use of soft law instruments such as the OMC and less reliance of hard law. As subsequent chapters show, the increased use of soft law, especially in the field of employment, has produced mixed results thus far, so it is not clear that this reorientation of policy priorities (from 'rights' to 'employment promotion') will deliver improvements in social conditions.

Chapter 4

Social Security and Pensions

Social security and pensions intersect with the European integration process in several ways:

1. They are core aspects of employment and thus deeply implicated in the internal market for labour. This means that EU laws concerning labour mobility and the equal treatment of men and women in employment are important areas of EU social policy legislation.
2. Privately organized occupational pension funds are increasingly part of a single market for financial services. Although the funded occupational pension sector is small relative to public schemes in most member states, it is growing in importance, and in several member states occupational pension assets exceed 50% of GDP.
3. The financial costs associated with public pension schemes – and the threat these costs purportedly pose to public budgets and EMU – has prompted the EU to use soft law to promote pension reform in the member states, largely via the open method of coordination (OMC).

This chapter considers the impact of these areas of EU legislative activity on social security and pension policy-making at the supranational level and in the member states. The chapter analyses EU policies that affect statutory social security as well as occupational schemes, particularly occupational pensions. The bulk of the chapter analyses the impact of 'hard law' on statutory and occupational social security, but it also includes a discussion of the recent introduction of the OMC and the role of 'soft law' in the process of reforming public pensions and other types of social security. Beginning in the 1990s, the Commission and Council have pushed for the modernization of social protection in response to demographic and economic shifts. Since the introduction of the Lisbon Strategy in 2000, EU social policy-making increasingly relies on 'new governance' tools designed to facilitate and encourage social policy reforms in the member states, not least the reform of public pensions.

The insurance of employment-related risks has important implications for the EU's guarantee of free movement because of the diversity of social security provision in EU member states. If free movement is to live up to its promise, workers and their families must be able to live and work in other EU countries without suffering disadvantage in terms of their social security coverage. This means that individuals must be able to take their employment-related benefits with them if they move to another member state, and they must be treated the same as nationals in access to social security. To promote free movement, the EU has adopted a number of key regulations and directives to ensure the coordination of social security benefits when an individual lives and works in more than one member state.

Social security is also inextricably linked to EU legal provisions concerning equality between men and women. Article 157 TFEU's (ex Article 141 EC) guarantee of equal pay between men and women has far-reaching implications for social security and pensions because social security benefits and occupationally based fringe benefits are based on wages. Indeed, social security, whether statutory or occupational, is a key component of the employment contract. Workers not only earn wages, they also earn entitlement to insurance for periods of unemployment, sickness, disability, parenthood and retirement. ECJ interpretations of primary legislation and subsequent EU legislation require the member states to ensure that men and women are paid equal wages for the same jobs, and they also have to guarantee that the social security benefits and occupational social provisions based on these wages are the same for men and women.

Governments increasingly share the function of providing social security with private actors. Occupational social policy has always been part of the social protection packages of most European workers, with occupational schemes usually supplementing state-provided social security. Indeed, the importance of occupational social security has increased since the EU was founded in 1957, especially in the field of pensions. While state-provided social security dominates the coverage of unemployment, sickness and disability, the role of occupational pension schemes in overall retirement provision has increased. EU legislation targets two aspects of occupational pension provision: the rules governing the operation of pension funds (institutions for occupational retirement provision, IORPs) and the portability of occupational pension rights. These legislative initiatives are based on primary law concerning the internal market. This chapter also discusses the impact of European legislation on privately organized social security in the member states.

Despite the very real influence of EU legislation on social security in the member states, we cannot speak of a common EU social security regime. EU legislation leaves national social security schemes in place; it only requires member states to treat nationals from other member states the same as their own nationals, and it requires member states to ensure the equal treatment of men and women in their social security schemes. Thus, social security coordination is a classic case of negative integration and the use of regulatory instruments to achieve social and economic goals. In contrast, EU action in the area of gender equality has been much more active. We can speak of an equality regime at EU level (von Wahl, 2006), and it has had a substantial impact on the basis for entitlement in the member states' social security schemes.

In contrast to the EU's efforts to guarantee labour mobility and gender equality by the use of hard law, the EU's recent efforts to promote the modernization of social protection represent a much more active policy orientation that relies on soft law. Here, the goal is not to ensure labour mobility and the equal treatment of men and women, but to reform social protection, especially pension policy, so that it is financially and demographically sustainable and promotes social inclusion.

The chapter begins with a conceptual discussion of social security and its organization. Section two discusses free movement. Section three analyses gender equality law. Sections four and five analyse pensions, in terms of creating a single market for supplementary pensions via hard law and the OMC process.

What is social insurance?

'Social security' is an umbrella term that includes social policies that provide income protection for individuals who leave the labour market temporarily or permanently because of sickness, unemployment, disability, pregnancy, care obligations, or old age. Social security schemes can be financed by earnings-related contributions paid by employers, employees (or both), or by general tax revenues.

Benefits are usually based on the length of insurance (either residence or employment) and/or contributions, as well as on previous income from employment. For some minimum income schemes, including pensions, benefits may be flat rate. As noted, governments are not the only actors in the business of social insurance: schemes may be run by the state, or organized as part of the employment contract at the firm or sectorial level.

Based on these basic attributes, the social policy literature typically distinguishes social security schemes along two dimensions: public versus private provision and flat-rate versus earnings-related benefits. To make things slightly more complicated, benefits may also be based on individual entitlement or family status. EU law affects all these aspects of social security to varying degrees. Table 4.1 captures these two dimensions, which result in four types:

1. Beveridgean social insurance (top-left quadrant) combines state sponsorship and flat-rate benefits, usually granted on the basis of residence. Flat-rate basic pensions in the UK, the Netherlands and the Nordic countries are clear examples.
2. Company-based and sectorial schemes (top-right quadrant) combine private sponsorship and flat-rate benefits. This type of benefit is possible in theory but there are few real-world examples; a good example is flat-rate benefits for work-related risks like old age and unemployment.
3. Bismarckian social insurance (bottom-left quadrant) is best represented by the public pension schemes in Germany, France and Italy. Public schemes cover most workers, benefits are based on previous earnings, and financing is based on wage-related contributions usually shared between employers and employees.
4. In company-based and sectorial social security (bottom-right quadrant), employers and groups of employers organized by sector provide employment-based social security, often as part of collective agreements. The large Dutch, Danish, Irish and UK occupational pension sectors are key examples.

All four types of social security are subject to EU law concerning free movement. Indeed, the Beveridgean countries have modified their pension schemes to prevent 'welfare tourism'. The citizenship pensions in Denmark, Finland and Sweden were replaced with residence-based pensions when these countries became EU members. All other publically organized social security schemes are subject to

Table 4.1 *Types of social security schemes*

	Public	Private
Flat rate	Beveridgean social insurance	Company and sectorial benefits
Earnings related	Bismarckian social insurance	Company and sectorial social security

EU rules concerning the coordination and portability of benefits, and EU legislation in this area constituted the earliest intervention into the sphere of social policy. Even privately provided social security is subject to EU law concerning free movement. Similarly, the institutionalization of EU law concerning equal pay has had far-reaching effects on national social security schemes. As the chapter shows, the member states sometimes adopted substantial changes in their social security legislation in order to comply with EU equality law. The EU's ongoing agenda for modernizing social protection has already started to affect the balance between public and private forms of social security. Because of the rising costs of social security, especially pensions, EU actors have turned to soft law, particularly the OMC, to push the member states to reform their public pension systems. These reform processes in the member states have usually included explicit attempts to increase the role of private social provision in order to compensate for reductions in public provision. This applies most directly to public pensions. Finally, the EU's efforts to construct a single market for financial services has been the basis for modest legislation affecting funded occupational pensions.

Free movement and the coordination of social security

The coordination of the social security provisions of migrant workers has been an important goal since the founding of the EU. As Chapter 1 stresses, the Treaty of Rome conceived of social policy as a by-product of economic integration, thus obviating the need for any strong role for European institutions in social policy. And as Chapter 2 emphasizes, the diversity of social policy institutions in the member states poses a challenge for positive integration because the member states are not likely to relinquish social policy-making authority to EU institutions. Given these constraints, the creation of a European market that included mobile workers required some way of allowing an individual from one member state to work in another one without giving up social security rights. Moreover, labour mobility within the EU required some mechanism through which individuals could aggregate social security rights earned in one or more member states during their working life. The most obvious example of this is pensions. An EU citizen might work in one or several member states before retiring. For labour mobility to mean anything, the EU citizen would need to be able to accumulate pension rights in more than one member state, and they would need to be able to draw pension benefits in any member state regardless of where those pension rights were earned. EU regulations concerning the coordination of social security are designed to solve these problems.

Primary legislation

The formative period of the EU focused on the construction of a common market, including the free movement of labour. The treaties declared that the removal of obstacles to free movement was necessary for achieving the overarching goals of the EU, originally formulated as including

> a harmonious development of economic activities, a continuous and balanced expansion, an increased stability, an accelerated raising of the standard of living, and closer relations between its member states. (Article 2 EEC)

Free movement thus acquired a status equal to key policies like the Common Agricultural Policy, the elimination of customs duties between the member states, and the creation of the European Social Fund. Article 7 EEC prohibited discrimination on the grounds of nationality for the activities encompassed by the treaty, and it empowered the Council to adopt relevant rules on the basis of QMV.

During the EU's founding years, the chief advocate of free movement was Italy, because it was the only member state that faced persistent unemployment at the time. Free movement would mean that Italian surplus labour could be redeployed in more prosperous member states. The other five member states had no strong preference concerning labour mobility, although Germany was starting to experience labour shortages (Collins, 1975; Hantrais, 2007) and would soon become one of the chief destinations of Italian workers within the newly formed EC. The guarantee of free movement of labour was thus intended to solve two problems at the same time, and contribute to the construction of the common market.

Like other elements of the common market, free movement of workers was phased in gradually after the Treaty of Rome took effect. Four specific articles (Articles 48–51 EEC, Articles 45–48 TFEU) provide content to the principles laid out in Articles 3 and 7 EEC:

- Article 48 EEC (Article 45 TFEU) guarantees non-nationals the same rights as nationals regarding 'employment, remuneration and other working conditions', including the right to seek and accept employment in any member state, the right to reside in the member state where one is employed, and to continue living there (subject to some limitations) after the termination of employment.
- Article 49 EEC (Article 46 TFEU) gave the Council the right to adopt legislation based on Commission proposals and the advice of the Economic and Social Committee.
- Article 50 EEC (Article 47 TFEU) established an exchange programme for young workers.
- Article 51 EEC (Article 48 TFEU) empowered the Council to adopt legislation based on unanimity to make social security schemes compatible with free movement. This included guarantees that mobile workers would be covered by social security schemes in other member states, mobile workers' right to accumulate benefits in all member states, and their right to draw benefits in any member state.

In sum, the Treaty of Rome emphasized three issues central to free movement and social security:

1. the right of workers to take up employment anywhere in the EC on terms equal to nationals
2. the right of workers to aggregate social security benefits earned in any member state
3. the right of workers to receive benefits anywhere in the EC.

The directives and regulations adopted in the first two decades of the EC provided content to these principles (see next section). Each of the subsequent treaty revisions reiterated and strengthened the core provisions described above.

Revisions of the Treaty of Rome have strengthened the principle of free movement (Hantrais, 2007). The Single European Act (SEA), however, changed little in the existing primary legislation on social security, despite its stated goal of removing the remaining barriers to free movement. Certainly, the SEA extended QMV to many areas related to the internal market, including workplace health and safety (see Chapter 8), but the free movement of persons was specifically excluded (Barnard, 2006; Hantrais, 2007). Despite this barrier, the SEA introduced new procedures (Articles 62, 67, 251 EC) for side-stepping unanimity (Hantrais, 2007).

The Community Charter of the Fundamental Social Rights of Workers adopted in 1989 confirms the principle of free movement (Articles 1–3). However, because of the resistance of the UK to the expansion of EU competences in social policy, the charter remained a declaratory document, so there was little concrete progress on expanding the free movement of labour. The sections of the charter dealing with social policy were placed in a Protocol and Agreement on Social Policy (also known as the Social Charter), which was appended to the Maastricht Treaty signed in 1992. Despite the UK's opposition, the charter was the basis for several legislative initiatives in the 1990s (see below; the rights outlined in the charter were incorporated into the Charter of Fundamental Rights of the European Union, which was incorporated into the 2009 Treaty of Lisbon).

Despite the setback concerning the Social Charter, the Maastricht Treaty gave free movement new momentum with the establishment of European citizenship (Article 20 TFEU). With the internal market nearly complete, the Maastricht Treaty focused on developing the political dimensions of European integration, including developing the social dimension and citizenship. Crucially, the establishment of European citizenship strengthened the status of mobile workers and their families and extended individual rights beyond the sphere of employment. EU citizens now gained the right to vote and compete for office in municipal elections and European Parliament elections. More importantly for present purposes, EU citizens now had the right to work and reside in any member state. The Treaty of Amsterdam amended the definition of European citizenship by defining it as a complement to, rather than a replacement of, national citizenship. The treaty also strengthened EU competences in combating non-discrimination on the basis of nationality, and it formally integrated the Agreement on Social Policy into the treaty. The 2001 Treaty of Nice introduced QMV for issues concerning European citizenship. The 2007 Treaty of Lisbon provides more rhetorical justification for the EU's social dimension but added few competences in the area of free movement.

In sum, the development of primary law has strengthened the principle of free movement beyond its initial, rather narrow definition. In the early years of the EU, workers could seek employment and live in other member states, with their families, under rather limited conditions. The introduction of European citizenship and the extension of the rights of mobile workers have meant a substantial expansion of the principle of free movement from one that applied only to the gainfully employed to one that includes the economically inactive. The next section details how secondary legislation and the jurisprudence of the ECJ have interpreted and often expanded these rights.

Secondary legislation

The story of free movement is one of the progressive erosion of member state control over the rules governing the residence and employment of nationals of other member states within their borders. Treaty amendments and especially ECJ rulings have broadened the scope of free movement, and the ECJ has played an important role in defining who qualifies as a worker for the purposes of free movement and the status of economically non-active persons such as former workers and job-seekers (Tomkin, 2009).

Article 51 EEC (Article 48 TFEU) provided the legal basis for legislation concerning the role of social security for free movement. Despite this seemingly firm treaty basis, the EU was slow to adopt legislation facilitating free movement (Geyer, 2000). Two regulations adopted in 1958 (Regulations 3/58 and 4/58; updated later by Regulations 1408/71 and 883/2004) were the first pieces of legislation to set out the rights of migrant workers (Martinsen, 2007). This legislation was among the earliest EU legislative interventions in the realm of social policy.

The 1960s was a period of consolidating and expanding EU legislation concerning free movement and national social security schemes:

- Regulation 15 of 16 August 1961 covered the mobility rights of workers, including the right of family members to join the employee in another member state, access to housing, and the integration of family members into the host member state (Collins, 1975).
- Regulation 38/1964 of 25 March 1964 was adopted in the second stage of the implementation of free movement and set out the conditions under which family members could join a worker in another member state.
- Regulation 1612/1968 (amended by Regulation 2434/92) of 15 October 1968 marked the end of the transitional phase and regulated the social and tax aspects of employment, as well as access to vocational training, in another member state. An important aspect of this legislation was Article 7(2) requiring the member states to grant migrant workers and their families the same social and tax advantages as nationals, including access to subordinate activities. Family members who were not EC nationals also enjoyed these rights. ECJ decisions have expanded the definition of social advantages to include some aspects of social assistance on the basis of Article 49 EEC (Article 46 TFEU).
- Directive 68/360/EEC of 15 October 1969 abolished restrictions on the movement and residence of workers and their families.
- Regulation 1251/70 of 29 June 1970 concerns a worker's right to stay in a member state after the termination of employment.

Thus, by 1970, the internal market for labour was more or less complete.

Despite early legislation on the rights of migrant workers, the member states were slow to adjust their national legal frameworks to the legal reality of free movement. Until 1968, EC nationals seeking residence in another member state in order to work were required to apply for residence (on the same terms as other non-citizens) according to national legislation, and this usually meant dealing with immigration authorities. The member states could and did refuse residence until European legislation made this impossible (Baldoni, 2003).

The ECJ has played a major role in interpreting the meaning of free movement of labour (Martinsen, 2007, 2011). After a series of ECJ decisions interpreting the meaning of treaty provisions and early regulations concerning free movement, the Council adopted Regulation 1408/71/EEC in 1971, supplemented by Regulation

574/72/EEC, which contained detailed implementation measures. Regulation 1408/71 and its successor are based on the following principles:

- *Equal treatment:* EU nationals (and citizens of Norway, Switzerland, Iceland and Lichtenstein) must be treated the same as nationals for the purposes of social security. Swiss nationals were covered under the EU-Swiss Agreement.
- *Aggregation:* Social security benefits are based on previous insurance periods in other member states.
- *Benefits may not overlap:* A worker is covered by only one social security system, and double contributions are not allowed.
- *Exportability:* Benefits are portable.

Regulation 1408/71 codified the most important elements of ECJ jurisprudence during the previous decade pertaining to free movement and remained the key legislative instrument concerning social security coordination until the European Parliament and Council adopted Regulation 883/2004. Regulation 883/2004 updated and modernized Regulation 1408/71 by expanding the scope of the regulation to all insured persons; previously, the rules applied only to those who were economically active and their families. Thus, under the new rules, students have a stronger position. A second innovation is the inclusion of additional social security benefits, such as pre-retirement benefits, under the rubric of social security provisions subject to EU law concerning free movement. Finally, the updated rules modify the provisions concerning unemployment. Unemployed individuals may now draw benefits for six instead of three months while they look for a job in another member state.

Directives adopted in the 1990s significantly expand the meaning of free movement to include categories of the economically inactive such as students and the unemployed. The directives allow these groups to reside in other member states if they have resources sufficient to guarantee that they will not become a burden on the host member state (Directives 90/364, 90/365, 90/366, 93/96 and 2004/38).

Legislative activity in the 2000s dramatically expanded the scope of free movement. Directive 2004/38 concerns access to social assistance. It distinguished between EU citizens who reside in a member state for three months or less, between three months and five years, and more than five years. A member state is not required to provide social assistance to a national from another EU member state if the person has been resident for three months or less. Citizens may continue to reside in another member state if they are employed, self-employed, or have sufficient resources so that they are not an 'unreasonable burden'. After five years of residence, EU citizens are granted permanent residence, and the requirement of having sufficient resources no longer applies. The latter rule substantially extends the principle of free movement because it further uncouples social security rights from employment. The member states are now obligated to provide social assistance benefits to all permanent residents who are citizens of the EU.

Directive 2004/38 caused several kinds of transposition problems, largely because of the difficulty of defining 'unreasonable burden' and the mismatch between national legislation and the content of the directive. For example, the Netherlands amended its social legislation so that any person entering the Netherlands was not entitled to social assistance for three months. This applied to Dutch citizens and conflicted with the Dutch Constitution (Minderhoud, 2013).

In sum, EU legislation has played an important role in expanding the scope of free movement beyond workers to include persons. Now, family members, even non-EU citizens enjoy the same rights as EU nationals. Non-economically active persons like the unemployed, pensioners and students are also included. The member states used to have complete control over who could enter and reside/work, and now they do not.

Equal pay and primary legislation

There is a large literature on the impact of EU law concerning gender equality on the public policies of the member states (Hoskyns, 1996; Caporaso and Jupille, 2001; Martinsen, 2007; van der Vleuten, 2007). As noted, the Treaty of Rome included provisions to safeguard equal pay between men and women, at French insistence. This treaty article lay dormant until the 1970s, when a series of court cases pushed equal pay to a prominent place on the EU legislative and legal agenda. The ECJ's interpretation of Article 157 TFEU established the status of statutory social security (pensions, unemployment insurance, sick pay and so on) as a form of pay, making it a violation of European law to discriminate between men and women in statutory social security schemes. ECJ decisions in the 1990s concerning occupational social protection have had a similar effect.

Article 157 TFEU requires the member states to ensure that women and men received equal pay for equal work, and they had until the end of 1961 to implement this. Implementation was, however, slow (van der Vleuten, 2007). The member states could not agree on the definition of equal work, and women continued to be paid wages much lower than men in all member states. Full implementation was postponed until 1964. Again, the member states failed to meet the deadline and the Commission threatened to initiate infringement proceedings against those that failed to comply by July 1973. The issue would not be settled in terms of legislation until several years later. In February 1975, the Council proposed the Equal Pay Directive (75/117/EC) with a July 1976 deadline.

The *Defrenne* cases from the 1970s brought the issue of equal pay to a head. Defrenne was a flight attendant for the Belgian airline, Sabena. At the time, Sabena's female employees not only received lower wages than men, but they were also forced to retire at age 40 (compared to age 55 for men), and they were not eligible for an occupational pension (which male colleagues received). In her first case, Defrenne brought a suit in a Belgian court under Article 157 TFEU, charging that her exclusion from Sabena's pension scheme violated EC law concerning equal pay. The Belgian court referred her case to the ECJ for a preliminary ruling. The ECJ's decision, announced in 1971 (Case 80/70), stated that Article 157 TFEU did not apply to Sabena's occupational pension scheme, because Sabena was a state-subsidized airline, so the pension was not considered part of pay. The ECJ argued instead that the pension was a form of social policy because it was governed by national legislation.

Undeterred, Defrenne brought a second suit, this time concerning differences in the mandatory retirement ages for men and women. Again, the Belgian court referred the case to the ECJ for a preliminary ruling. The ECJ's decision in this case (Case 43/75), issued in 1976, shattered any beliefs that the ECJ would remain passive on the issue of equal pay. The ECJ dropped the bombshell that Article 157 TFEU was directly applicable in national law. Martinsen (2007) calls the ECJ's ruling 'radical', because it declared that the principle of equal pay was directly applicable. Private parties could now rely on Article 157 TFEU in their interactions with other private parties. Thus, the decision gave individuals directly enforceable rights.

In justifying its decision, the ECJ acknowledged the economic and social goals of the EU. Additionally, EU citizens could rely on EU sex discrimination law even in the absence of relevant national law. It is worth emphasizing that in 1976, no member state had laws on the books that provided more protection than that which the direct effect of Article 157 TFEU promised. Despite these gains for women on the issue of equal pay, the ECJ ruled that the effect of the decision could not be applied retroactively, thus limiting the financial consequences of the ruling. In 1978, in the *Defrenne III* case (Case 149/77, concerning occupational pensions), the ECJ built on its previous decisions and extended the principle of equal treatment into a fundamental right.

The *Defrenne* rulings set the stage for further challenges to national law concerning equal pay and pension rights. In 1982, the *Bilka* case (Case 170/84) extended the principle of equal pay to occupational pension schemes. In *Bilka*, the ECJ ruled that occupational pensions were a form of pay, so employers could not exclude a group, for example part-time workers, consisting mainly of women. The Bilka store had excluded part-time employees, mainly women, from membership of its occupational scheme. The *Bilka* case quickly led to a new directive on occupational pensions (discussed in the next section) in order to limit the effects of the ruling. Directive 86/378 granted the member states seven years (until 1993) to comply with the new legal definition of equal treatment, and it excluded survivors' pensions and actuarially based differences in pension benefits from the reach of the new equal treatment doctrine. The directive also gave the member states more time to phase in the requirement of equal pension ages for men and women.

The *Barber* case was the next step in this tug of war between the member states and the ECJ. In *Barber* (Case 262/88), the ECJ ruled that different retirement ages for men and women in pension schemes violated Article 157 TFEU, thus overturning an important aspect of Directive 86/378. The member states responded with a protocol to the Maastricht Treaty that limited the retroactivity of the ruling. Subsequent decisions (*Ten Oever*, Case 109/91, *Vroege*, Case 57/93 and *Fisscher*, Case 128/93) clarified the implications of the new doctrine for occupational pension schemes (see Garrett et al., 1998, pp. 165–8 for an analysis).

Equal pay in statutory and occupational social security: secondary legislation

Once the principle of equal pay was established, the pace of legislative activity in this area quickened considerably. As Martinsen (2007) notes, five directives were adopted between 1975 and 1986 concerning equal pay. The first broadened the definition of equal pay to include equal work and work of equal value. A second directive concerned equal treatment to include not just pay, but also access to vocational training and employment. Directives 79/7/EEC and 86/378/EEC required the member states to ensure the equal treatment of men and women in statutory and occupational social security schemes. They prohibited the member states from discriminating in terms of access, the calculation and payment of contributions, and the calculation of benefits. They also created substantial pressure for those member states with 'breadwinner'-based social security schemes that excluded married women (because a breadwinner benefit was available only to the husband) or unmarried women (because the assumption was that they would get married at some later point and benefit from their husbands' benefits). Finally, equal treatment was extended to self-employment.

Martinsen's (2007) analysis of the implementation of these directives shows that European legislation and jurisprudence did not have immediate effects in the member states. Indeed, Defrenne's employer, Sabena, made several attempts to get around the new legal requirements. There were substantial delays and problems in implementation, particularly concerning the male–female wage gap, with obvious implications for earnings-related social security, including pensions.

The internal market and occupational pensions

Most member state pension systems are based on a division of labour between state and non-state actors concerning retirement provision: statutory schemes provide the bulk of pension income for retirees, while occupational schemes that are part of the employment contract provide supplementary income in retirement. To capture the division of labour between different providers of pension income, it has become commonplace to conceptualize national pension systems in terms of the relationship between 'pillars' (World Bank, 1994). Statutory pensions constitute the first pillar, privately organized occupational pensions form the second pillar, and individual, private pension savings make up the third pillar. First pillar, or public schemes dominate pension provision in all member states, whereas the size of the second pillar varies dramatically. Only three member states have occupational pension sectors that cover at least 90% of the workforce: the Netherlands, Denmark and Sweden. Despite the large size of the UK occupational pension sector, coverage is far below 90%. However, most member states have sizable workplace pension sectors, even if statutory provision dominates (Immergut et al., 2007; Ebbinghaus, 2011; Hennessy, 2014).

The involvement of non-state actors in the business of pension provision makes these schemes natural targets for internal market legislation, not only because companies are offering financial products in a common market, but also because occupational pension provision affects labour mobility. Workers' decisions about whether to take up employment in another member state are influenced by things like whether they will keep (or lose) their social benefits. The aggregation and portability of statutory social security have been guaranteed since the 1960s, but the regulation of occupational social benefits has been slow and conflictual. This is surprising, given the importance of occupational pensions to different dimensions of the internal market. This section analyses EU attempts at regulating cross-border occupational pension schemes and the individual portability of occupational pensions.

The absence of a single market for occupational pensions means that employers operating in more than one member state do not benefit from the economies of scale offered by a single pension scheme operating across national borders. For example, a multinational company like Royal Dutch Shell or Unilever, with operations in several member states, would have to maintain different occupational pension schemes in each member state it does business in. Wide variations in the structure of occupational pension schemes in the member states are an important brake on EU regulation, so EU law concerning a 'single market for supplementary pensions' matters in very different ways in the member states.

There are generally three ways to organize occupational pensions. The first two ways, life insurance and pension funds, rely on funding. The third type, book reserves, does not rely on capital funding. In life insurance and pension fund arrangements, employers (often in negotiation with unions) set money aside in dedicated savings arrangements in order to fund future occupational pensions.

Both types of arrangement are complicated, but for present purposes, the key difference is that pension schemes based on life insurance principles have higher capital requirements than pension funds. This means that pension schemes based on life insurance need to have more 'money in the bank' to fund their pension obligations than schemes based on pension fund principles. To put it another way, life insurance-based pension schemes are subject to tough regulation concerning the funding of their accumulated pension promises, whereas pension funds have more flexibility. Finally, book reserves are an entirely different construction, because they are not based on capital funding at all. In book reserve schemes, employers do not set funds aside in dedicated accounts to cover the costs of occupational pensions. Instead, employers simply record the pension liability on their balance sheets. Occupational pensions are then paid out of current firm revenues, rather than on accumulated savings (Anderson, 2010).

There is wide variation concerning occupational pension provision in the member states. As noted, some have highly developed schemes, while others have very little occupational pension provision. Among member states with significant occupational pension provision, the differential reliance on life insurance, pension funds and book reserves means it is difficult for the EU to pursue a robust policy concerning occupational pensions. In Denmark and Sweden, funded occupational pensions are mainly organized according to life insurance principles. In the Netherlands and the UK, a pension fund, or trust, arrangement is much more common. Book reserve schemes are common in Germany (Anderson, 2010).

The IORP Directive

The choice of legal vehicle for workplace pensions (life insurance, pension fund or book reserves) has important implications for the impact of EU legislation on member state workplace pension sectors. The EU has a long history of regulation concerning life insurance products, but before 2003, there was no EU legislation covering pension funds. Book reserve schemes remain outside the scope of EU legislation. The completion of the internal market and the emergence of funded pension provision (as a component of pension reform) meant that occupational pension regulation took on new salience in the EU, and the Commission introduced pension fund legislation in 2000 under the treaty provisions concerning the internal market, as part of the *Financial Services Action Plan* (Commission, 1999a). The proposed directive continued the process of financial market liberalization because it would grant pension funds (IORPs) the freedom to operate cross-border, something that other financial institutions, like insurance companies, could already do. The proposal included regulations concerning investment mix, financial oversight, and the definition of full funding (the level of assets considered to be sufficient to cover current and future liabilities). Book reserve schemes were excluded from the IORP Directive (2003/41/EC), and there was no mention of biometric risks (Haverland, 2007; Hennessy, 2008; Anderson, 2010).

The final version of the IORP Directive was the result of more than 10 years of negotiations among the member states. Hennessy (2008) highlights the line of conflict between the Bismarckian countries (Germany, France, Italy and Spain), which combine generous earnings-related statutory pension schemes with relatively small occupational pension sectors, and the Beveridgean countries (the UK, Ireland, the Netherlands and Denmark) with basic statutory provision and extensive funded occupational pension sectors. A pro-risk equity culture characterizes the Beveridgean countries, whereas a risk-averse insurance culture marks the Bismarckian countries. Moreover, the Bismarckian countries – especially Germany – were more likely to use book reserves to finance occupational pensions. These key differences shaped member state bargaining about the IORP Directive, leading to delay and the removal of controversial provisions. Indeed, the Bismarckian countries succeeded in keeping book reserve schemes out of the directive. Hennessy (2008) argues that the introduction of the final stage of EMU in 2002 made it more difficult for the Bismarckian countries to continue opposing key aspects of the directive, because 'EMU changed the level of Bismarckian governments implicit and explicit debt obligations and, as such, influenced the perception of their solvency' (Hennessy, 2008, p. 115). The IORP Directive (2003/41/EC) was adopted in 2003 and entered into force in October 2005.

The IORP Directive has not contributed significantly to the emergence of a single market for supplementary pensions. In 2012, there were only 87 IORPs operating in more than one member state (EIOPA, 2012). The chief reason for this is that the directive only applies to a small part of the occupational pensions sector. Most employers do not operate in more than one member state, and many schemes are not funded and thus do not fall under the scope of the directive. The promise of a single market for supplementary pensions thus appears to be limited.

Occupational pension portability

If member state compromise on cross-border occupational pension funds was difficult, agreement on occupational pension portability has been nearly impossible. Despite the importance of occupational pension portability for the internal market, however, agreement on legislation has been difficult. Like the IORP Directive, portability legislation has been on the Commission agenda for several years and took on new salience with the Lisbon Strategy's focus on increasing employment by promoting worker mobility. In October 2005, the Commission (2005a) proposed portability legislation but the proposal soon attracted strong opposition from the member states, particularly the Netherlands and Germany. The 2005 proposal included provisions allowing workers to take accrued pension rights (that is, capital) with them to a new job after a vesting period of two years. The proposal also included rules for safeguarding the value of dormant pension rights (pension rights for workers not currently in employment).

Dutch and German opposition was rooted in the structure of each country's occupational pension sector. The Netherlands has the largest funded occupational pensions sector in the EU, with assets totalling more than 100% of GDP, while Germany has a modest occupational pensions sector dominated by book reserves. Dutch opposition mainly concerned the directive's provisions in relation to the transferability of accrued pension rights, which would have meant the transfer of pension assets out of the Netherlands to other member states. Indeed, Dutch opposition was so strong that the Dutch minister threatened to veto the directive in Council. The transfer of pension assets outside the Netherlands would mean large potential losses of tax revenue. German concerns were based on the widespread use of unfunded book reserves in their relatively small occupational pension sector. In particular, German occupational pension providers feared that the transfer of pension assets required by pension portability would lead to high costs for German pension schemes, because unfunded pension rights would have to monetized in order to be portable. German employers thus pushed for the exclusion of book reserves and PAYG schemes from the directive (Hennessy, 2008; Mabbett, 2009), because capitalizing accrued benefits would be too costly.

Because of member state opposition (and the requirement of unanimity on the Council), the pensions portability directive was stalled in Council until 2013, when the Commission amended several key provisions in a bid to reach a compromise. Moreover, the post-Lisbon decision-making rules in the Council meant that unanimity was no longer required. The Commission's proposal reduced the maximum vesting period to three years and dropped the transferability of pension rights. The member states agreed on the watered-down proposal in late 2013, and the European Parliament adopted the directive in 2014 (Commission, 2014). One of the most difficult items to negotiate was the relationship between cross-border portability and internal portability. In many member states, occupational pensions are not even portable within domestic borders. Employers use waiting periods, vesting rights and rules governing the valuation of dormant pension rights to reward employee loyalty and the acquisition of firm-specific skills. This is especially true in Bismarckian countries (Mabbett, 2009).

The revised proposal included a maximum vesting period of three years. As noted, Germany has fiercely opposed shorter vesting periods, because German firms use occupational pensions as a tool for worker recruitment and retention. German domestic legislation continues to allow a minimum vesting period of five years, and German stakeholders (German Employers Association, the Occupational Pension Fund Association and Mercer, a pensions consultancy) have claimed that the directive is an attempt to harmonize German vesting periods through the back door (Ottawa, 2013). The revised proposal also protects dormant pension rights, but it excludes provisions concerning the transferability of pension rights between schemes, a concession to countries with large funded occupational pension schemes, like the Netherlands.

Soft law and the modernization of pensions

Apart from the aspects of statutory pensions already discussed, such as free movement and equal pay, there is no legal basis for binding EU intervention in the field of statutory pensions. However, the introduction of EMU has changed this because of the importance of fiscal discipline. The 1997 Stability and Growth Pact (SGP) mandated strict rules for member state public deficits, and social spending became increasingly implicated in efforts to meet deficit targets. Public pensions are typically the largest item in member state budgets, so they increasingly became targets of criticism at EU level. Specifically, EU policy-makers worried that growing pension spending because of ageing would endanger the success of EMU. Growing awareness of the link between social spending and the success of EMU led to support for new modes of governance that would encourage the member states to maintain budget discipline. This was the background to the decision adopted at the 2001 Stockholm European Council to apply the OMC to pensions in order to promote pension system modernization as part of the overall strategy of reforming social protection to support the Lisbon Strategy (Eckardt, 2005).

The focus on public pensions is not surprising, as typically they are the largest item in member states' budgets and account for a large share of member states' economies, averaging about 13% of GDP in the EU 28 in 2010 (see Figure 4.1). Moreover, public pension costs will grow as European societies age. The modernization of social protection schemes, particularly pension schemes, has been an important item on the EU's agenda since 2000, largely because of the well-known financing problems associated with mature public pension schemes like the ones in the EU 15.

The dramatic ageing of populations creates unprecedented pressure on social protection institutions, which were designed for a high fertility, high employment, high growth socioeconomic context. According to the most recent projections of the EU, the old age dependency ratio (the ratio of the size of the population aged 65 and over to the size of the working age population) will increase from 26.8% (about four workers per pensioner) in the EU 27 to 52.6% (about two workers per pensioner) for the EU 28 in 2060 (Eurostat, 2013). These demographic and economic shifts have undermined the essential preconditions of public PAYG systems because the taxes and social security contributions of a shrinking number of workers will need to finance a growing number of retirees. Population ageing coincides with a second challenge: rapidly changing labour markets and employment patterns. Full employment for standard, full-time workers seems to be a thing of the past. Instead, 'dual' or 'segmented' labour markets have emerged in many European economies (Palier and Thelen, 2010), characterized by high levels of youth unemployment, the expansion of part-time and atypical work, and persistent long-term unemployment.

These demographic shifts threatened to derail EMU. The Maastricht convergence criteria and the SGP created fairly tough

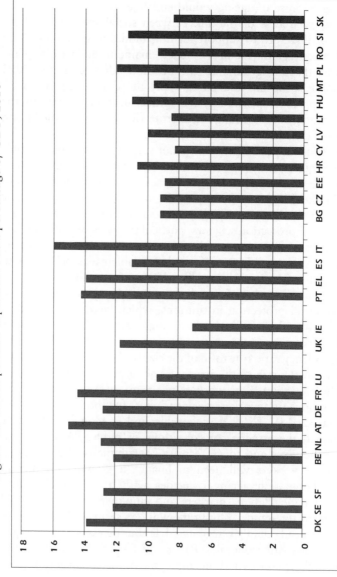

Figure 4.1 *Public pension expenditure as a percentage of GDP, 2010*

Source: Data compiled from www.epp.eurostat.ec.europa.eu (2010)
Note: Includes early retirement pensions and disability pensions

constraints on public spending, so projections of increasing pension spending alarmed EU policy-makers. By definition, public pensions involve long-term benefit commitments, which make them difficult to reform. One of the first activities of the OMC process in pensions was to gather systematic information about the nature of the 'pension crisis' in the member states in order to increase awareness of the future fiscal implications of PAYG pension liabilities. Proponents of the pensions OMC hoped to prod member states with large public pension commitments to reform their systems so as to prevent runaway pension spending in the future.

The increasing cost of public pensions was not the only concern of OMC advocates. Pro-reform actors pointed to the contribution of public pensions to high non-wage labour costs, as well as the lack of fit between pension schemes and changing employment and family patterns. The Commission was a key actor in this process, pointing to the negative effects of member state pension systems on work incentives and worker mobility (Eckhardt, 2005).

These criticisms of member state pension policy soon formed the core of a fairly coherent EU reform template (Stepan and Anderson, 2014). Financial actors within the Commission took the first steps at constructing this template. In May 1998, the Economic and Financial Affairs Council urged 'addressing all aspects of social security systems in view of ageing populations' (ECOFIN, 1998). ECOFIN argued that population ageing would lead to unsustainable levels of pension spending that would threaten the viability of EMU. Given the seriousness of this challenge, in 1999 ECOFIN set up a working group for ageing populations to study these issues and make recommendations. The group included representatives of the ministers of finance and the Directorate-General for Economic and Financial Affairs of the European Commission. The more socially minded actors at EU level were slower to respond to this challenge. In 2000, a Social Protection Committee (SPC) was appointed to complement the activities of the new working group. The SPC includes representatives of the EU member states' social security ministries and the corresponding directorate-general of the European Commission. In the field of pensions, the Commission invited the member states, in cooperation with the European Commission, to begin analysing and discussing pension reform. The involvement of the Economic Policy Committee (EPC) and the SPC means that the EU's pension agenda contains both economic and social goals promoting the adequacy and financial sustainability of public pensions (Commission, 2000).

To achieve these goals, the strategy introduced by the Stockholm European Council in 2001 encourages the member states to rapidly reduce public debt, increase employment and productivity, and reform pensions, health care and long-term care systems.

The entry into force of the Treaty of Nice in 2003 bolstered these efforts because of stronger treaty provisions concerning the EU's role in promoting social protection via soft law. Specifically, the Treaty of Nice (Article 137(2)(a)) assigned the European Council the task of:

> adopt[ing] measures designed to encourage cooperation between member states through initiatives aimed at improving knowledge, developing exchanges of information and best practices, promoting innovative approaches and evaluating experiences.

The Commission and Council's 2003 joint report on pensions was the first in a series of reports highlighting the EU's soft governance approach to pension reform (Commission, 2003). The joint report emphasized the interdependence of financial sustainability and the adequacy of public pensions. If the member states did not undertake reforms to improve financial sustainability, the adequacy of public pensions would be endangered. Population ageing would lead to substantial financial pressure on member state pension systems, necessitating comprehensive reforms. The report set out 11 objectives to guide pension reforms, including improving incentives for older workers to remain longer in the labour market, strengthening the link between contributions and benefits, and increasing public and private funding.

The EPC has played an important role in providing data and analysis to demonstrate the challenges facing member state pension systems, particularly the long-term effects of demographic changes on public expenditure in member states. The EPC's first important study, published in 2001, contained long-term forecasts (until 2050) of the effect of ageing on age-related public expenditure projections until 2050 (Commission, 2001a). By highlighting the negative consequences of not undertaking pension reform, the report was important in shaping consensus at EU level about the necessity of pension reform. Besides forecasting the long-term fiscal implications of pension systems, it included recommendations: the promotion of funded occupational pension provision and increasing the role of the occupational and private pensions sectors (Stepan and Anderson, 2014). The Presidency Conclusions from the 2001 Stockholm European Council that launched the pensions OMC reflect the emerging consensus concerning the EU's pension reform template:

> The Council should regularly review the long-term sustainability of public finances, including the expected strains caused by the demographic changes ahead. This should be done both under the guidelines and in the context of stability and convergence programme. (Council, 2001a)

Given these challenges, the Presidency Conclusions exhorted the member states to:

- reduce public debt as quickly as possible
- raise employment rates and productivity
- reform pension, health care and long-term care systems.

The pensions OMC has gone through three cycles (starting in 2001, 2005 and 2008), and has been integrated into the social OMC since 2005. The social OMC is now part of the EU's new growth strategy, Europe 2020.

The most recent Commission report on pensions, the 2010 *Joint Report on Pensions*, catalogues the progress achieved thus far and the challenges presented by the current financial crisis. It also presented the updated European agenda for adequate and fiscally sustainable pensions (Commission, 2010a).

In order to achieve the targets set out in the Europe 2020 strategy, member state policies are coordinated at EU level in the European Semester process (see Chapter 3). The cycle begins with the Commission's publication of the Annual Growth Survey. The Council and the European Council then formulate policy priorities, and the member states draw up their stability or convergence programmes and National Reform Programmes. The EPC, the SPC and the Employment Committee analyse developments in the member states and the EU. The Commission then proposes country-specific recommendations, which are then approved by the European Council.

Pensions played a prominent role in the Annual Growth Surveys for 2011 and 2012. These surveys contain specific recommendations concerning pensions, which were also reflected in the recommendations to member states:

- linking the retirement age to life expectancy
- restricting early exit
- promoting longer working lives
- standardizing the pension age for men and women
- supporting the development of second and third pillar pensions.

The importance of pension reform for the success of EMU and the role of occupational pensions in the internal market were the background to the Commission's renewed commitment to pension reform in 2010 with its Green Paper on pensions (Commission, 2010b). The Green Paper reiterated the messages of earlier policy statements, emphasizing the importance of reforming member state pension systems to deal with the consequences of population ageing. The Green Paper echoed earlier policy prescriptions: extending working lives and linking the retirement age to changes in life expectancy. The onset of the financial crisis in 2008, however, added a new dimension to the pension reform debate at EU level. Funded pensions, particularly in the second pillar, experienced heavy losses as a result of financial market turbulence. According to the Commission, these developments highlighted the need for improved governance of funded pensions. The Green Paper thus combined its previous emphasis on public pension reform with a renewed agenda for the governance of funded occupational pensions. In addition, it reiterated earlier policy statements about the importance of expanding second and third pillar pensions to complement public schemes. The issues outlined in the Green Paper were key elements of the Europe 2020 strategy. The White Paper on pensions, released in 2012, contained detailed proposals that addressed the issues raised in the Green Paper: linking retirement age to life expectancy, increasing employment, and strengthening second and third pillar pensions (Commission, 2012a).

To sum up, EU soft law initiatives in pension policy represent a coherent reform template for the member states. The central elements of this template are:

- actuarially fair statutory pensions that provide adequate income in retirement
- minimum pensions for those with insufficient employment-related pension rights
- measures to increase working lives
- linking retirement age to life expectancy

- promoting the expansion and security of the second and third pension pillar.

This template cannot be imposed on the member states within the framework of the OMC, but it serves as a reference point and model for pension reform.

Despite the emergence of a coherent reform template, the OMC process has had little demonstrable impact on pension reform processes in the member states (Eckardt, 2005; Natali, 2009). The OMC is particularly effective at calling attention to policy problems and advocating preferred solutions, but in the absence of binding policy instruments, it is bound to have little influence on substantive policy change. Even if the member states benefit from mutual learning and awareness of policy problems, this is no guarantee that national politicians can push difficult pension reforms through the national political decision-making process. In addition, actors at EU level involved in the OMC pension process have often worked at cross-purposes. ECOFIN has promoted financial sustainability, while the Directorate-General for Employment, Social Affairs and Inclusion has pushed pension adequacy (de la Porte and Pochet, 2002b).

What can we conclude about the role of the OMC in the modernization of member state pension systems? It is difficult to attribute the many substantial pension reforms in the member states to the OMC process (see Immergut et al., 2007 for an analysis of pension reforms). The Lisbon Strategy and the OMC process in pensions cannot force any member state to reform pension provision. The OMC only offers incentives and a forum for mutual learning through the exchange of best practices that provide the context for national-level debates and decisions concerning pension reform. But given that pension reform will occupy national political agendas for many years, it would be unwise to ignore the normative force and specific content of the OMC pension agenda. Indeed, perhaps the most important function of the OMC pension process is the collection of data concerning current and projected future pension spending in the context of population ageing. If nothing else, these statistics frame pension reform debates at EU and member state level.

The sovereign debt crisis and pension reform

The emergence of the sovereign debt crisis in 2009 pushed pension reform to the top of the national political agenda in the most affected member states: Greece, Spain, Portugal, Italy and Ireland. Greece and Spain were particularly hard hit because of their dependence on loans from the EU Commission, ECB and IMF (the troika) in order to finance growing government deficits. Loan packages negotiated between the member states and the troika were conditional on the borrowing state's willingness and capacity to undertake tough reforms specified by the troika. The terms of this 'conditionality' included labour market reform, social insurance reform, and other measures designed to reduce public indebtedness and, in the troika's view, lay the foundations for economic growth.

The effects of conditionality have been swift and radical, especially in Greece. The Greek pension system exemplifies the Southern European model of social provision, with a large number of schemes providing generous, income-related benefits to different occupational groups. Despite rising costs, Greek governments were slow to undertake reforms (Triantafillou, 2007). The euro crisis changed this. Greece negotiated two loan packages with the troika, in May 2010 and February 2012, for a total of €240 billion. The troika made the loans conditional on tough pension reforms and monitored progress quarterly. Troika representatives pointed to the projections made as part of the OMC process that showed substantial long-term increases in pension expenditure. Representatives of the troika specified the content of pension reforms, so Greek policymakers had little choice but to implement them. Despite massive political opposition, Greek governments adopted reforms that harmonized the more than 130 pension funds, raised the retirement age, and reduced earnings-related benefits. In addition, a basic pension aimed at poverty reduction was introduced (Matsaganis, 2011; Stepan and Anderson, 2014).

Conditionality has had less effect on pension reform in the two other countries that turned to the troika for loan assistance: Portugal and Ireland. Portugal had already taken steps to improve the financial sustainability of its pension system prior to the outbreak of the crisis in 2008 (Chuliá and Asensio, 2007) so the troika demanded only modest reforms in order to reduce short-term public deficits – a pension freeze and modest cuts for higher income pensioners (Hinrichs and Brosig, 2013). Similarly, the Irish pension system was not a target for radical reform because forecasts showed that the system was reasonably sustainable in the long term (Schulze and Moran, 2007). However, the Irish loan deal contained instructions to raise the retirement age, increase public workers' financing of their occupational pensions, and suspend basic pension indexation (Hinrichs and Brosig, 2013).

Other member states also felt the effects of the crisis on their pension systems. Even though Italy did not require loan assistance, Italian governments introduced several cuts in pension generosity between 2008 and 2012 in order to reduce public deficits and calm financial markets. In addition, several Central and Eastern European member states adopted pension cuts as elements of fiscal consolidation packages (Hinrichs and Brosig, 2013).

Conclusion

Despite the centrality of social security and pensions in national welfare states, EU regulation now reaches into nearly all aspects of these policy areas. The EU has few explicit, binding legislative competences concerning social insurance and pensions, but the EU's market-building project provided an opening for the ECJ and Commission to use equality law and internal market law to create regulatory principles that shape national policy development. Indeed, the impact of law concerning equal treatment highlights the tug of war between the Council and ECJ concerning the scope of European law. The extension of social insurance rights to some categories of the economically non-active is another example of the expanded reach of EU regulation.

Even as the EU has encroached into core aspects of pension provision, attempts to bring private, occupational pension provision into a single market for supplementary pensions have produced mixed results. There is now binding legislation concerning the activities of cross-border occupational pension funds, but the decision-making process was conflictual, resulting in fairly weak regulation. Important aspects of occupational pension provision, such as vesting rights and the status of book reserves, remain largely under member state control. Similarly, efforts to regulate occupational pension portability were hindered by intense member state preferences for the status quo because of institutional diversity.

The limits to soft coordination of member state social policies are also revealed by the absence of discernible progress in the OMC pension process. Certainly, the OMC pension process has done much to frame pension reform debates by generating detailed statistical analyses of the effects of population ageing and labour market changes on the sustainability and adequacy of public pensions in the member states. In this sense, the pensions OMC has succeeded in pushing public pension reform to the top of the EU policy agenda. However, the OMC pension process is not backed up by binding instruments, resulting in domestic reform processes largely shaped by electoral politics. Ironically, it took the euro crisis and the strict conditions linked to loan assistance to move member states such as Greece to reform their public pension systems. Although reform advocates may applaud difficult reforms because they serve sustainability and adequacy, the reforms were only possible because the domestic democratic process was largely suspended.

Chapter 5

Employment Policy

Labour markets are an important vehicle for EU social policy-making because of the centrality of the employment relationship in the market-making process. As other chapters in this book demonstrate, the construction of the internal market and the guarantee of labour mobility are key routes through which European integration influences social policy at EU level and in the member states. With the deepening of the integration process in the 1980s and 90s, however, the scope of EU action concerning employment took on new salience. The completion of the internal market sparked concerns that employment would be sacrificed, or at least de-emphasized, in the process of market-building. Many centre-left political actors feared a Europe dominated by the concerns of business, with potentially disastrous consequences for large groups of ordinary workers. The introduction of the European Employment Strategy (EES) in 1997 was a direct response to these concerns. At the same time, the development of EU law and jurisprudence concerning equal rights for men and women in the workplace spurred a flurry of policy activity concerning women's employment, especially the reconciliation of work and family. In contrast to the progressive orientation of EU law concerning equality, recent jurisprudence (the *Laval*, *Viking* and *Rüffert* judgements) concerning labour law subordinates the social policy functions of labour agreements to the market-making process. This chapter considers these central elements of EU employment policies.

The inclusion of a separate employment title in the Treaty of Amsterdam was important in two respects:

1. It marked the extension of EU-level efforts to promote higher levels of employment as well as 'better' employment conditions.
2. It signalled the substantial expansion of the use of the open method of coordination (OMC) for social policy-making at the EU level.

The chapter also assesses the extent to which the EES has been successful in terms of concrete policy impact (more and better jobs) and 'output-oriented legitimacy' (Scharpf, 1999; Büchs, 2007).

The European Employment Strategy

The EU has long been active in regulating specific aspects of the employment relationship. As Chapter 4 discusses, EU law concerning equal pay between men and women was the impetus for major changes in the social security policies in the member states. And as Chapter 7 shows, treaty provisions concerning health and safety at work have been the basis for legislation in these areas. Aside from the limited initiatives available under the auspices of the European Social Fund (ESF), the EU has never pursued a true employment policy in the sense of stimulating job creation and improving the quality of employment. Indeed, the Treaty of Rome assumed that economic integration would, on its own, lead to rising standards of living and the expansion of employment. After the unemployment shocks of the 1970s and the completion of the internal market, there were calls for a more concerted employment policy at EU level. Monetary union would remove some of the most important tools of employment policy from member states' toolboxes: the European Central Bank would control monetary policy, and the 3% limit on annual budget deficits would constrain the use of expansionary fiscal policy in a recession. To make matters worse, the status quo bias of European decision-making institutions and the difficulty for the member states to agree on common employment policy virtually guaranteed that the EU would not be able to embark on any bold initiatives based on hard law in pursuit of full employment.

The emergence of persistently high unemployment in the 1970s prompted several EU initiatives in employment. Directives on collective redundancies (Council, 1975, later replaced by Council, 1998) and employee protection in the case of firm insolvency (Council, 1980, later replaced by Council and Parliament, 2008) were adopted. In addition, a tripartite Standing Committee on Employment was established in 1970, staffed by the social partners (ETUC, CEEP and UNICE), the Commission and ministers of labour in the member states. It was charged with facilitating the coordination of national employment policies so that they would support EU goals. However, the new committee was beset with problems from the outset: national ministers were sceptical of

EU-level coordination, and the UNICE opposed meaningful cooperation (Goetschy, 1999). In the wake of this failure, attention
shifted to the role of the Structural Funds in fighting unemployment. Despite the use of structural funding to promote employment
for vulnerable groups (women, the long-term unemployed, youths),
results were mixed.

The 1993 White Paper *Growth, Competitiveness, Employment*
was an important step in the development of the EES. The White
Paper attributed the EU's economic malaise to structural problems
such as the absence of active labour market policies (Commission,
1993). The White Paper emphasized supply-side measures –
improving training and education, making workplaces more flexible, and reducing non-wage labour costs – combined with
deregulation as the remedy for Europe's economic malaise. The
White Paper was the prelude to more far-reaching statements about
the future of employment policy at EU level at the December 1994
European Council at Essen. With the third stage of EMU set to
begin in 1999, there was growing concern that the EU needed to
take policy action to offset the potentially negative effects of EMU
on national and European labour markets. With the transfer of
monetary policy to the European Central Bank, the member states
would lose an important tool for managing their economies. A
vigorous EU policy to promote employment would help to quell
fears about the deleterious effects of EMU on employment
(Goetschy, 2003). The Essen Summit also set out a multilateral
monitoring procedure, whereby the member states would report
their progress on agreed goals to each other and the Commission.

The Essen Council formulated five central goals for achieving
higher employment:

1. The creation of human capital through vocational training
2. Wage moderation to facilitate investment
3. Increasing the efficiency of the labour market
4. Locally based schemes for job creation
5. Increasing labour market participation of youths, women and
   the long-term unemployed.

Essen was thus the prelude and model for the EES. However,
declaring a commitment to raising employment is merely symbolic
politics in the absence of concrete EU competences and resources to
back them up. Social democratic and Christian democratic parties

participated in government in most member states in the mid-1990s, and they used the 1994 Essen Summit to build support for a more comprehensive EU role in employment policy. Social democratic party leaders working in the Party of European Socialists (PES) had already introduced the European Employment Initiative in December 1993 with the publication of the Larsson Report, and the Essen Summit provided momentum for further collaboration across national boundaries. The Larsson Report analysed how to formulate a common social democratic programme for fighting unemployment that would combine national and European strategies (PES, 1994). An alliance of social democratic party politicians, union leaders and representatives of the Commission (supported by Commission President Jacques Delors) worked to keep employment policy on the EU agenda after the Essen Summit (Johansson, 1999). Rhodes (2005) credits the entrepreneurial efforts of the Commission with creating the impetus for the EES. The Commission saw an opening when there were enough social democratic governments in the Council in the mid-1990s, and it used European Council meetings – Madrid in 1995 and Dublin in 1996 were particularly important – to move the employment agenda forward. The Commission tried to create a critical mass in favour of some sort of employment strategy by appealing to social democratic governments and trying to convince other member states to go along.

Social democratic and Commission efforts paid off. At the June 1997 Amsterdam Summit, the member states agreed to make employment a 'common concern' of the EU and to include a separate chapter on employment in the Amsterdam Treaty (Articles 125–130 EC, Articles 145–150 TFEU). Indeed, the treaty now specifically cites the promotion of employment as one of the EU's objectives. As the treaty states:

> the duties of the member states and the European Community are to develop a coordinated strategy for employment and particularly for promoting a skilled, trained and adaptable workforce and labour markets responsive to economic change. (Article 125 EC, Article 145 TFEU)

The treaty also requires the member states to pursue an employment policy in line with the economic policies adopted under Article 145 TFEU (Article 126 EC), and to treat employment as a matter of common concern (Article 3 TEU, Article 2 EC). In addition, the treaty specifies the roles and duties of EU institutions in employment policy-making, allows the Council to adopt (via co-decision) measures to support employment policies in member states and authorizes the Council (with the approval of Parliament) to create an Employment Committee (EMCO) to support the work of the Council and Commission. This new committee is charged with the tasks of monitoring employment conditions and policies. It formulates opinions, but its role is purely advisory. The member states and the Commission appoint two representatives each to the committee (Article TFEU 150, Article 130 EC).

As originally conceived, the EES was based on four pillars:

1. *Employability:* to achieve a high level of employment in the economy and for all groups in the labour market.
2. *Entrepreneurship:* to move away from a passive fight against unemployment towards promoting sustainable employability and job creation.
3. *Adaptability:* to promote a new approach to work organization so that EU firms can deal with economic change while reconciling security and adaptability and allowing individuals to participate in lifelong training.
4. *Equal opportunities:* to provide equal opportunities for everyone in the labour market to participate and have access to work.

The content of the pillars demonstrates the supply-side orientation of the EES. The EES envisaged active labour market policies designed to upgrade workers' skills, activate groups with weak attachments to the labour market (youths, women, older workers), and encourage job growth. In short, the EES marked a clear break with the passive labour market policies that dominated the policy approaches of many member states. Rather than providing cash benefits for the unemployed, the EES would encourage the member states to adopt policies that increased employment for all groups and emphasize the take-up of paid employment over labour market withdrawal.

The 1997 Luxembourg European Council, also known as the 'Jobs Summit', formally launched the EES, even though the Treaty of Amsterdam had not yet taken effect. The heart of the EES is a multilateral surveillance framework, the OMC, which encourages the member states to coordinate their employment policies in pursuit of full employment. The OMC is based on soft law; the member states are encouraged to meet specific targets, and the process works via benchmarking, monitoring, the diffusion of good practices and peer pressure (Borrás and Jacobsson, 2004).

In its current form, the annual EES policy cycle begins with the Commission's formulation of the employment guidelines, which the member states are obliged to consider in national policy-making. The Council adopts the employment guidelines by QMV. The member states are required to submit a National Reform Programme (NRP; formerly National Action Plans, NAPs). The NRPs are peer reviewed by EMCO, which then reports its findings to the Council. The Council and Commission then formulate a joint report, which is submitted to the European Council. The Council may also adopt by QMV a recommendation (formulated by the Commission) to a specific member state.

Recommendations are the Commission's and Council's only instrument to call attention to a member state's failure to comply with the employment guidelines. Unlike the warnings that are part of the Stability and Growth Pact, employment policy recommendations carry no sanction. Moreover, the member states in the Council make the final decision about recommendations, so the recommendations are almost always rather weak (Barnard, 2012, p. 94). The Commission and rotating presidency have the greatest impact on the content of the guidelines. The European Parliament plays no specific role in the policy cycle, except for being consulted on the formulation of the guidelines (Article 128 EC, Article 148 TFEU).

The early years of the EES were marked by optimism. In 2000, 13 of the15 member state governments were led or co-governed by social democratic parties. The introduction in 2000 of the Lisbon Strategy, intended to relaunch the European economy and social model, also boosted the early development of the EES. The Lisbon Strategy aimed for the EU to become 'the most competitive and dynamic knowledge-based economy in the world' by 2010. An ambitious social agenda underpinned the pursuit of competitiveness, including the modernization of the European social model and the goal of full employment. Lisbon also put meat on the bones of the EES by laying out the mechanisms for the OMC in the Presidency Conclusions (Council, 2000a). The EES was to be a core element in the Lisbon Strategy. The Lisbon Strategy thus updated and strengthened the nascent EES by integrating it into a broad framework of economic and social policy coordination.

The Commission's evaluation of the EES in 2002 was cautiously optimistic, noting the improvement in EU labour market performance and 'clear convergence towards the common EU objectives set out in the EES policy guidelines' (Commission, 2002, p. 2). This convergence could be seen in the increasing emphasis on active labour market policies:

- the reorientation of employment exchanges towards prevention and activation
- the implementation of gender mainstreaming in employment policies
- efforts to make tax systems more employment friendly
- the promotion of lifelong learning.

Moreover, the Commission emphasized that 10 million jobs had been created between 1997 and 2002.

By the mid-2000s, the Commission and the member states started to modify EES procedures. As originally designed, the EES followed an annual policy cycle and was based on the four pillars and 18–20 guidelines. The Commission's 2002 review of the EES reported that participants found the EES structure cumbersome (Commission, 2002), and the procedure was streamlined in 2004; the pillar structure was dropped and the number of guidelines reduced. Three comprehensive goals – full employment, productive high-quality work, and social cohesion – replaced the pillar structure. The EES was also more closely integrated with economic policy coordination. Starting in 2005, the European economic guidelines were integrated with the broad economic policy guidelines to become 24 integrated guidelines for growth and jobs. Ten of these were related to employment, and they mirrored the content of the guidelines before the overhaul. By now, the guidelines also contained more specific targets. For example, Barnard (2012) notes that the 2003 guidelines specified the goal of 25% participation by the long-term unemployed in a labour market programme (training and so on) by 2010, and 85% of persons 22 or older should have an upper secondary degree by 2010. The revamped procedure allowed for more focus on jobs, growth and 'flexicurity' (flexibility and security) and to make the process less cumbersome. Instead of an annual cycle, there is now a triennial cycle. The EES NAPs and the Joint Employment Report were also merged to become NRPs. The first cycle using the revamped procedures was 2005–08.

Other developments also pushed the EES away from its original design. The European Employment Taskforce sharply criticized the effectiveness of the EES in its 2003 report and shifted the EES in a more supply-side direction favouring 'flexicurity' (Kok, 2003). The growing number of non-socialist governments in the member states reinforced this policy orientation in the Council, and it was further strengthened by the installation of the Barroso Commission in 2004.

Prior to the 2004 revamp, there was widespread dissatisfaction among the member states about the use of recommendations to call attention to inadequate implementation in the member states. Many member states were not pleased about being singled out for criticism, and this reignited decades-old concerns about the growing influence of the Commission vis-à-vis the member states and the involuntary surrender of sovereignty by the member states (Rhodes, 2005). In addition, there was uncertainty about whether the EES produced concrete policy results; it was not clear that the EES added anything to what member states were already doing. Moreover, social partner involvement in the NAPs was uneven (Goetschy, 2003).

Despite the role of the Commission in shaping the employment guidelines, the member states dominate the EES. Subsidiarity plays a key role, because even though employment is a matter of EU competence, EU institutions can only support member state efforts (Barnard, 2012). Moreover, the European Parliament plays a small role, and the ECJ is virtually absent. Indeed, the EES process depends on the central role of the member states, because it is the voluntary actions of the member states in coordinating their employment policies that is supposed to produce the desired results.

How does the soft law foundation of the EES compare to the use of the Community method – the procedure for adopting binding legislation (regulations and directives)? As in the process of making hard law, the OMC is characterized by member state attempts to upload their own policies to the EU level (Büchs, 2007). In contrast to hard legislation, however, the OMC foresees member state consultation of relevant stakeholders. But soft law is non-binding; the employment guidelines are not obligatory, and there are no sanctions if a member state fails to reach specified targets. This means that the member states can use the EES as a justification for carrying out reforms that were already planned, or they can simply ignore EES guidelines and recommendations that are undesirable or unfeasible.

The inherent weaknesses of the OMC are arguably the cause of the disappointing performance of the EES. After the launch of the Lisbon Strategy, the Stockholm European Council (March 2001) set goals of overall employment rate of 70% by 2010, 60% female labour market participation (LMP), and an LMP rate for older workers of 50% (Commission, 2001b). The mid-term review of the Lisbon Strategy in 2005 was not optimistic about reaching these goals, and the 2006 relaunch of the Lisbon Strategy meant a downgrade of the importance of the EES because social protection was now subordinate to growth and jobs. Since 2006, the EES has been less visible (see Zeitlin, 2008), and few policy-makers view it as a powerful tool for increasing employment. The weakness of the Lisbon Strategy added to this perception. By 2010, it was clear that the Lisbon Strategy was a failure, not only because of overly ambitious goals and weak policy instruments, but also because of the onset of the financial crisis in 2008. The exhaustion of the Lisbon Strategy further weakened the EES as an effective tool for promoting employment at the EU level. The Europe 2020 strategy replaced the Lisbon Strategy, emphasizing smart, sustainable, inclusive growth.

It is not clear whether the EES will continue to stagnate or will play a more prominent role. The overhaul of the EU's economic governance structures as part of Europe 2020 included modifications in the EES. As discussed in Chapter 3, Europe 2020 is intended to spur 'smart' economic growth and employment by improving the EU's procedures for policy coordination, mutual learning and surveillance. Indeed, one of Europe 2020's headline targets is to raise the proportion of people aged 20–64 in employment to 75%.

The EES is now embedded in the European Semester (see Chapter 3), so the annual cycle begins with the publication of the employment guidelines, EMCO's evaluation of member state NRPs, and the European Council's country-specific recommendations. The latter two elements are included in the Joint Employment Report, which also includes an assessment of EU-wide employment. The most recent EES cycle (2013/2014) was based on guidelines adopted in 2010, which emphasized:

- raising labour market participation and reducing structural unemployment
- promoting the development of a skilled workforce responsive to labour market needs
- the promotion of 'quality' jobs
- lifelong learning (Commission, 2013a).

The integration of the EES into Europe 2020 has already provided opportunities for innovation within the EES. There is now an employment scoreboard built into Europe 2020, which aims to improve the monitoring and awareness of the links between social and employment policies and EMU. The employment scorecard is flanked by a social scorecard, and both are used in drafting the Joint Employment Report. A second innovation is the introduction of high-profile policy initiatives within the EES and Europe 2020. The Commission proposed a Youth Employment Package in December 2012 to address the growing number of jobless among those aged 25 or younger (it was the result of a request by the Council and Parliament). The package relies on the familiar instruments of labour market policy within the EU's multilevel governance structure. The member states were asked to submit proposals for programmes that would give young people training, education or an offer of employment. The Youth Guarantee is a key element of the package: member state programmes funded by the package are intended to give young people a job or education/ training offer within four months of leaving school or becoming unemployed. The ESF provides funding for the package, and monitoring takes place within the European Semester. The Council soon followed with a related programme, the Youth Employment Initiative, launched in February 2013 and financed with an additional €6 billion (€3 billion would come from the ESF) to support additional programmes in 2014–20 aimed at curbing youth unemployment (Commission, 2013b; Council, 2013).

What difference does the European Employment Strategy make?

The ambition of the EES and its innovative governance mechanisms have generated a large literature evaluating its effectiveness. Rhodes (2005) calls the EES a 'radical departure' from the Community method and social dialogue because of the substantial shift in EU goals that the EES implies: now the EU is involved in efforts to create jobs, not just protecting those already in employment, even if the instruments are only soft law. Other analysts emphasize the potential of the EES to overcome policy-making inertia at EU level by using soft policy instruments designed to accommodate diversity, experiment with new policy approaches, learn from past policy experiences and other member state's experience, and above all, to use the OMC to avoid the kinds of conflicts caused by heterogeneous member state interests that prevented agreement on hard law initiatives. Moreover, using the OMC was supposed to increase the democratic legitimacy of EU policy-making in this area because of its emphasis on stakeholder involvement (Büchs, 2007).

Despite the use of the OMC, the EES is prone to many of the same problems that plague traditional policy-making using hard law. The member states (in the Council) still compete with the Commission to define the policy agenda, and subsidiarity makes it difficult for EU-level actors to promote substantial policy change (Rhodes, 2005). Moreover, it is particularly difficult to trace the impact of the EES on national reforms (Büchs, 2007). Copeland and ter Haar (2013) analyse the effectiveness of the EES in 10 member states for the period 2005–09 and conclude that the use of the OMC for the EES is a 'toothless governance tool'. The EES was most successful when an employment guideline matched what a member state already planned to do, although this does not rule out 'policy learning' in terms of policy-makers in the member states absorbing new policy priorities. Similarly, Buchs (2007) finds that the OMC influences national policy-making in ways that cannot be classified as top-down or bottom-up. Instead, the member states use the OMC strategically, attempting to shape the formulation of policy goals at EU level and then strategically using OMC procedures in national policy-making. Finally, Jacobsson and Vifell (2005) conclude that the EES has not been effective at reshaping national employment policies. National governments pay lip service to the EES but then ignore it at home.

Analysts have also criticized the EES as a tool of 'experimental governance'. One of the advantages of using the OMC in employment policy-making was that it was supposed to increase the democratic legitimacy of EU initiatives by including domestic stakeholders and respecting the institutional diversity of employment policies in the member states. The OMC was also intended to encourage policy experimentation as the member states learned from each other and tried new policy approaches in their efforts to boost employment. In practice, however, the OMC is less democratic and experimental than many analysts hoped. National and European parliamentary influence on the EES is minimal. Indeed, the Commission and Council are the key players, resulting in a policy cycle that is relatively insulated from outside pressure and dominated by a small number of experts (Rhodes, 2005).

To sum up, there is much to criticize in the EES, and there is no real support for strengthening the EES or constitutionalizing it. However, it would be a mistake to conclude that the EES has had no influence on employment policies in the member states. Even if it is difficult to link specific reforms in the member states to the EES, the OMC policy cycle has put concrete policy problems and goals on the EU agenda and backed them up with a wide range of quantitative indicators to assess whether the member states meet commonly agreed targets. After 15 years' experience with the EES, European and national policy-makers now have a clear frame of reference, specific categories, and indicators for communicating about employment. Even if the member states resist – for whatever reason – reforms that would allow them to meet EES targets, they cannot ignore the discourse embedded in the EES. The EES as a process is based on a supply-side perspective that emphasizes activation even for groups that have often been excluded or less present on EU labour markets: women, older workers and the disabled. The EES encourages policy-makers to adjust the 'mental maps' that steer their approach to policy (Visser, 2009), and it changes the process by which employment policy is made at the domestic level (Heidenreich and Zeitlin, 2009). For many member states, the EES means thinking about employment policy in ways that clash with previous policy prescriptions and solutions, and this may turn out to be a revolution in itself.

A judicial revolution in labour law?

Recent ECJ rulings on labour law and the internal market have potentially far-reaching implications for established patterns of industrial relations. Particularly in the EU 15, organized labour and employer organizations negotiate the terms of the employment contract. These collective agreements play an important role in labour markets, because they shape wage levels, collective social provision and, ultimately, employment levels. It is important to recognize that, by definition, collective agreements restrict competition. Unions and employer organizations are essentially cartels, which negotiate on behalf of their members. In many cases, workers and employers have little or no choice about whether they fall under a collective agreement. Collective agreements thus have a social function that is achieved by restricting competition.

Until recently, few believed that EU law would impinge on collective agreements. The treaties implicitly recognized the right of the social partners to conclude collective agreements (via provisions concerning the social dialogue), and the ECJ had ruled in relevant cases that collective agreements did not violate EU law. For example, in the 1997 *Albany* ruling, the ECJ 'ring-fenced' national labour law by finding that EU competition law (Article 101(1) TFEU) had to consider EU treaty provisions concerning social policy, in this case collective action and the social dialogue (Barnard, 2012). The *Albany* case (Case 67/96) concerned a Dutch supplementary pension scheme that was compulsory for all firms in a particular sector. The advocate-general ruled that collective action – making collective agreements compulsory for all firms in a sector – served social policy goals, so this specific kind of restriction on competition did not violate EU competition law.

The much-contested Services Directive (2006/123) also seemed to strengthen the wall that protected collective bargaining from EU competition law. The Monti I clause (Article 1(7) of the directive) confirmed the exclusion of national systems of collective bargaining from the reach of the directive. At the same time, ECJ jurisprudence concerning the role of 'solidarity' in excluding national social policies from the scope of competition law seemed to bolster the argument that collective bargaining should also be excluded because of its social character. The principle is that activities based on national solidarity are not economic activities and therefore not subject to competition law (Barnard, 2012). Thus, social policy goals in collective agreements seemed to be beyond the reach of EU law.

The ECJ seems to be departing from the principle established in *Albany* concerning the freedom of establishment and the right to take industrial action. The *Viking* ruling of 2007 (Case 438/05) was the first sign that the ECJ had shifted course. Viking, a Finnish ferry company, wanted to change the registration of one of its ships, the *Rosella*, from Finland to Estonia in order to save labour costs by employing an Estonian rather than a Finnish crew. The Finnish Seaman's Union and the International Transport Workers' Federation (ITF) opposed the move, arguing that Finnish law must apply even if vessels were reflagged within the EU. The Finnish Seamen's Union requested relevant third parties to respect its right to negotiate wages and working conditions on the *Rosella*, and it threatened to strike if Viking went through with its plans. The ITF supported the Finnish union by calling for a boycott of Viking. Viking responded by requesting an injunction from an English court (ITF's home was England), which would prevent the Finnish

Seamen's Union and the ITF from taking industrial action to stop the reflagging of the ship and the negotiation of a new collective agreement. Viking relied on Article 43 EC (Article 49 TFEU), arguing that the union's industrial action was illegal because it prevented Viking from exercising its right to freedom of establishment under EU law. The English High Court sided with Viking in June 2005, citing Article 43 EC (Article 49 TFEU) on the freedom of businesses to relocate their operations within the EU.

The basic legal issue at stake was 'freedom of establishment'. Article 43 EC (Article 49 TFEU) permits firms from any member state to set up shop in another member state. The host state may not hinder this freedom, unless there is a legitimate reason for doing so that is compatible with EU and serves 'overriding reasons of the public interest'. Moreover, EU law requires that the restriction be proportionate.

The unions appealed, arguing that the injunction was a violation of their right to take industrial action. The English Court of Appeal lifted the injunction, ruling that Viking's rights under EU law must be balanced with the union's right to strike under national legislation. The Court of Appeal referred the case to the ECJ for a preliminary ruling. One of the key questions that the Court of Appeal referred to the ECJ was how conflicting fundamental rights should be decided. Besides the freedom of establishment, the *Viking* case involved the right of unions to take industrial action, guaranteed by both Finnish Law and Article 28 of the Charter of Fundamental Rights of the EU. Fourteen member states and Norway submitted briefs, and the ETUC submitted its own brief. The new member states and the UK lined up in favour of EU law, while the old member states advocated keeping EU law out of national systems of industrial relations (see Bercusson, 2007, for an analysis). The ECJ ruled that EU law did apply; it therefore decided not to ring-fence national labour law and did not recognize a fundamental right to strike. Thus, the *Viking* decision seems to say that strikes have to comply with both national and EU law (Barnard, 2012).

The *Laval* case (Case 341/05) involved issues similar to *Viking*. Laval is a Latvian construction firm that ran several construction projects in Sweden using Latvian workers employed under the provisions of the Posted Workers Directive (PWD, 96/71/EC). The Swedish Construction Workers Union tried to get Laval's workers included in their own collective agreement, and when this failed, they blockaded Laval's worksites in Sweden. Laval sued in the

Swedish Labour Court under Article 49 EC (Article 56 TFEU) and the PWD (the lawsuit was financed by the Swedish Employers Organization), and the Swedish court referred the case to the ECJ for a preliminary ruling. Like *Viking*, the key issue was whether industrial action fell under EU law, and whether Laval's actions violated the provisions of the PWD (Barnard, 2012). The advocate-general argued that Swedish union actions did not violate the PWD. However, the ECJ overturned the advocate-general's opinion, ruling that industrial action violated Laval's right to provide services. The ECJ argued that Laval did not violate any rules about minimum wages and other provisions, because these do not exist in Sweden. The Swedish system of industrial relations is based on strong unions and employers that negotiate wages and other working conditions without state interference. This means that there is no legislation on minimum wages and related benefits (like supplementary insurance). The PWD specifies a hard nucleus of legal provisions (minimum wage, working conditions and so on) that undertakings from other member states must adhere to. However, in *Laval*, the union's industrial action was aimed at getting Laval to sign a collective agreement that regulated provisions beyond those required by the PWD in this case. The ruling chipped away at *Albany*, in the sense that it did not acknowledge that collective bargaining and industrial action were beyond the scope of EU law. Indeed, the ECJ emphasized that industrial action was a fundamental right, subject to the requirements of EU law. This meant that the ECJ confirmed the right of unions to take industrial action, but only after meeting rather rigorous standards in terms of whether the public interest was endangered and only if the PWD was strictly followed.

The *Rüffert* ruling (Case 346/06) also dealt a dangerous blow to industrial relations practices. The case concerned the compatibility of public procurement law with the freedom to provide services. The case involved the German state of Lower Saxony, which had a law on the books that required undertakings carrying out public tenders to adhere to state law concerning the minimum acceptable wage. Germany does not have a statutory minimum wage; in this case, the minimum wage was determined by collective agreement at the worksite.

The *Rüffert* case involved a Polish firm carrying out a public tender with 53 posted workers (from Poland) earning less than half of the collectively bargained wage rate at the worksite in Lower

Saxony. The state cancelled the contract and fined the company. The company later went bankrupt, and in the course of the bankruptcy proceedings, its representative, Rüffert, took legal action against the government of Lower Saxony. In July 2006, the German Court of Appeal referred the case to the ECJ for a preliminary ruling. The key issue was whether Lower Saxony's public procurement rules were compatible with EU law concerning the freedom to provide services in the EU and whether service providers from another member state had to pay wages determined in a local collective agreement in order to comply with the requirement in the PWD that wages paid to posted workers meet minimum standards. The ECJ ruled in April 2008 that public procurement legislation that requires service providers to pay wages set in local collective agreements violated Article 49 EC (Article 56 TFEU), because the requirement could not be justified by the goal of worker protection.

The *Rüffert* case, like *Laval* and *Viking*, seriously threatens the position of trade unions because it undermines their freedom to negotiate wages and make sure that all workers in a sector or firm are paid the negotiated rate. It is no accident that all three cases concern those member states that have no statutory minimum wage. Indeed, the reason for this is that the state has delegated wage-setting to unions and employers in Germany, Sweden and Finland. In *Laval*, *Viking* and *Rüffert*, the absence of a statutory minimum wage or a collective agreement that is universally applicable allowed a loophole to emerge that permitted foreign service providers to pay wages lower than locally bargained rates. In essence, the ECJ rulings in these cases state that only a statutory minimum wage or a universally applicable collective agreement is the relevant reference for determining whether posted workers are paid too little. Thus, these ECJ rulings make it much more difficult for trade unions to negotiate the best deal they can for their members because the ECJ rulings effectively create a ceiling on posted workers' wages. That ceiling is determined by the statutory minimum wage or universally applicable collective agreements. Even where statutory minimum wages exist, unions often try to negotiate a higher wage rate, especially in sectors dominated by skilled labour. Moreover, collective bargaining in most countries is usually marked by some heterogeneity: there are often different collective agreements (with different wage rates) in the same sector. The ECJ's interpretation of the requirements of Article 49 EC

(Article 56 TFEU) and the PWD implies that unions have lost some of their influence on wage formation because they are not free to bargain for wage rates above the ceilings that the *Viking, Laval* and *Rüffert* rulings have set.

The *Viking, Laval* and *Rüffert* rulings appear to constitute a shift in the ECJ's view of the relationship between the social and economic aspects of European integration. Since the 1970s, ECJ jurisprudence has emphasized individuals' right to equal treatment (mainly on the basis of gender and nationality), even when undertakings' economic interests were at stake. In contrast, the *Viking, Laval* and *Rüffert* cases appear to signal that the right of undertakings to market access now trumps national labour law and practices under some circumstances. In other words, the 'fence around' national labour laws and practices is no longer impenetrable. Unions can still take industrial action, but the circumstances under which they may do so are now more restricted. The effect of the rulings is not to prohibit industrial action against foreign service providers; however, unions may not demand that foreign undertakings sign the same collective agreements that domestic undertakings do. This means that in autonomous bargaining models like Sweden's and Denmark's, unions cannot prevent low-wage competition (Malmberg and Sigeman, 2008). Although this is certainly a blow to the strong labour movements in the high-wage countries of Northern Europe, it is a boon to the accession states, with their lower labour costs and weaker industrial relations systems (Barnard, 2012, p. 208). Unions in Northern Europe are justifiably concerned about the impact of *Viking, Laval* and *Rüffert* on their industrial relations systems. The ETUC and other union actors are now lobbying for the inclusion of a provision in EU law that would require social issues to take precedence over economic ones if there were conflict between the two.

The uproar following the *Viking, Laval* and *Rüffert* rulings prompted the Commission to try to repair some of the damage by proposing the so-called 'Monti II' regulation in March 2012 (Commission, 2012b). The heart of the proposal was to establish that the freedom to provide services or establish a business did not supersede the right to take industrial action, as long as that action was proportionate. The Commission withdrew the proposal in September 2012 after widespread member state opposition and uncertainty about whether the European Parliament and Council would support it.

Reconciliation of work and family

This section considers EU policies that aim to make it easier for workers to combine work with family responsibilities, particularly child-rearing. Reconciliation policies, that is, policies that promote work–life balance, include:

- leave schemes that allow parents to take time off from work to care for a new baby or child
- protection for pregnant workers
- access to affordable childcare
- flexible working time arrangements that allow working parents to respond to the needs of their families.

There is tremendous variation across the member states concerning female labour force participation rate (see Figure 2.3) and the availability of reconciliation policies. The Nordic countries have the highest levels of female LMP and typically offer the most generous policies. Many conservative and liberal welfare regimes offer little support for working parents (Morgan, 2006).

EU policy initiatives in this area have only emerged in the past two decades; indeed, the founding treaties never foresaw any role for EU legislation concerning issues related to the family. Policies regulating the employment of mothers were left to the member states, along with most other social policies. Three developments changed this:

- the political mobilization of women beginning in the 1960s and 70s
- the expansion of individual employment-related rights
- EU policies for increasing employment.

The first EU initiatives concerned with the reconciliation of employment and family obligations, including the Equal Treatment Directive of 1976 (Council, 1976, later updated by Council and Parliament, 2006), were based on Article 119 EEC (Article 157 TFEU) concerning equal pay between men and women. The slowness of the member states to honour their commitments under Article 157 TFEU foreshadowed the lack of interest at member state and EU level in what were considered to be women's issues, such as the reconciliation of work and family. Indeed, in the 1950s and 60s, it was not uncommon in the original six member states for women to be required to leave employment when they got married (as in the Netherlands until 1956) or for married women to be legally required to ask their husbands for permission to work outside the home (Germany). Moreover, wages and social security benefits were usually based on the breadwinner principle, and single women's wages were often lower than men's (Sainsbury, 1996). In short, women's work was a sensitive issue, and the member states had no expectation or desire for the EU to intervene in this sphere.

In the following decades, the ECJ refused to consider the organization of the family in its rulings (Caracciolo di Torella and Masselot, 2010). In spite of this, women's political mobilization across Europe had some effect at EU level: the 1974 Social Action Programme (SAP) included the concept of work and family reconciliation for the first time, albeit in a way that was hardly revolutionary. The reference to work and family reconciliation was vague, and it implied that reconciliation applied only to women (Commission, 1974a). Incremental steps continued to follow, and the reconciliation goal was restated in the Community Charter of the Fundamental Social Rights of Workers in 1989 as well as in two SAPs on equal opportunities. Thus, by the beginning of the 1990s, the reconciliation of work and family was firmly on the EU policy agenda, but only supported with weak policy instruments.

The first substantial proposal concerning reconciliation was a proposed directive concerning parental leave in 1983 (Commission, 1983). The proposal would have given either parent three months of paid leave for a child under the age of three, but it fell victim to the UK's veto several times between 1983 and 1986 (van der Vleuten, 2007). A modified version of the proposal was adopted in 1993, after treaty reform made it possible to neutralize the UK veto (see below).

The Treaty of Maastricht was a major boost for reconciliation policies in four ways:

1. The adoption of the Agreement on Social Policy allowed the EU to move forward in social policy without the assent of the UK.
2. It elevated social protection to one of the EU's central aims.
3. It expanded the EU's social policy remit to include things like the equality of men and women in employment.
4. It gave the social partners a formal role in EU social policy decision-making (Caracciolo di Torella and Masselot, 2010).

The Commission and Council were quick to take advantage of these new policy competences. For example, a Council Recommendation on childcare adopted in 1992 identified four categories in which measures should be introduced:

- childcare services
- leave for employed parents
- family-friendly policies at the workplace
- encouraging the participation of men in the upbringing of children (Council, 1992).

The Commission's 1994 White Paper *European Social Policy* illustrates this orientation by stating that labour market participation should be improved by promoting 'greater solidarity between men and women' (Commission, 1994a; see Lewis, 2006).

A series of directives concerning the reconciliation of work and family were adopted starting in 1992. The Pregnant Workers Directive, adopted in 1992 (Directive 92/85), was based on the 1989 Framework Directive on Health and Safety (Directive 89/391/EEC). It established minimum standards for the workplace to protect the health of pregnant workers and new mothers, provided employment protection for pregnant workers and new mothers, and established minimum leave provisions for both groups. The proposal was actually introduced in 1990 on the basis of Article 153 TFEU so QMV applied. The UK objected that the original proposal would be too expensive for employers, resulting in a somewhat watered-down compromise. The European Parliament, backed by the Commission, tried to strengthen the proposal (concerning the level of compensation to be paid during leave), but failed after difficult negotiations in the Council (Falkner et al., 2005).

The Maastricht provisions for framework directives based on agreements by the social partners resulted in the Parental Leave Directive, the Part-time Work Directive and the Fixed-term Work Directive:

- The Parental Leave Directive (96/34, replaced by Directive 2010/18/UE) was relatively easy to negotiate compared to the Pregnant Workers Directive. The Council simply ratified the text adopted by the European organizations representing employers and unions (UNICE, CEEP and ETUC). The directive sets out minimum requirements for parental leave and time off for other family reasons. Workers have the right to at least four months (originally three months) of parental leave, they may not be dismissed for taking parental leave, and their jobs are protected while they are on leave.

- The Part-time Work Directive (97/81) establishes minimum standards concerning working time in order to remove discrimination against part-time workers.
- The Fixed-term Work Directive (99/70) forbids employers from treating fixed-term workers differently from permanent employees (unless there are objective reasons for doing so). Employers may also not abuse fixed-term contracts to avoid giving an employee a permanent contract.

These directives contain modest provisions concerning the rights of pregnant workers and parents of young children. However, they do mark the beginnings of an integrated EU policy to protect the employment rights of parents and make it easier for workers to combine parenthood and employment.

By the end of the 1990s, the emphasis on women as workers began to shift towards a human rights perspective emphasizing the rights of women. Articles 2 and 3 of the Treaty of Amsterdam (Article 3 TEU) explicitly state that the EU should promote equality and 'prohibit inequality between men and women in all areas'. In addition, the ECJ started to incorporate the principle of equality independent from market provisions in its rulings. Both the *Gerster* (C-1/95) and *Hill* (C-243/95) cases frame reconciliation as a right not only for women, but also for men. Moreover, the *Hill* case states that the goal of EU policy is to 'encourage and, if possible, adapt working conditions to family responsibilities'. In addition, EU law recognizes that women and men have the right to protection in their professional and family lives as a 'natural corollary of the equality between men and women'.

The introduction of the employment title in the Amsterdam Treaty and the subsequent Lisbon Strategy in 2000 gave the EU more competences to shape national employment policies, and reconciliation policies quickly became an important element in both. The EES explicitly addresses the need for better reconciliation of work and family. For example, one of original four pillars of the EES, equal opportunities, included the promotion of 'flexicurity' as a means to enhance the reconciliation of work and family by having atypical employment in combination with some degree of security (Caracciolo di Torella and Masselot, 2010).

The EES and Lisbon Strategy's emphasis on increasing employment requires a significant increase in female LMP, and reconciliation policies have become increasingly important for achieving this. The Lisbon Strategy (and EES) aimed at an employment rate of 70% and a female employment rate of 60%. The Europe 2020 strategy also explicitly recognizes reconciliation policies as key elements in its strategy for smart, sustainable and inclusive growth. Indeed, one of the central goals of Europe 2020 is a 75% employment rate by 2020, and reconciliation policies are emphasized as important elements in achieving this goal. In 2009, the employment rate in the EU 27 was 64.6%, slightly lower than the 2008 figure of 65.9%. The employment rate for women was 58.6% in 2009.

Besides these headline initiatives, the Commission and Council have stepped up their efforts to use soft law instruments to promote reconciliation policies in the 2000s and 2010s. Important initiatives include the adoption of a Council resolution on the balanced participation of men and women in family life (Council, 2000b) and the Commission's work–life balance package of 2008 (Commission, 2008a). The work–life balance package explicitly emphasizes the role of reconciliation policies in promoting gender equality. The European Pact for gender equality for 2011–20, annexed to the Council Conclusions from March 2011, reiterates this perspective and calls on member states to take steps to increase the availability of affordable childcare and flexible work arrangements. The June 2011 Luxembourg Council Conclusions contain a particularly strong statement on the role of reconciliation policies in promoting gender equality, but also emphasize how reconciliation policies, because they facilitate female employment, can help to meet the challenge of demographic change (Council, 2011a).

Conclusion

Policies concerning employment, collective bargaining, and the reconciliation of work and family are now important elements of the multilevel structure of EU social policy. This is not surprising, given the centrality of labour markets and labour mobility for the EU project. The constraints created by EMU were the impetus for a coordinated EU policy to promote employment, and the steady progress of individual rights concerning employment inspired EU initiatives concerning the reconciliation of work and family. What is surprising, however, is the recent judicial turn towards the primacy of the internal market over national social arrangements like collective bargaining. The European integration project has always been based on a bargain between the member states and European institutions, which guarantees that the four freedoms would not imperil member state social policies. In other words, the internal market was never supposed to lead to the weakening or even dismantling of domestic arrangements like collective bargaining. This seems to be exactly what is happening as a result of recent ECJ decisions. It is, however, too early to tell whether these decisions are anomalies or part of a larger trend (cf. Höpner and Schäfer, 2010).

The performance of the EES has not lived up to expectations. High hopes accompanied the launch of the Luxembourg process in 1997, but the worldwide financial crisis and the sovereign debt crisis have overwhelmed the weak policy instruments associated with the OMC. Even if the EES has resulted in a shift in national reform agendas, awareness of new policy solutions among domestic actors, and a change in cognitive understandings of the causes and consequences of unemployment, it has not prevented the dramatic deterioration in employment since 2008. In August 2014, the EU 28 unemployment rate was 10.1%, and it was even higher in the eurozone, at 11.5% (Eurostat, 2014b). These averages mask large variations among the member states. Greece and Spain recorded the highest unemployment levels, at 27% and 24.4% respectively (Greek data is for June 2014). Austria and Germany had the lowest unemployment rates, at 4.7 and 4.9% respectively (Eurostat, 2014b). Certainly, the EES was not designed to handle an economic shock of the magnitude associated with the economic and sovereign debt crises. The danger is, however, that these crises will undermine remaining support for positive action at EU level to promote employment. As discussed in Chapter 3, the EU's poor recent performance in promoting employment and the subordination of employment policy to the imperatives of EMU during the sovereign debt crisis have contributed to a decline in public support for European integration. This does not augur well for the future of EU employment policies.

Chapter 6

Vocational Training and Higher Education

The Treaty of Rome envisioned the EU's role in vocational education and training (VET) as a vehicle for helping the member states to retrain workers displaced by the establishment of the common market. If the treaty saw VET as a tool of market-building, it was completely silent concerning higher education. Despite these early constraints, a developmental process similar to harmonization has taken place in both fields. The member states now share a common two-cycle degree structure in higher education (the European Education Area created by the Bologna Process) where none existed before, and they have introduced a European Qualifications Framework (EQF) designed to make vocational qualifications comparable and transferable across national borders. Secondary legislation and non-binding tools of social policy-making have also shaped the development of other aspects of EU education and training policy. The EU has used hard law to facilitate the mutual recognition of professional qualifications, and there is a long tradition of using action programmes, recommendations and other soft law instruments to nudge member state policies in specific directions. Moreover, the European Social Fund has been an important source of funding and, more recently, innovation in VET policies.

As in other areas of social policy, the development of EU policies in education and vocational training has been marked by the incremental increase of EU competence and policy activity. Although the entrepreneurial efforts of supranational institutions, especially the Commission, have been important, intergovernmental bargaining has shaped the emergence of the European Education Area and the EQF. The Commission's early attempts to create a common VET policy did not come to much, but the onset of structural unemployment in the 1970s pushed higher education and VET to the top of the EU agenda. Before the arrival of persistent unemployment, EU

134

efforts focused on retraining in order to channel surplus labour to regions with labour shortages. The increasing awareness at EU and member state level of the importance of skill formation to economic growth and competitiveness was also the impetus for the inclusion of an article on 'Education, vocational training and youth' in the Maastricht Treaty (Articles 126 and 127 EEC, Article 145 TFEU), which gave EU institutions the power to introduce incentive measures. By the 1990s and 2000s, education and vocational training were implicated in several EU goals:

• helping the member states fight unemployment and adapt to structural economic change
• promoting EU identity and understanding of other cultures
• promoting human capital formation in order to enhance competitiveness.

The Bologna Process and the Copenhagen Process that created the EQF are core elements of all three goals. Thus, one of the keys to understanding the remarkable development of higher education and VET policies at the European level is the elevation of knowledge, skills and lifelong learning to core status in the EU's growth and employment strategies since the 1990s.

Varieties of skill formation

The growing literature on skill systems points to two broad approaches to skill formation:

• coordinated, collective skills systems that largely provide specific skills in tertiary education
• uncoordinated or 'liberal' systems that provide general skills.

Collectively organized systems also vary according to the role of school-based education in relation to work-based training like apprenticeships (Hall and Soskice, 2001; Busemeyer and Trampusch, 2012). Germany is the prototype of a collective, employer-based system, while France exemplifies the collective, school-based approach. These collective systems rely on the provision of the theoretical knowledge and skills required for specific occupations. Employers, unions and usually the state jointly determine the content of VET and are in charge of skill certification. As Brockmann et al. (2008) argue, these systems emphasize 'inputs': specific courses of study and periods of apprenticeship that prepare students for a lifelong career in a specific occupation. The uncoordinated general skills model exemplified by the UK and Ireland functions differently because it emphasizes 'outputs', or learning outcomes, rather than inputs. The demand for and certification of skills are largely determined by the market, rather than by coordination among employers, unions and the state. Instead, students acquire general education that they supplement with more narrowly defined training. Thus, the uncoordinated systems focus on the production of 'competences' or 'outputs' that ensure employability in broadly defined occupations, while collective systems produce certification for specific, regulated occupations.

National systems of skills provision, like other areas of social policy, are often objects of intense political contestation, so changing them is not easy. Education and training policies are often central elements in the competitive strategies of firms, especially in coordinated skills regimes, so employers and unions often have strong preferences for the status quo. For example, firms in collective skill systems like Germany absorb much of the cost of vocational training through the apprenticeship system, and many firms understandably prefer rules that allow them to recoup some of their investment in worker training. In liberal skills regimes, employers invest less in training programmes, because school-based education and training provides graduates with a much more general skill set. The direction of EU policy in VET challenges some of the core features of coordinated models such as Germany's (Brockmann et al., 2008; Trampusch, 2009). The last section of the chapter addresses this issue.

Early development of the EU's VET policy

The ambiguous legal basis for EU action in vocational training and member state hesitance to give the Commission any power constrained early attempts to formulate a coherent policy at the EU level. Article 128 (Article 148 TFEU) of the Treaty of Rome seemed to provide the basis for a common vocational training policy because it empowered the Council to establish general principles for a common policy of occupational training. However, the treaty was silent on the issue of how this should be accomplished (Collins, 1975). Similarly, little came of the provisions of Article 118 EEC (Article 156 TFEU) concerning the promotion of 'close collaboration in the social field', including occupational training. In the absence of a clear legal basis, the Commission and Council could agree on very little concerning VET in the early years of the EU. As in other areas of social policy, the Commission tried to fill the vacuum created by legal ambiguity (O'Grada, 1969), but the member states blocked these attempts. Moreover, the treaty provisions on vocational training contradicted other parts of the treaty that guaranteed member state supremacy in social policy (O'Grada, 1969). Thus, the first decade of the EEC was marked by the near absence of activities in education and training, despite the opening provided by Article 128 EEC (Article 148 TFEU).

The Commission got its chance when its proposal for a common VET policy was adopted by the Council in 1963. The Council decision set out 10 general principles for a common vocational training policy based on Article 128 EEC (Council, 1963). The common policy was intended to spur the member states to undertake collaborative action based on an aggregate assessment of manpower needs in the EU in order to estimate the need for different kinds of labour and train people to supply those skills. In 1960, the Commission had initiated annual surveys of 'manpower trends in the Community' that detailed labour shortages and surpluses. The Commission now urged the member states to cooperate in vocational training and promoting mobility so that surplus labour could move to areas experiencing shortages. Thus, by 1963, the Commission was proposing cooperation with the member states to relieve labour shortages by undertaking joint actions to train skilled workers (Commission, 1964).

Decision-making on the general principles foreshadowed the kinds of conflicts that continue to plague EU social policy-making. The final version of the proposal was weaker than what the Commission and the European Parliament wanted. The main points of disagreement with the Council concerned the role of European-level institutions. The Parliament wanted more involvement from European institutions, and the Council wanted to reserve implementation of general principles for the member states. The Council also resisted calls for the harmonization of levels of training, preferring instead a much weaker formulation and weakened provisions for common financing (O'Grada, 1969).

Thus, the issue of competence doomed the general principles to weakness. The member states simply did not want to give the Commission meaningful competence in vocational training

(O'Grada, 1969). Nevertheless, the Commission now had a mandate to:

- propose 'appropriate measures' in support of the goals set out in the decision
- carry out research
- assemble an inventory of training institutions in the member states
- promote the harmonization of training levels
- contribute to the improvement of VET instructors.

However, the member states retained control; indeed, the first principle stated:

> A common vocational training policy means a coherent and progressive common action which entails that each member state shall draw up programmes and shall ensure that these are put into effect in accordance with the general principles contained in this Decision and with the resulting measures taken to apply them. (Council, 1963, p. 2)

O'Grada (1969) argues that the general principles had 'little potential' and reflected the Council's hesitant view of VET.

Despite these constraints, the Commission formulated an action programme on vocational training policy to implement the general principles, and it was approved by the newly formed tripartite Advisory Committee on Vocational Training (O'Grada, 1969). The action programme focused on occupations that met three criteria:

1. occupations that were important for the European economy
2. occupations where there was some degree of mobility
3. occupations where there were labour shortages.

One of the most important components of the action programme was the attempt to harmonize training levels in occupations such as metalworking. One of the first attempts to create a European skill profile concerned the metalworking sector, but the initiative was unsuccessful.

The Commission continued its work on the harmonization of training levels, which expanded to include occupations in the building and transport sectors. The idea was to create a European career brief based on common training standards that individuals could use to gain access to the labour market in any member state – an idea that foreshadowed the EQF more than four decades later. At the same time, the Commission (1965) also started to push for a more active labour market policy that would not only train people for jobs in other member states but also for jobs in other economic sectors. Building on these efforts, the Commission proposed its first joint programme in vocational training to the Council in 1965, including plans to reskill 3,000 Italian workers in the building, metalworking and hotel sectors. The Council's response, predictably, was negative (because of joint financing and decreasing labour shortages) and the Commission (1967) withdrew the proposal.

These initial attempts to construct a European vocational training policy were piecemeal and largely without impact. The Commission had insufficient resources, both financially and in terms of staff, to promote an ambitious agenda. Indeed, the Council consistently rebuffed Commission efforts to expand EU activities in VET. The member states were wary of EU involvement in vocational training not only because of their general unwillingness to transfer competences in VET to the European level, but also because of the diversity of VET institutions in the member states. As discussed earlier, the member states differed in terms of the degree of specialization in their occupational training procedures and the role of workplace-based and school-based training and skill certification. These fundamental differences would make harmonization difficult, as the member states obviously preferred their own institutional template (collective or liberal skills regime) and had little interest in adjusting to a different system of providing and certifying vocational skills.

The European Social Fund

Despite the inability of the Commission to muster Council support for active EU intervention in VET, it could draw on the resources of the European Social Fund (ESF) to further EU involvement in VET. Article 123 EEC (Article 162 TFEU) established the ESF to promote 'the employment of workers' and enhance 'their geographical and occupational mobility within the Community'. In contrast to the regulatory bias of most EU social policy, the ESF has an explicitly redistributive basis. Unlike national entitlement-based social policies, however, the ESF does not redistribute among individuals or households, it redistributes across territories – the member states and the regions within them.

The ESF was introduced as part of the ECSC and was an explicit element in the Treaty of Rome because of the recognition that economic development would result in regional winners and losers. The ESF is now part of a broader set of policies, known as Cohesion Policy, and is one of five Structural and Investment Funds that help to finance and implement the policy. The two other main funds are the European Regional Development Fund (ERDF), which mainly finances infrastructure projects, and the Cohesion Fund, which complements the activities of the ESF and ERDF by financing projects (typically environmental and transport infrastructure) in those member states whose GDP is less than 90% of the EU average. Two smaller funds, the European Agricultural Fund for Rural Development and the European Maritime and Fisheries Fund, are targeted at agriculture and fisheries. For the programming period 2014–10, the EU allocated €351.8 billion, or 32.5% of the EU budget, to the Cohesion Policy. About €80 billion of this has been earmarked for the ESF, €63.5 billion for the Cohesion Fund, and €140 billion for the ERDF (Allen, 2010; Commission, 2014).

As the next sections show, the ESF has developed into an important vehicle for the EU's vocational training policies since the 1970s. The establishment of the ERDF in 1975 and the Cohesion Fund in 1994, as well as several reforms of the Cohesion Policy in the 1990s and 2000s, means that the EU, in partnership with the member states, now plays an important role in vocational training, but at the regional and not the individual level (Bachtler and Mendez, 2007). EU policies, however, do not create individual actionable rights to training.

The provisions in the Treaty of Rome concerning the ESF were sources of ambiguity and clarity. Article 123 EEC (Article 162 TFEU) is fairly open-ended, stating that the task of the ESF was to make the employment of workers easier and increase workers' geographical and occupational mobility. In contrast, Article 125 EEC (amended by Article 164 TFEU) explicitly mandated the ESF to reimburse the member states for 50% of the costs associated with training and relocating workers who became unemployed. Taken together, the treaty bases for the ESF seemed to assign an important policy-making function to the fund, while limiting its role to the task of reimbursing member states' costs.

Despite the legal ambiguity of the ESF, it played an important part in the first decade of the EEC by facilitating labour migration, especially from Italy to other member states. The newly formed

EEC allowed those member states with labour shortages to absorb workers with surplus labour. Once this initial phase of moving surplus labour to expanding regions was complete, the Commission increasingly focused on the effects of structural economic change on labour markets in the member states, advocating active labour market policies (O'Grada, 1969; Collins, 1983). Indeed, the Commission's first report on the activities of the Community (Commission, 1958) discusses the ESF in the same paragraph as the common vocational training policy and emphasizes the urgency of European policies that would coordinate member states' vocational training activities.

Although the ESF was up and running in 1961, it soon became clear that it would only play an intermediary role and not the more active role the Commission advocated. The Commission argued that it was not supposed to be a reactive institution that merely compensated the member states for the costs of relocation and retraining, but that it should promote the expansion of employment by 'reinforcing' member state policies intended to fight structural unemployment (Commission, 1961, p. 158, para. 153). As early as 1962, the Commission proposed expanding the ESF's activities, advocating pilot programmes in the member states in vocational training (Commission, 1963). The Commission also began to link labour surpluses in some countries to the low level of skills among the unemployed. To remedy this, the Commission (1963) advocated collecting more data on the distribution of skills and labour mismatches. The Commission's 'Initiative 1964' illustrates this orientation by setting out a range of proactive ideas about using the ESF as part of vocational training policy and labour market policy. The Council, however, consistently resisted any initiative that would expand the competence of the ESF and the role of the Commission in administering it (Collins, 1983).

Despite disagreement about the direction of ESF activities, it played an important role in the first decade of the EEC's effort to build a common labour market by addressing regional labour market imbalances. Between September 1960 and the end of 1973, about 1 million workers received vocational training co-financed by the ESF, and 700,000 were resettled with ESF co-financing. Of these 1.7 million workers, 65% were Italian and 25.5% were German. Moreover, many Italian workers receiving ESF-financed training did so in Germany, France and Belgium (Commission, 1998).

To sum up, the first decade of the ESF was marked by a tug of war between the Commission and Council concerning the ESF's remit. Despite the Commission's numerous attempts to use the ESF as a platform for a more active EU vocational training policy, the ESF remained firmly in member state control. The Council could exploit treaty provisions to rein in the Commission: Article 125 EEC called for the ESF to reimburse member state costs for training and resettlement, and the Council stuck to this minimal definition. This simply reinforced existing member state policies, rather than creating a foundation for more active EU intervention led by the Commission. It was completely up to the discretion of national authorities whether and how they used the ESF, and the ESF was reduced to writing cheques made out to the member states.

Reforming the European Social Fund

Article 126 EEC called for an evaluation of the activities of the ESF at the end of the 12-year transitional period for the establishment of the common market. Besides the legal obligation to review the ESF, there was growing concern that the ESF was not functioning as intended. By 1967, Germany had become the largest beneficiary of ESF financing, prompting concerns about its redistributive impact. In addition, there was growing concern in the Council and Commission that the market-building process itself was contributing to unemployment. The Commission's advocacy of an EU manpower policy within the remit of the ESF gained support in this context. Discussions about reforming the ESF were also linked to parallel discussions about whether to give the EU more power. The Commission took the reform initiative, presenting its ideas about ESF reform in 1969. The Council supported many of the principles proposed by the Commission, adopting a new set of ESF regulations in 1971 (Council, 1971; Collins, 1983; Commission, 1998).

The 1971 reform of the ESF was a watershed, in the sense that it reduced the Council's virtual monopoly over the ESF. The reform broke with the past in three ways:

1. The scope of the ESF's remit expanded. Rather than being a passive intermediary, the ESF would now be able take action if EC policies adversely affected employment, or if there were requests for joint action to improve the match between the supply and demand of labour in the EU. The ESF would also continue

to finance policies carried out in the member states, including vocational training.

2. The 1971 reform abolished the existing forms of retroactive grants (under Article 125 EEC), replacing them with advance grants. Now, the objectives outlined in the treaty would guide the ESF's operations; existing member state policies concerning training would no longer structure ESF activities. The ESF could channel resources to specific occupational groups, and the Commission was empowered to issue guidelines and priorities rather than simply processing member state applications for reimbursement of resettlement and training costs.

3. Under the new regime, the member states or the Commission would submit applications for support in advance to the Council (the Commission could also request the Commission to apply). This meant a more active role for the ESF; the Commission got more power because it could steer the programming, and it controlled the budget (Collins, 1983; Commission, 1998).

The EU's first enlargement in 1973 and mounting pressure to develop the social aspects of integration were the impetus for another reform of the ESF in 1977. As discussed in Chapter 1, the 1972 Paris Summit was the scene of intense negotiations concerning the social policy of the EU, resulting in the EU's first Social Action Programme. As Collins (1983, p. 15) put it:

> The high point of community political commitment to regional and social development was the Paris summit of 1972 which accepted the need to deal with regional and structural imbalances, the need to coordinate regional policies and to create a community fund to assist in both agricultural and industrial changes.

Rapidly rising unemployment also added to the pressure to reform the ESF so that it could be used as a more active instrument for promoting employment via training and other measures.

By now, the Commission had begun to view the ESF as the main instrument of EC social policy and began to press for more resources and the establishment of active labour market policy. The introduction of the ERDF in 1975 at the insistence of Italy and the UK responded to these concerns, and the Commission now viewed the ESF as an instrument of vocational training and the ERDF as an instrument of regional development. At the same time, the 1974 Paris Summit reinforced the idea of a coordinated EC-level employment policy in which the ESF would play a large part (Collins, 1983).

The emergence of high levels of youth unemployment also prompted calls for a more active ESF role. In 1982, EU-wide unemployment reached 10.5%, with 42% of the unemployed younger than 25. The ESF had already initiated programming that dealt with youth unemployment, channelling 44% of ESF resources to it in 1982. However, there was growing awareness that existing ESF programme rules were not suited to the needs of youths, because many young unemployed persons lacked even basic skills (Commission, 1998). The 1983 reform of the ESF (Council, 1983) thus redirected ESF policies to the goal of fighting youth unemployment and helping less developed regions. The ESF was to concentrate on upgrading the skills of young people with few qualifications and the long-term unemployed over the age of 25. Disadvantaged groups were also specifically targeted, including women, migrants and the disabled. As later sections show, high unemployment, especially among youths, continues to plague the EU, empowering actors who advocate a stronger role for European solutions to such problems.

The adoption of the Single European Act (SEA) in 1985 signalled another shift in ESF programming. The SEA's focus on economic and social cohesion in the context of Spanish, Portuguese and Greek accession led to a reorientation in the ESF. An important part of this process was the transformation of the ESF from an instrument of resettlement and vocational training into one of the three Structural Funds charged with promoting economic and social cohesion: the ESF, the ERDF and the Cohesion Fund. A 1988 reform streamlined the coordination of the three funds and doubled the overall cohesion budget. Cohesion Policy is now based on strategic, multiannual programmes, with EU funding intended to complement, rather than replace, national sources of finance. Cohesion programmes also operate on the partnership principle: supranational, national and subnational actors cooperate in planning and executing programmes (Hooghe, 1996; Bachtler and Mendez, 2007). Under the new rules, the Commission plays an important role, but it shares decision-making power with the Council and Parliament. The principle of 'concentration' allows the Commission to specify a limited number of goals and regions to guide Cohesion Policy. However, the Council (and later the

Parliament, via co-decision) allocates financial resources among the member states.

Since 1988, there have been four multiannual Cohesion Programmes (1988–93, 1994–99, 2000–2006, 2007–13). In late 2013, the Council and Parliament approved the current programme that runs from 2014 to 2020. Since the integration of the ESF into Cohesion Policy, it has continued to be an important vehicle for vocational training policies. It is, however, less clear what impact these policies have actually had. Certainly, the Commission plays a much more strategic role than it did prior to 1988, and it does so in partnership with national and subnational actors. As Marks (1996) argues, Cohesion Policy, including the ESF and its training initiatives, is the clearest example of multilevel governance in practice. Moreover, the goals driving ESF VET policies have shifted; the embedding of the ESF's training policies within the overall goals of Cohesion Policy means that social inclusion and social cohesion have shaped ESF training programming since 1988.

The principles of partnership and concentration have spawned a good deal of policy innovation (Brine, 2004). Civil society actors interact with national governments and the Commission in the design of the implementation of ESF projects. Under the partnership principle, the Commission negotiates with the member states on operational programmes partially financed by the ESF. This gives the member states considerable flexibility in designing training initiatives under the auspices of the ESF (Welbers, 2011). The Commission, Parliament and Council decide the amount of funding and the overall objectives, whereas the Commission and the member states hammer out the details of programmes. In the last programming period, the ESF:

- co-financed programmes that provided counselling and coaching to disadvantaged students
- offered initial vocational training
- expanded workplace training
- involved stakeholders from local communities in vocational training.

There is some evidence that the ESF has influenced the content and direction of member state policies. In Belgium, for example, ESF programming helped to spur policy innovation in the area of activation policies, including vocational training (Verschraegen et al., 2011).

Towards a more integrated approach

The primarily intergovernmental, unintegrated approach to VET began to change at the end of the 1960s. Pépin (2006) calls the period 1969–84 'the founding years' of the EU's education and training policy. The member states agreed on the outlines of non-binding cooperation in November 1971, and education ministers met at EU level for the first time. As in other areas of social policy, the challenge was to find a way to promote cooperation in a sensitive area. The accession of the UK, Ireland and Denmark in 1973 promised to make member state agreement on common policies more difficult, largely because Denmark objected to EU actions that lacked an explicit treaty basis.

Another sign of the growing commitment to EU policy in VET was the increase in resources in the Commission. The status of this policy field was elevated in 1973 with the establishment of a separate Directorate for Education and Training within the DG for Research and Science, and the founding of the European Centre for the Development of Vocational Training (Cedefop) in 1974 as part of the Social Action Plan (Commission, 1974a). The Commission also began to devote more resources to soft law. In March 1974, the Commission adopted a Communication laying out the guidelines for cooperation in education and training. The Communication identified the areas in which cooperation was desirable and provided for the creation of the Education Committee charged with providing content to the agreed areas of cooperation (Commission, 1974b). This marked the emergence of cooperation at EU level that presaged the adoption of the OMC in the 1990s: the member states would adhere to EU procedures, but they were not obligated to cooperate because of the absence of an explicit treaty basis (Pépin, 2006).

As noted in previous sections, rising unemployment created pressure for more EU involvement in education and training. In December 1975, the Council and the ministers of education agreed on their first action programme, and it was adopted as a Council resolution on 9 February 1976 (Council, 1976). The resolution identified six priority areas:

• education of migrant workers' children
• closer relations between national education systems
• gathering of information and statistics

- higher education
- foreign language teaching
- equal opportunities.

The resolution led to several small-scale programmes, but the tenuousness of the treaty basis for EC action led to stalemate between 1978 and 1980, largely because of Danish opposition. In the wake of member state intransigence, the Commission shifted focus, relocating education and training to the DG for Social Affairs and Employment and focusing on the links between education/training and social and economic policy. The adoption of the SEA in 1985 strengthened these efforts, partly because the implementation of the internal market raised the issue of the mutual recognition of educational and professional qualifications. In the absence of common standards, a single European labour market would remain elusive. In 1984, the Fontainebleau European Council agreed a flexible set of procedures that would later be set out in two directives to speed up this process (Directives 89/48 and 92/51). Stakeholders gave up on the old idea of harmonizing training systems and instead agreed to a new system based on the comparability of training.

This period also saw the establishment of several other specific programmes to promote student exchange:

- Community Programme in Education and Training for Technology (Comett)
- European Community Action Scheme for the Mobility of University Students (Erasmus)
- Programme for the Vocational Training of Young People and their Preparation for Adult and Working Life (PETRA)
- Youth for Europe
- Lingua
- Action Programme to Promote Innovation in the Field of Vocational Training Resulting from Technological Change in the European Community (Eurotecnet).

These programmes benefited from a renewed emphasis on a 'people's Europe' as well as efforts to achieve the single market. ECJ jurisprudence strengthened these developments: the ECJ's ruling in *Gravier* (Case 293/83) in 1985 expanded the scope of Article 7 EEC (Article 6 TFEU) and Article 59 EEC (Article 165 TFEU) on vocational training to include education more broadly. This made it possible to include higher education within the scope of the treaty and for Comett, Erasmus and other exchange programmes to move forward. At the same time, experiments with a European Credit System for Vocational Education and Training (ECVET) created the conditions for enhanced student mobility.

The 1992 Maastricht Treaty specifically included education for the first time (Article 126 EEC), reflecting the key role of education for the internal market as well as efforts to specifically clarify the treaty basis of higher education after the conflicts of the 1970s. The Maastricht Treaty also introduced the concept of 'subsidiarity' – the principle that the EU should only act when EU action is more effective than member state action (except in areas for which the EU has exclusive competence). The treaty specifically ruled out the harmonization of higher education and training systems, requiring that EU initiatives 'support and supplement' member state activities. It also gave the European Parliament more powers in the field of higher education and training by extending co-decision to these areas.

The period 1993–99 was characterized by the increasing integration of education and training policies as the EU began to emphasize the importance of creating a 'knowledge-based society'. The emphasis of the newly adopted European Employment Strategy (see Chapter 5) on employability included a prominent role for education and training. The first set of employment guidelines thus included concrete benchmarks linking training to employment: the guidelines exhorted the member states to offer training or some other measure within 12 months of the onset of unemployment, but 6 months for young people (Council, 1997). EU policies concerning VET, including ESF programming, thus became important elements in the EU's attempt to promote active employment policies in the member states.

The completion of the internal market added momentum to the EU's education and training policies. The 1993 White Paper *Growth, Competitiveness, Employment* emphasized the central role of education and training in creating jobs and economic growth, and it specifically emphasized lifelong learning (Commission, 1993a). A White Paper followed in 1995, *Teaching and Learning: Towards the Learning Society* (Commission, 1995), which identified the major challenges to education and training systems: globalization, the rise of the information society, and technological change. For the Commission, the answers to these challenges were lifelong learning and skills. More importantly, the White Paper rejected the distinction between education and training, and outlined a renewed agenda in this area. The Commission supported this new orientation by declaring 1996 the 'European Year of Lifelong Learning'. Such actions are largely symbolic, but they do help to call attention to issues and solutions by framing policy problems and solutions.

Long-term policy coordination: the Lisbon and Europe 2020 growth strategies

The 1993 *Growth, Competitiveness, Employment* White Paper and the emphasis on education and training as central elements for the EU's growth strategy set the stage for a more long-term integrated approach. The launch of the Lisbon Strategy in 2000 strengthened European cooperation in education and training further by emphasizing the central importance of education and training in adapting to the knowledge society. Thus, the Lisbon Presidency Conclusions included, for the first time, concrete goals in education and training (Council, 2000a):

1. increased resources for investments in human capital
2. halving (by 2010) the number of 18- to 24-year-olds with lower secondary education who are not in further education or training
3. transforming schools and training facilities into multipurpose 'local learning centres'
4. formulating a definition of 'basic new skills' to be acquired through lifelong learning, including ICT, foreign languages, business skills and social skills
5. improvements in student and teacher mobility
6. development of a voluntary common format for CVs to facilitate mobility.

With education and training now key elements in the EU's growth and employment strategy, the 2001 Stockholm European Council identified common objectives in VET and education to be met by 2010, and commissioned a work programme to achieve them, Education and Training 2010 (known as ET 2010). The Education Council adopted five benchmarks to be achieved using the OMC, including the following goals (Council, 2001b):

- increase the quality and effectiveness of education and training systems in the EU
- improve access to education and training
- improve the accessibility of education and training systems for those outside the EU.

In 2003, these goals were translated into the following five quantitative goals to be achieved by 2010:

1. 85% of 20- to 24-year-olds should have an upper secondary education
2. 12.5% of 25- to 64-year-olds should be engaged in lifelong learning
3. the number of graduates in mathematics, science and technology should increase by 15%; the gender imbalance among graduates should decrease
4. the average number of early school leavers in the EU should not exceed 10% of 18- to 24-year-olds
5. the percentage of low achievers in reading should decrease by at least 20% compared to 2000.

In keeping with the OMC, the Commission monitored the implementation of ET 2010, and the first joint report evaluating progress was presented at the spring 2004 European Council. In the Presidency Conclusions of the 2002 Barcelona European Council, the EU heads of government extended the goals of ET 2010 to include 'making these educative and training systems a world quality reference by 2010' (Council, 2002) and promoting cooperation in vocational education and training akin to the Bologna Process (see below). This mandate was the basis for the Copenhagen Process discussed below. In May 2009, the Council adopted an updated set of benchmarks to guide activities until 2020 and renamed the programme Education and Training 2020 (known as ET 2020). ET 2020 targets build on ET 2010 but are more ambitious. The emphasis on reducing the number of early leavers and increasing tertiary level attainment and adult participation in lifelong learning remains, but ET 2020 also ventures into fairly new territory by including targets for early childhood education, achievement in basic skills, employability (the number of graduates in employment), and study abroad.

The performance of ET 2010 and 2020 has been mixed. Certainly, the application of the OMC has greatly increased awareness and expertise at EU and member state level concerning education and training outcomes. However, the programme has made little concrete progress in achieving its most important goals. Progress on Europe 2020 headline targets demonstrate this:

- the share of early leavers from education and training was 12.7% in 2012, well above the target of 10%
- tertiary educational attainment was 35.7% in 2012, well below the target of 40% (Commission, 2013c).

Intergovernmental initiatives: the Bologna Process and the European Qualifications Framework

Intergovernmental bargaining largely outside EU institutions has led to the adoption of far-reaching reforms of higher education. The Bologna Process, initiated in 1999, created a higher education area in Europe that includes, but is not limited to, EU member states. Participants in the Bologna Process now share the same two-cycle degree structure, cooperate in quality assurance, ensure the transparency and transferability of degrees, and guarantee the mutual recognition of study abroad periods. Before Bologna, the EU and the rest of Europe were home to a wide variety of higher education institutions. The UK and Ireland used the two-cycle system (bachelor and master), while higher education systems on the Continent and in Nordic countries were based on the single degree system. Today, 47 countries share the same basic degree structure and grant comparable degrees that are transferable across the member states.

The Bologna Process originated in intergovernmental discussions about how to improve the compatibility of higher education institutions in Europe. In May 1998, four European ministers of education issued the Sorbonne Declaration calling for the harmonization of higher education institutions in Europe (Sorbonne Declaration, 1998). The underlying idea was to create a European higher education area that would promote European universities and culture, as well as increase competitiveness. The declaration emphasized the non-economic aspects of European integration, stating that the EU 'must be a Europe of knowledge' besides promoting the internal market and common currency. In short, the four signatories (France, Germany, Italy and the UK) set out to create the conditions for a higher education area in Europe that would enhance individual mobility and employability.

The comparability and transferability of higher education degrees were key elements in the process that led from Sorbonne to Bologna. One element of this was the introduction of the Diploma Supplement in all signatory countries. This is designed to facilitate employability and increase the attractiveness of European higher education because it provides graduates with an easily recognizable and accepted method of translating their degree into a European equivalent. Equally important, the Bologna signatories signalled their willingness to introduce a two-cycle degree structure. The first degree, usually the bachelor, would be the standard entrance qualification for the labour market, whereas the second degree, the master, would represent a more advanced qualification. Bologna would also promote student mobility by setting up a credit system that would be used throughout Europe (with the existing ECVET as the model).

The Commission has largely been a bystander throughout the negotiations leading to the Bologna Process. Additionally, the Bologna Process retains the status of an international treaty. Although the EU has incorporated the Bologna Process into its policy-making in education, especially the Lisbon Strategy and Europe 2020, the Bologna Process is administered largely outside the EU's machinery. The Bologna governance structure includes representatives from the participating countries, as well as representatives from the European Commission and European higher education organizations. However, the key decision-makers are the education ministers from the signatory countries. This means that the member countries pursue the convergence of higher education systems within a framework that allows them to steer the implementation and monitoring and preserve the autonomy of their universities. Ravinet (2008, p. 354) argues that 'it is no longer possible to create national higher education policies that are anti-Bologna' because the follow-up and monitoring procedures create incentives for the participating countries to comply.

The success of the Bologna Process is remarkable when we consider that it is the result of member state attempts to circumvent EU policy-making institutions. The Bologna Process commits signatories to comply with its provisions, but crucially, signatories do not give up any control over higher education to supranational institutions. Bologna's architects were also motivated by domestic considerations. Hoareau (2012) argues that the four founding ministers' attempts to overcome domestic opposition to educational reforms were important causes of the Bologna Process. Jürgen Rütt-gers, German minister of education, was particularly influential. Rüttgers wanted to simplify the German higher education degree structure and reduce the federal state's influence on higher education. The 16 German states (*Länder*) are responsible for higher education, but federal government influence on education had increased somewhat. The Bologna framework allowed Rüttgers to pursue two goals simultaneously: reduce federal influence on education and avoid EU interference, thereby preserving *Länder* control over higher education. The 16 *Länder* would use existing institutions for federal–state cooperation to request the federal government to sign the Bologna Declaration, the guiding document of the Bologna Process, and they would retain the right to request the federal government to withdraw from it in the future. In short, the multilateral structure of the Bologna Process allowed the German *Länder* to consolidate their control over higher education.

The Copenhagen Process and the EQF

Like the Bologna Process, the Copenhagen Process is intended to promote cooperation in the field of tertiary education, especially concerning mobility and improving the transparency and transferability of vocational qualifications. Unlike Bologna, however, the impetus for the Copenhagen Process came from within the EU. After the successful launch of the Bologna Process and the introduction of the Lisbon Strategy, the Barcelona European Council in March 2002 called for increased cooperation in VET. In November 2002, the Education Council adopted a resolution calling for increased European cooperation in VET that later became the foundation for the Copenhagen Declaration, signed a few weeks later by 31 national ministers (including non-EU members and candidate countries) responsible for VET, the Commission, and the European social partners. The Copenhagen Process is intended to improve the performance, quality and attractiveness of VET in Europe, and is a central element of Europe 2010 and Europe 2020 (Heyes and Rainbird, 2007).

The Copenhagen Process is based on the OMC, relying on benchmarking, information sharing, mutual learning, and the identification of good practices to promote common objectives. The goal is to create uniform indicators for measuring qualifications by creating national qualification frameworks that form the basis for the EQF.

There are eight qualification levels that facilitate the comparability of skill levels across national systems. Each participating country in the Copenhagen Process agreed to link its national qualification framework to the 8-level EQF. Like other OMCs, the Copenhagen Process includes procedures for monitoring progress towards meeting the objectives. The Maastricht Communiqué set out priorities in 2004, including the establishment of the EQF. Additional evaluations were conducted in 2006 (the Helsinki Communiqué) and 2010 (the Bruges Communiqué). By the end of 2012, 16 countries had linked their national qualifications levels to EQF levels by December 2012 (Cedefop, 2013). In sum, the goal was not to harmonize systems of vocational qualification but to accept national differences within a standardized European system (Heyes and Rainbird, 2007; Powell and Trampusch, 2012).

The implementation of the EQF has not been smooth in all participating countries. As Powell and Trampusch (2012) argue, the EQF challenges the 'vocational principle' underlying VET in the input-oriented, collective skills regimes in countries like Germany and Austria. The vocational principle means that individuals are trained to carry out specific, legally recognized occupations. Firms typically play an important role in training, and skill acquisition is organized around the needs of specific occupations. In contrast, liberal or uncoordinated skills regimes typically rely on skill acquisition organized in modules, rather than in integrated vocational training programmes lasting several years. The EQF's emphasis on learning outcomes rather than vocational orientation thus threatens the logic of collective skills regimes. The implementation of the EQF has been conflictual in Germany, precisely because of the important of the vocational principle. In contrast, the EQF has been consensual in those member states where school-based VET dominates and the vocational principle is weaker, including the Netherlands, Austria and Denmark (Powell and Trampusch, 2012).

Conclusion

The development of higher education and VET policies at the European level has been marked by the steady increase of European competences and policy activism. The European Social Fund has been transformed from a passive financial supporter of member state VET policies targeted at a narrow group of displaced workers to an active partner in multilevel policies aimed at upgrading the skills of a broad range of target groups. Treaty revisions and Commission entrepreneurship have expanded the EU's remit in education and training to include all levels of instruction. Higher education and vocational training are now core components in EU policies for fighting social exclusion (see Chapter 8) and enhancing economic competitiveness, especially in knowledge-based sectors. Finally, intergovernmental cooperation outside the EU's decision-making channels has led to the harmonization of higher education degree structures, whereas soft governance within EU institutions drove the emergence of the European Qualifications Framework.

The development of the internal market has been an important driver of these developments. The construction of a common labour market and the effects of the market-building process on employment created incentives for the EU to expand its education and training policies. In this sense, 'functional spillovers' from the market-making process are an important explanation for the expansion of EU education and training policies. Efforts to harmonize education and training are designed to promote the transparency and transferability of degrees and qualifications across national borders, thereby facilitating labour mobility and enhancing EU competitiveness. As the Bologna Process demonstrates, however, domestic political conflicts concerning the direction of reform also shaped policy development at European level.

The process of harmonizing degree structures and qualification levels in VET has produced a complex picture of winners and losers. Students are clearly the chief beneficiaries of the Bologna Process, because of the transparency and transferability of degrees. It is too early to tell, however, whether the adoption of the two-cycle structure outside the UK and Ireland will result in the acceptance of the bachelor degree as an initial labour market qualification. Despite the advantages of Bologna for universities, the adjustment costs have not been minimal. In many participant countries, the implementation of the two-cycle degree structure involved high adjustment costs, especially in terms of teaching loads and administrative procedures. As discussed above, the implementation of the EQF has also produced winners and losers. The implementation phase has sometimes been conflictual, with stakeholders exploiting the implementation process to push institutional change in their preferred direction.

Europe 2020 and the Social Investment Package announced in early 2013 are likely to increase the salience of EU policies concerning education and training. Europe 2020 is based on 'smart growth' and the Social Investment Package emphasizes skilling and reskilling as essential elements of smart growth. This reorientation places education and training at the centre of social protection and economic growth. At the same time, however, the worldwide economic crisis and the EU sovereign debt crisis place limits on the EU's capacity to expand education and training policies. The deflationary effects of the crises mean that the EU and the member states have fewer resources to devote to education and training. More ominously, the employment effects of the crises mean that many recent graduates cannot find jobs and many experienced workers remain out of work. In the context of high unemployment, supply-side policies like education and training have limited effect.

Chapter 7

Health Policy

Health policy is a field where European integration was never supposed to have much influence, except for measures related to migrant workers and occupational health and safety. When the founding treaties were negotiated, the member states naturally assumed that they would remain firmly in control of health policy, especially their health care systems. The limited provisions in the founding treaties concerning health policy were, nonetheless, the basis for modest EU interventions in public health as well as occupational health and safety in the 1960s, 70s and 80s. Just as the EU's founders intended, the member states seemed to be firmly in control of health care policy during this period, and they showed little inclination to transfer any more health policy competences to the European level other than the limited ones already in place. The reinvigoration of the integration process in the 1980s and the adoption of the Single European Act (SEA) in 1986 signalled the beginning of a new phase of EU health policy activism by including a modest expansion of EU competence in public health. The Maastricht and Amsterdam Treaties extended EU competence in public health in important ways, but these advances did not appear to represent a strong threat to member state autonomy in health policy. A series of ECJ rulings since the late 1990s concerning the applicability of internal market rules to health care marked a radical shift in the development of EU health policy. Since then, the member states have woken up to the harsh reality that core elements of their public health care systems may be subject to EU law concerning the freedom to provide services and the freedom of European patients to purchase medical services and products (like glasses) in other member states. ECJ activism has prompted efforts by the member states to use the Council to claw back some of the control over national health care they lost as a result of ECJ rulings.

This chapter analyses how the development of the internal market, in conjunction with the emergence of coherent EU policies in public health and occupational health and safety, has brought forth the beginnings of a truly European approach to health policy. The hallmarks of this approach are European policies on public health that complement and coordinate member state policies, a binding set of minimum standards for occupational health and safety, and a potentially far-reaching intrusion of internal market legislation into national health care systems. These policies, especially those concerning health care, impinge on member states' ability to organize their health care systems on a purely national basis and pursue autonomous public health policies.

The chapter begins with a conceptual discussion, distinguishing between three elements of health policy: health care, public health, and occupational health and safety. Section two discusses health care, section three analyses public health and section four analyses occupational health and safety. Each of the policy sections discusses the role of primary and secondary law, as well as the role of ECJ case law in shaping health policy at EU level and in the member states. The bulk of the chapter deals with health care policy because it is here where most is at stake: the health care systems in the member states are enormously complicated, expensive bundles of policy that represent decades of political contestation.

Conceptualizing health care

Health policy is a broad field, encompassing not only health care, but also public health and occupational health and safety:

1. *Health care policy* is the most important subfield of health policy, at least in terms of health spending and impact on individual wellbeing. The member states spend a total of 9% of GDP on health care – second only to pensions – and EU residents interact with health care providers frequently throughout their lives. For the purposes of this chapter, health care is defined as the set of policies that regulate the three central dimensions of health care systems:
   - the range of health care benefits available to individuals as well as access to them
   - the administration of health care services
   - the financing of health care services.
   An analysis of health care policy thus includes:

- attention to the structure of health care coverage, either via social health insurance funds or national health care systems
- the actors and institutions who provide health care services – doctors and other medical professionals and the hospitals and clinics they work in
- the insurance funds or national health care budgets that finance care.

2. *Public health policy* encompasses initiatives designed to prevent and control the spread of disease, promote healthy behaviour, and ensure a healthy human environment.

3. *Occupational health and safety policy* includes legislative measures that regulate working conditions to ensure worker safety.

The development of EU law and policy shapes what the member states do in each of these three areas, but in different ways. The EU has a tangible but limited legal mandate in occupational health and safety and public health because of the EU's core concern with labour markets within the larger EU internal market and the mainstreaming of public health with the Amsterdam Treaty. In the field of public health, the Directorate-General for Health and Consumers has been able to use fairly specific treaty provisions to promote the development of a genuinely European public health policy that complements member state policies. In the field of health care, there is no specific treaty basis for EU action. EU health care policy is largely based on the rules governing the internal market and the ECJ's interpretation of this legislation (Mossialos et al., 2010; Lamping, 2012; Greer and Kurzer, 2013; cf. Buch-Hansen and Wigger, 2011).

EU policies in the field of health do not affect the health policies of the member states uniformly, so it is necessary to understand the most important dimensions of institutional variation in health policies. Whereas public health and occupational health and safety are regulatory policies involving relatively modest financial resources, a limited number of actors and little redistribution, health care is a much more complicated policy area. There is little meaningful variation across the member states in their approaches to public health; all member states pursue policies designed to prevent and control the spread of disease, but there is variation concerning the level of government responsible for implementing some aspects of public health policy. Federal systems like Germany divide authority for public health between the central and regional governments, creating an additional layer of complexity in the negotiation and implementation of EU public health policies. In occupational health and safety, the key dimension of variation is between those member states with regulated labour markets and those with relatively less regulated labour markets. Member states like France, Germany and Italy have extensive regulations on issues related to occupational health and safety, such as working time. Member states like the UK and some of the new member states have less regulation in this area. This division between the member states in terms of workplace regulation shapes negotiations at EU level concerning occupational health and safety, as well as implementation.

Health care policy is much more complicated than public health and occupational health and safety because of the resources and institutions involved, which makes the political salience of this policy area that much stronger. Despite decades of research on typologies of welfare regimes (Esping-Andersen, 1990), there is little conceptual clarity concerning health policy, particularly health care systems. Indeed, the most influential attempts to identify the key elements of health care systems borrow from the literature on social insurance that emphasizes the Bismarck/Beveridge dichotomy rather than Esping-Andersen's three worlds of welfare capitalism. As noted above, the three key dimensions of variation in health care systems are the basis of entitlement, the mode of financing, and the method of administration or provision. Table 7.1 captures these dimensions of variation for the Bismarckian and Beveridgean clusters, which are as follows:

1. *Beveridgean* systems provide access to health care based on residence, general taxation finances the health care systems, and public hospitals and medical providers predominate. Thus, Beveridgean systems offer 'benefits-in-kind' to all residents regardless of occupational status, medical history or ability to pay. The 'national health care' systems of the UK, the Nordic countries and Southern Europe belong to this cluster.
2. *Bismarckian* systems also provide universal access to health care, but the institutional arrangements that accomplish this are very different from those in the Beveridgean cluster. Bismarckian systems are based on social insurance linked to occupational status, with separate schemes for those who lack employment-based coverage (the unemployed, pensioners and so on). Dependent family members are co-insured. Bismarckian systems

Table 7.1 *A typology of health care systems*

	Beveridge	*Bismarck*
Basis of entitlement	Citizenship or residence	Occupational or family status
Mode of financing	General taxation	Social insurance contributions
Method of administration	Public health care providers	Public, semi-public and private providers

are financed with earnings-related insurance contributions, often with some form of state grant to supplement insurance revenues. Institutions and providers (hospitals, clinics, doctors, nurses) are usually semi-public or private, but their services are strongly regulated by national fee schedules and rules about access.

Hervey (2011) emphasizes that solidarity is a key organizing principle of all health care systems in the EU, regardless of whether they are based on Bismarckian or Beveridgean principles. All EU member states guarantee coverage to those residing within their borders, and all health care systems contain some elements of risk pooling so that all individuals have the same or similar access to health care, regardless of their health status or ability to pay. This also means that health care financing is not related to health status; individuals who are 'bad' risks do not pay more for their coverage than those who are healthy. Even those member states with large private health care sectors have policy mechanisms in place that promote risk pooling and solidaristic financing. Thus, even private actors like private insurance companies are constrained, in that they usually cannot exclude bad risks and cannot charge higher rates for those with health problems.

Primary and secondary legislation

The most important aspect of EU involvement in health care policy is that the internal market has encroached on national health care systems in ways that the architects of the founding treaties never intended. It is not formal EU competences but rather the ECJ's interpretation of internal market legislation that shapes health policies in the member states. As Leibfried (2010) puts it, health policy exemplifies how EU social policy is made by judges and markets. Greer (2006) calls the Europeanization of health care 'uninvited Europeanization'.

Despite the inroads that the internal market has made into health care, there is little support for European intervention into this policy field. It is above all the Commission and the ECJ who are the prime movers behind health policy at EU level, and they have 'effectively created EU health policy without any demand for it' (Greer, 2009, p. 3). Thus, EU legislation influences health care policy less via treaty articles and legislation than through other parts of the treaties, especially internal market regulation, competition law, worker mobility, the mutual recognition of diplomas, and public procurement (Greer, 2009). The ECJ's activist interpretations of the application of internal market provisions to health care have been an unwelcome intrusion into national competences for the member states. Indeed, Article 168 TFEU recognizes that the member states have primary responsibility for their health policies and the 'organization and delivery of health services and medical care', and ECJ decisions affecting health care routinely emphasize member state control in this area. Formally, the member states look as if they are the key players, but the ECJ has repeatedly ruled that member state control of health care does not mean that treaty provisions concerning the internal market can be ignored. ECJ jurisprudence has established that many of the principles governing the internal market apply to health care.

Before discussing the court cases that form the foundation of the ECJ's legal policy-making, it is necessary to review the treaty provisions and secondary legislation that apply to health care, even if these have not been especially powerful. If we look at the first key element of health care systems – the structure and accessibility of health care benefits – the EU's regulation of the social security rights of migrant workers has important implications for health care. Article 48 TFEU assigns the EU the power to adopt rules that guarantee the coordination of social security policies across the member states, and Article 5 TFEU empowers the EU to take measures to ensure the coordination of social policies. A series of regulations adopted since 1967 govern the health care rights of migrant workers. It should be obvious that the mobility of migrant workers does not make much sense if the host country does not allow for the health insurance coverage of migrant workers. Regulation 1408/71, replaced by Regulation 883/2004, grants migrant workers and their families access to emergency health care while residing, even temporarily, in another member state and access to the public health care system of the host state while employed there. Regulation 1408/71 has implications for national health care systems because in those member states with Bismarckian systems, health care is part of the public social security system and thus falls under the scope of the regulation. With the adoption of Regulation 883/2004, European citizens and those with permanent residence now have a European health insurance card. Private health insurance systems are subject to different rules. In principle, any European citizen with private health insurance may seek treatment in another member state because private health care services are services in the meaning of the treaties.

Turning to the second key aspect of health care systems – the administration of health care – there is little in the treaties that directly addresses how health care is administered in the member states. As noted, the member states remain formally in charge of their health care systems: EU law does not dictate whether medical providers should be public or private. However, EU law concerning the internal market permits the EU to regulate two areas central to how health care systems are administered: the trade in medical products and the mobility of medical professionals. The Treaty of Rome (Articles 9–16 and 30–36) included medical products among the goods subject to legislation concerning the internal market. Article 36 allows for exceptions to free movement if these are 'justified on grounds of the protection of health and life of humans'. Hervey (1998) observes that the ECJ has allowed much latitude to the member states in interpreting what this means.

Directive 65/65/EEC is the first piece of legislation dealing with the safety of medical products, and it required the member states to mandate regulatory supervision of new medical products (amended by, for example, Regulation 2309/93/EEC and Directive 93/39/EEC). National regulatory bodies still control approval of most new medical products, but mutual recognition applies unless the member states provide a compelling reason to exclude medical products approved for sale in other member states. One of the core elements of the legislation is that producers of medical goods can seek regulatory product approval in member states other than the one where they are located. European-level approval is also possible for certain medical products. National legislation concerning pharmacies, especially vendors allowed to sell prescription drugs, however, has survived the internal market.

Freedom of movement also allows health care workers to move to other member states to practise their profession (Articles 46–66 TFEU). Because of variations in medical training, there are directives that deal with the mutual recognition of qualifications for professions like doctors, dentists, pharmacists, nurses and midwives (Directive 2005/36/EEC). The basic principle guiding the legislation is that the relevant institutions in the member states that certify health professionals are required to accept the qualifications obtained in another member state. Health care professions that do not fall into the categories covered by these directives are regulated by legislation that covers the recognition of higher education diplomas (Directive 89/48/EEC). Hervey (1998) notes that migration by health professionals is low except for those member states with the same language or located close to each other.

There is nothing in the treaties or secondary legislation that directly impinges on the third key dimension of health care systems – the structure of financing. The member states are free to choose between social security financing (wage-based contributions), general taxation, regulated private insurance, or a combination of these elements, as the basis for financing health care. As the preceding discussion demonstrates, however, EU legislation concerning the four freedoms cracked open the door to EU influence on the functioning of health care systems in the member states. In a series of decisions beginning in the 1990s, the ECJ has progressively pulled that door open wider, and the member states have responded by trying to wrest control back from the ECJ. The next section deals with these court cases and the tug of war between the member states and European institutions about control over health care.

The internal market and health care

Patient mobility

In a series of foundational cases, the ECJ shocked the health care policy community by ruling that Article 49 EC (Article 56 TFEU) concerning the freedom to provide services gives individuals the right to publicly funded cross-border health care services. Before the ECJ's rulings, national-level regulations largely determined access to health care. Certainly, health care systems in the member states offered universal access to care, but they did not pay for treatment received by individuals in other member states, except in the situations detailed in Regulation 1408/71:

1. Individuals insured under the public health care system in one member state could receive emergency treatment in the public health care system of another member state.
2. Individuals insured under the public health care system of one member state could receive medical care in another member state if the treatment had been pre-authorized.

These two rather restrictive provisions would become the centre of controversy in several important court cases concerning patient mobility.

The first case, *Decker* (Case 120/95), involved the purchase of medical equipment in another member state. Decker, a resident of Luxembourg, purchased prescription glasses in Belgium, but his request for reimbursement was denied because his sickness insurance fund argued that Regulation 1408/71 did not require reimbursement. According to Regulation 1408/71, persons wishing to receive non-emergency medical care in another member state required pre-authorization from their insurance fund, which Decker had not sought. Decker appealed several times in the Luxembourg courts and lost. The sickness funds argued, and Luxembourg social security courts confirmed, that non-emergency medical care received abroad was subject to social security law and not treaty provisions concerning free movement. The case reached the Luxembourg Social Security Tribunal, which referred a question to the ECJ for a preliminary ruling. The tribunal asked whether Luxembourg social security law violated Articles 30 EEC and 36 EEC (Articles 34 and 36 TFEU) of the treaty. By now, the Commission had joined Decker's side in the case, and both argued that Luxembourg law was an 'unjustified barrier to the free movement of goods' (para. 17 of *Decker* ruling). The Belgian, French and UK governments joined Luxembourg in arguing that Articles 30 EEC and 36 EEC did not apply. The German, Spanish and Dutch governments agreed with Luxembourg, Belgium, France and the UK that Regulation 1408/71 should apply. The ECJ ruled that Articles 30 EEC and 36 EEC applied, arguing that this was consistent with earlier rulings that found that national implementation of Regulation 1408/71 did not mean that the member states could violate treaty provisions concerning the free movement of goods. The ECJ reasoned that national rules requiring nationals to receive glasses from domestic providers discriminated against suppliers in other member states and therefore constituted a barrier to free movement.

The *Kohll* case (Case 158/96) also originated in Luxembourg and concerned an individual's right to seek orthodontic care in another member state, Germany. Kohll's daughter received orthodontic care in Germany, but Kohll's health insurance fund denied the claim for reimbursement because Kohll did not seek prior authorization from the competent social security institution. Kohll appealed several times and the case finally reached the highest social security court in Luxembourg. Because Kohll argued that his health insurance fund was subject to Articles 59 EEC and 60 EEC (Articles 56 and 57 TFEU), and not just to Regulation 1408/71, the court asked the ECJ for a preliminary ruling. Greece and the UK joined Luxembourg's side in the proceedings, and Germany, France and Austria agreed with Luxembourg that pre-authorization should be allowed to continue. The Commission sided with Kohll but did allow that the freedom to provide services could be restricted if there were 'overriding reasons relating to the general interest' (*Kohll*, para. 14). The ECJ found that there was no compelling justification based on general interest, cost control or public health and ruled that member state rules that precluded reimbursement without pre-authorization were a violation of Articles 59 and 60 EEC.

The importance of the *Kohll* and *Decker* cases is that the principle of freedom of movement of goods and services now applied to public health care systems. To put it another way, patients could now purchase medical goods and services in another member state and receive reimbursement on the same terms as those that apply to national providers. Thus, patients gained new rights in terms of cross-border medical treatment, and the member states lost some control over their own social security schemes. The rulings left several issues open, however, and created uncertainty about the extent to which internal market legislation could apply to health care systems (Nickless, 2001; Obermeier, 2009).

The *Vanbraekel* and *Geraets-Smits* and *Pereboom* cases expanded the principles outlined in *Kohll* and *Decker* and reduced some of the uncertainty created by those rulings. *Vanbraekel* (Case 368/98) concerned a Belgian who, despite not having pre-authorization from her health insurance fund, received orthopaedic surgery in

France. The patient's Belgian insurer denied the claim for reimbursement, but later decided to grant pre-authorization. Thus, the case turned on the level of reimbursement rather than the issue of pre-authorization. The key issue became whether the Belgian insurer had to reimburse at the Belgian or home state level (which was higher), or the level in the member state where treatment was received, in this case France (which was lower). The ECJ ruled in July 2001 – in line with *Kohll* – that Articles 59 EEC and 60 EEC (Articles 56 and 57 TFEU) applied to hospital treatment covered by national social security schemes. It also ruled that Regulation 1408/71 required reimbursement at the (higher) home state level for patients who received ex post authorization.

The *Geraets-Smits* and *Peerbooms* cases (Joint Cases 157/99) were similar to *Vanbraekel* in that a person insured in one member state, in this case the Netherlands, was refused reimbursement for inpatient care received in another member state, in these cases Germany and Austria. The Dutch insurers had no contract with the German and Austrian providers and did not pre-authorize the treatments. The Dutch insurers argued that EC law concerning the freedom to provide services did not apply in this case because the treatment was an in-kind benefit; the patient did not pay for treatment and providers did not make a profit. The ECJ disagreed, ruling that the in-kind provision of medical care was a service in the context of Article 57 TFEU. The ECJ allowed that barriers to freedom to provide services could be allowed on grounds of public health and other matters. The ECJ acknowledged member state concerns by recognizing the special character of hospital care in terms of planning and providing access to care; in other words, the member states could reasonably require pre-authorization for treatment in another member state in the interest of maintaining a high-quality, accessible hospital system. The ECJ confirmed that prior authorization is allowable for hospital care but can only be enforced if there are no unreasonable delays in providing treatment to the patient.

The ruling in *Geraets-Smits* and *Peerbooms* is a logical, but not inevitable, extension of ECJ jurisprudence because it extends Articles 56 and 57 TFEU to inpatient care in in-kind benefit systems, that is, Beveridgean systems. The ruling thus builds on the principles established in *Kohll* and *Decker* that apply Articles 56 and 57 TFEU to outpatient care in Bismarckian, or reimbursement-based systems and the *Vanbraekel* ruling's extension of Articles 56 and 57 TFEU to inpatient care in reimbursement systems. The *Geraets-*

Smits and *Peerbooms* cases left several issues unanswered, however. What would happen to outpatient care in in-kind systems (Obermeier, 2009)? The *Müller-Fauré/van Riet* cases would address precisely this question.

The *Müller-Fauré/van Riet* cases (Case 385/99) originated in the Netherlands, a country with a Bismarckian, or public health insurance system providing in-kind benefits. Ms Müller-Fauré obtained outpatient dental care in Germany while on holiday there and applied for reimbursement from her Dutch health insurance, which was denied. Similarly, Ms van Riet received an arthroscopy in Belgium after her Dutch insurance denied her request for pre-authorization on the grounds that the procedure could be performed in the Netherlands by a contracted provider. The ECJ's ruling in both cases introduced two important principles:

1. Articles 56 and 57 TFEU permit pre-authorization if treatment can be provided at a contracted facility without undue delay. Patients are entitled to seek hospital treatment in other member states if that leads to quicker treatment.
2. Articles 56 and 57 TFEU apply equally to health insurance systems based on reimbursement and those that offer in-kind benefits.

The *Müller-Fauré/van Riet* cases opened the door to a more expansive interpretation of the application of Articles 56 and 57 TFEU to Beveridgean systems: national health care systems that provide tax-financed, in-kind benefits to all residents. The ECJ issued this interpretation in the *Watts* case. *Watts* (Case 372/04) was the latest in a series of explosive rulings because it extended Articles 56 and 57 TFEU to countries with a Beveridgean national health system, and it had something to say about acceptable waiting times as well. Watts was an elderly woman in the UK who needed a hip replacement. Mrs Watts's primary care trust informed her that the wait would be one year (this was later shortened to four months). Watts requested pre-authorization for treatment in France, arguing that the waiting time was unnecessarily long. The UK NHS denied her request, reasoning that the waiting time was not unduly long and that EU law concerning patient mobility did not apply to in-kind systems. The ECJ's ruling shocked health policy-makers in the member states, especially those with Beveridgean in-kind systems, because it argued that earlier ECJ jurisprudence did apply to in-kind systems (Blomqvist and Larsson, 2009). The ruling is important not just because it extends EU law on patient mobility to Beveridgean systems, but also because it states that reimbursement should be based on the rates prevailing in the home state. Additionally, the ruling called for more transparency and precision in defining waiting periods for medical procedures.

According to Lamping (2013), the majority of national governments opposed the ECJ's activism concerning patient mobility. Even if the member states have lost some control over their health care systems, patients' rights have been strengthened somewhat. Taken together, ECJ jurisprudence harmonizes the rights of patients, thereby confirming patients' rights to seek care in another member state and to be reimbursed for that care from their health insurance institution at home. These principles apply no matter how the health care system is organized, that is, they apply equally to Bismarckian and Beveridgean systems.

The ECJ's activism concerning patient mobility spurred health policy-makers in the member states to action (see Hervey and Vanhercke, 2010). In 2003, the ministers of health requested the Commission to propose legislation on patient mobility in order to reduce legal uncertainty by clarifying some of the issues left unresolved after the *Kohll*, *Decker* and other cases. The Commission's original proposal for the Services Directive 2006/123, published in 2004, added to the urgency because the proposal included provisions that would have meant the far-reaching liberalization of health care. The European Parliament and Council stepped into the fray, opposing the inclusion of health care into the scope of the Services Directive. The Commission backed down, and health care was removed from the Services Directive, paving the way for the formulation of a less radical European policy regarding health care. The European Parliament was actively involved in this initial phase, producing analyses of patient mobility and the impact of the exclusion of health care from the Services Directive. The Council added a Statement on Common Values and Principles in EU Health Systems in June 2006, and 250 stakeholders submitted opinions on the issues raised by the Commission in the formulation of the proposed directive.

Lamping (2013) argues that the patient mobility directive (2011/24/EU) attempts to reconcile three principles:

1. ECJ's jurisprudence should be respected
2. member states need to remain in control of their own health care systems

3. patients need to have some clarity in terms of what they can expect when they move abroad for medical care.

The proposal permits EU citizens to receive non-hospital care in other member states, financed by their home system. However, pre-authorization would be required for hospital care, and reimbursement is based on fee schedules in the home states. Greer (2013) argues that the directive shows a shift in emphasis in EU policy because it focuses on patient rights rather than the rights of providers. The member states agreed to the directive because it clarifies and codifies existing legal principles and might slow the ECJ down.

Despite the proposal's origins in ECJ jurisprudence, the patient mobility directive attracted significant opposition in the member states and the European Parliament. Less affluent member states such as Portugal, Poland and Lithuania were concerned about potential negative consequences for their health systems, fearing that patients and medical providers would go to other member states for treatment and employment. The same group of countries also feared destabilizing inflows of patients from more affluent member states.

Approval of the patient mobility directive (2011/24/EU) took six years. Like most other social policy directives, this one explicitly stated that the member states remain responsible for the health care within their borders. It is also notable that it states that the application of the directive is not intended to lead to a citizen being encouraged to go to other member states for medical treatment. Finally, the directive emphasizes that the member states may limit reimbursement for cross-border health care if this is justified by 'overriding reasons of general interest relating to public health' (para. 11), such as maintaining the financial viability of health care institutions and ensuring the quality of care.

Despite the volume of high-profile litigation on patient mobility, the issue does not have substantial impact on member state health care systems (Hervey, 2011). According to one estimate, the member states do not spend more than 1% of their public health care budgets on cross-border health care (Lamping, 2013). The member states still have some control over patient mobility because it is the member states who decide which procedures are reimbursable and at what rate. So, the member states seem to comply at least at a superficial level but it is not clear whether the spillovers from the internal market will have a more significant effect than they have now. Other aspects of the internal market, however, have the potential for more far-reaching effects, as the next section discusses.

EU competition law

EU competition law forbids cartels – policies that lead to abuse of a dominant market position (Article 102 TFEU) – and state aid policies that distort competition (Articles 106–108 TFEU). These provisions can have far-reaching consequences for national social policies, especially national health care systems or health care insurers that occupy a privileged position in the domestic market. Exceptions to this competition regime are services of general economic interest, as defined in Article 14 TFEU, Article 106 (2) TFEU as well as in Protocol 26 on services of general interest. The application of competition regulation to health services hinges on three issues:

- whether a health care provider is considered to be an 'undertaking'
- whether a service of general economic interest is involved
- whether any restriction of competition is proportionate.

ECJ jurisprudence has established some of the principles under which competition law applies. If a health care system is based on social solidarity, then competition law does not apply. However, even a Beveridgean system like the UK health care system can fall under the competition regime if elements of competition have been introduced into that system. Under those circumstances, competition law applies (Hervey, 2011).

A recent court case illustrates the legal conflicts arising from the application of internal market law to health care systems. In the *FENIN* case (Case 205/03P), the ECJ ruled that organizations that are part of national health care systems are not undertakings for the purposes of EU law when they purchase medical products from private suppliers. The case involved FENIN, an association of companies that sold medical supplies and equipment to Spanish health care organizations. FENIN claimed that Spanish health care authorities abused their dominant market position by paying their invoices late. The Court of First Instance, and later the ECJ, ruled that FENIN was engaging in economic activity by offering goods for sale, but that the Spanish health authorities were not engaging in economic activity when they purchased goods. Because the

Spanish health care services were financed by taxes and social security contributions and provided free health care, they were operating on the basis of 'solidarity'. This meant that the Spanish health care organizations were not 'undertakings' for the purposes of EU law and therefore not subject to competition law.

Legal analysts observe that *FENIN* did not provide a definitive answer to the question of whether public health care actors are engaging in economic activity when they purchase goods and services from private actors. Hervey (2007) argues that the legal reasoning in *FENIN* leaves open the possibility that health care purchasing bodies in public systems could fall within the scope of EU competition law if they make contracts with private actors. If this reasoning prevails in the future, it would make it difficult or impossible for public health care systems to make exclusive contracts with private providers and fixed fee schedules.

Public health policy

The beginnings of a coherent public health policy were visible from the earliest days of the EU, even if formal policy competence would have to wait until the Maastricht Treaty was adopted. Article 36 EEC (Article 36 TFEU) of the Treaty of Rome permitted restrictions on imports and exports in order to safeguard human health and life, and Articles 117 and 118 EEC (Articles 151 and 156 TFEU) provided for EU authority in occupational health and safety (see below). The 1986 SEA took the first steps towards formal competence in public health with the inclusion of Article 100a EEC (Article 114 TFEU), which requires the EU to base its internal market legislation in the areas of health, safety, environmental protection and consumer protection on the goal of a 'high level of health protection'.

The absence of direct references to public health in the treaties did not prevent the EU from adopting two modest programmes in the area of public health. In 1989, the EU adopted the Europe Against Cancer programme at the initiative of the Council (Commission, 1986), which was the first of its kind. The programme was consistent with earlier policy initiatives, in that it centred on research and information about best practices in the member states. It focused on activities to promote cancer prevention and improve public information about cancer, and laid the groundwork for later proposals, such as a ban on smoking in public places, the regulation of tar content of cigarettes, and tobacco labelling and advertising.

The origins of the 1991 Europe Against AIDS programme are similar (Commission, 1994b). The increase in incidence of AIDS in the EU in the 1980s was the background to the adoption of several resolutions and smaller initiatives concerning AIDS. These developments culminated in the adoption of a Council Decision to ask the Commission to formulate a three-year action plan to prevent and control the spread of AIDS. Like the Europe Against Cancer programme, the AIDS programme contained measures to improve and promote the dissemination of information and awareness about AIDS, gather data on the 'knowledge, attitudes, and behaviour of the general public and target groups', prevent HIV transmission, and improve social support, counselling and medical treatment.

The 1992 Treaty of Maastricht was notable for the introduction of Article 129 EEC (Article 168 TFEU) on public health, giving the EU legal authority in public health for the first time. Article 129 gives the EU the responsibility to 'contribute towards ensuring a high level of human health protection by encouraging cooperation between member states and, if necessary, lending support to their action'. It also covers the prevention of major diseases, research on the causes and transmission of major diseases, and activities involving information and education. The Commission was given the task of acting as liaison among the member states in their cooperative efforts. As Hervey (1998) put it, Article 129 EEC amounts to a 'flanking policy' because it did not give the EU any new powers in terms of promoting harmonization; coordination meant that the member states and the Commission would work together in activities, especially research, aimed at disease prevention and cooperation in information campaigns. Article 129 also empowered the Commission to propose incentive measures to be approved by the Council and Parliament using co-decision, or to propose recommendations that the Council and Parliament could adopt using QMV.

There was much ambiguity in the public health provisions agreed at Maastricht (Hatzopoulos, 2010). The Commission stepped in to try to reduce this ambiguity with the publication of its framework for action in public health in 1993, identifying four criteria for EU action (Commission, 1993b). EU action is appropriate if:

1. There is a 'significant health problem' that can be addressed by 'appropriate preventive measures'.

2. EU action is consistent with the requirements of subsidiarity.
3. EU action supplements or promotes the aspects of other European policies related to health.
4. EU action is in line with the policies of other international organizations.

The Commission's health framework identified eight areas for EU initiatives: cancer, AIDS, health promotion via education and training, drug addiction, improved health monitoring, rare diseases, diseases caused by pollution, and accidental injury. The Council built on the Commission's work, adopting a resolution in June 1994 on public health that laid the groundwork for a Commission action programme (Commission, 1994b), which was adopted by co-decision in 1995. The programme, for the period 1995–99, prioritized problems like health promotion, education and information, fighting drug addiction and disease prevention.

The 1997 Treaty of Amsterdam built on these early initiatives. The expanded Title IV concerning health applied the precautionary principle to all community policies. This means that EU policies will take into account the goal of achieving a high level of human health protection. Article 152 EC (Article 168 TFEU) empowers the Commission to take steps to facilitate cooperation between the member states in the field of public health and foster cooperation with third countries and international organizations. Measures may be passed by co-decision or the Council may adopt recommendations by qualified majority after a proposal by the Commission. Article 152 also responded to member state concerns about growing EU competences by stating that subsidiarity clearly applies in the field of health care and that community activities 'shall fully respect the responsibilities of the member states for the organization and delivery of health care services and medical care'.

The EU's strengthened competence in public health led to the creation of a new Directorate-General for Health and Consumer Protection in 1999, which paved the way for a more coherent EU strategy concerning public health. There have been two public health programmes thus far, for 2003–08 (Decision No. 1786/2002/EC) and 2009–13 (Decision No. 1350/2007/EC). The 2003–08 programme, budgeted at €312 million, focused on increasing awareness and expertise about threats to public health, improving responses to immediate public health threats, and promoting disease prevention. The 2009–13 programme, at a cost of €366 million, went beyond the previous programme's priorities by emphasizing the need to reduce health inequalities, improve health security, and promote the generation of knowledge about health. Despite these moves forward, EU policy can only complement member state policies. As in other areas of health policy, EU initiatives are intended to respect member state responsibilities. Nevertheless, the exceptions to subsidiarity included in Article 152 EC have been used as the basis for directives on blood safety (Directive 2002/98/EC) and human tissue safety (Directive 2004/23/EC). The Lisbon Treaty pushes the mainstreaming of public health further with the adoption of Article 9 TFEU, which reiterates the requirement for all EU policies to consider the protection of human health, giving it 'greater legal weight' (McKee et al., 2010).

Despite the ambiguity of treaty provisions concerning public health, the Commission has pursued an activist agenda in the area of tobacco control. Soon after the entry into force of the SEA, the Commission proposed a ban on tobacco advertising. The proposal was framed as legislation related to the internal market because its goal was to harmonize national rules concerning product marketing. The Commission submitted its proposal to the Council in 1989, but it took the member states eight years of negotiations to reach agreement on the basis of QMV (Directive 1998/43/EC). Opponents of the proposal, led by Germany, argued that the directive had little to do with harmonizing advertising and interfered illegally in member states' public health policies. Germany challenged the directive's legality, and the ECJ agreed, overturning it in 2000. The Commission countered with a somewhat watered-down tobacco advertising directive (Directive 2003/33/EC), which was adopted in 2002 (Duina and Kurzer, 2004), banning the use of direct (but not indirect) advertising of tobacco products.

The Commission has also targeted the manufacture and sale of tobacco products. Two tobacco directives (Directive 2001/37/EC and Directive 2014/40/EU) tightly regulate the content, presentation and sale of tobacco products. Perhaps the most visible effect of this legislation is the requirement that health warning labels cover 65% of cigarette and rolling tobacco packages. The directives also required tobacco manufacturers to submit detailed reports concerning their products' ingredients, and manufacturers are not permitted to use 'characterizing flavours' in tobacco products.

Occupational health and safety

The EU has long been active in occupational health and safety. The ECSC and Euratom Treaties provided for EU involvement in worker health and safety in the mining and other extractive industries. More importantly, Article 118 EEC (Article 156 TFEU) of the Rome Treaty gave the Commission the authority to promote 'close cooperation between the member states' in social policy, including measures concerning worker health and safety. The Commission was charged with acting 'in close contact with member states by making studies, delivering opinions and arranging consultations both on problems arising at national level and on those of concern to international organisations' (Article 118 EEC). The 1974 Social Action Programme (SAP) set the goal of improving occupational health and safety and appointed an Advisory Committee on Safety, Hygiene and Health Protection at Work (Commission, 1974a), which was replaced by the Advisory Committee on Safety and Health at Work in 2003 (Council, 2003). The committee has a tripartite structure: there are three representatives from each member state, one each for the government, unions and employers. It advises the Commission on the formulation and implementation of action programmes concerning worker health and safety. Committee members serve for renewable three-year terms.

The 1974 SAP prompted the adoption of the first action programme concerning occupational health and safety in June 1978, followed by a second in February 1984. The 1974 SAP included provisions concerning industrial health and safety. The approach of the Commission at the time seems to have been to devote its resources to research and activities related to workplace health (Hantrais, 2007). But the programme also formed the basis for the adoption of directives to strengthen the protection of workers from chemical and biological substances, industrial accidents, and exposure to hazardous metals, asbestos and noise.

The SEA was a milestone in EU policy concerning occupational health and safety because it strengthened the EU's competence. Article 118a EC (Article 153 TFEU) requested the member states to 'pay particular attention to encouraging improvements, especially in the working environment, as regards the health and safety of workers'. QMV was introduced for this area. Article 118a EC was the basis for the Commission's 1987 programme on the safety, hygiene and health of workers at work and the European Health and Safety Directive (Directive 89/391/EEC – OSH Framework Directive). The framework directive set out general principles as the basis for more specific legislation in the future and called for employers to take a more active role in guaranteeing occupational health and safety (Falkner, 1998).

The 1989 Community Charter of the Fundamental Social Rights for Workers represented another opportunity to expand EU involvement in occupational health and safety. Occupational health and safety was one of the 12 fundamental social rights in the charter (Article 19). It also included provisions on the protection of children and young people, for example, concerning working hours and night work (Articles 20–23). The charter built on and strengthened policies developed in the previous 30 years (Hantrais, 2007). However, health and safety were restricted to the workplace.

Although the charter was not binding, the European Council requested the Commission to propose legislation and other measures based on the charter that were within EU competence, and the Commission responded with an action programme to implement the charter in November 1989 (Commission, 1989). By most accounts, progress was limited, but the action programme did lead to the adoption of six important social policy directives, including three related to occupational health and safety issues: working time, the safety of pregnant workers, and the safety of young workers.

In 1990, the Commission proposed a directive on working time under Article 118a (Article 153 TFEU) of the SEA. The decision rule was QMV, which allowed the Council to overcome fierce British opposition. The Working Time Directive (93/104/EEC) was adopted in November 1993 and set out the rules for rest periods as well as regulations for shift work, night work and rotating shifts:

- it set the minimum daily rest period at 11 consecutive hours for a 24-hour period, as well as minimum paid holidays of four weeks per annum
- it set a maximum working week of 48 hours on average
- derogations were allowed for collective agreements
- there were special provisions for doctors in training
- individual wage-earners were permitted to opt out of the maximum weekly limit on working time.

The proposed directive exposed deep divisions among the member states about labour market regulation. At the time, the UK had virtually no legislation regulating working time. In contrast, France had detailed legislation regarding working time and was one of the most vociferous proponents of the directive. The Commission strategically proposed the directive as part of the EU's competence in occupational health and safety (because of QMV in the Council) in order to circumvent British opposition (Falkner et al., 2005). Agreement on the directive was difficult. The UK was able to negotiate several exceptions (including the individual opt-out for weekly working time) to the regulations but nevertheless abstained in the final vote in the Council.

The Working Time Directive (WTD) had important implications for medical providers. Its provisions concerning the maximum length of the working week, overtime, mandatory rest periods and vacations conflict with many traditional procedures in health care systems. The *Jaeger* case (Case 151/02) concerned these issues. Jaeger, a doctor in Germany, filed a suit arguing that the time he spent on-call and resting at the hospital where he worked constituted working time. His employer disagreed, based on provisions in German law. In 2003, the advocate-general and later the ECJ ruled that time spent by hospital doctors who are physically at the hospital and on-call is working time even if the doctor is asleep for some or all of the time.

The provisions of the WTD are also problematic for doctors in training. These problems, in conjunction with the *Jaeger* ruling, were the background to the revision of the WTD (Directive 2003/88/EEC). The 2003 WTD strengthened regulations concerning maximum weekly working hours, minimum rest periods, annual leave, and the definition of working hours for professions such as medical doctors.

Further revision of the WTD has been on the Commission's agenda since 2003, but no agreement has been reached. In September 2004, the Commission presented a proposal for a revised directive after two rounds of consultation with the social partners at EU level. The proposed revision contained clarifications concerning on-call time and the individual opt-out. In its first reading of the proposal in May 2005, the European Parliament adopted extensive amendments, including the cancellation of the individual opt-out. Employers and unions attempted to negotiate an agreement in 2011 and 2012, but this failed.

Article 118 EEC (Article 156 TFEU) was also the basis for a directive to protect pregnant women at work, the Pregnant Workers Directive (92/85/EEC). This:

- regulated the exposure of pregnant workers or those who had just given birth to dangerous substances
- included provisions concerning leave, working hours and employment rights of pregnant workers and new mothers
- specified 14 mandatory minimum standards, including the right to take 14 weeks of paid maternity leave, dismissal protection, and the right to time off for medical examinations.

Unlike the WTD, few derogations are allowed.

Like the WTD, the Pregnant Workers Directive would not have been adopted under unanimity voting in the Council. The Commission issued its proposal in 1990, and the Conservative UK government quickly emerged as one of the fiercest opponents. During the co-decision process, the European Parliament proposed amendments that would have strengthened the draft directive, but the UK was able to take advantage of its EU presidency in the second half of 1992 to push the adoption of a weaker version of the proposal. Besides its general opposition to the proposal, the UK was concerned about the costs of implementing it, given the weak provisions concerning the health and safety of pregnant workers in UK law. The final version of the directive requires maternity leave to be compensated at the level of sickness pay – already fairly low in the UK – which eased UK concerns. The UK still abstained in Council voting, but it won important concessions.

The Young Workers Directive (94/33/EC), adopted in 1994, is also an important part of the EU's occupational health and safety regime. Its goal is to protect young workers from dangerous working conditions, for example by banning child labour, mandating rest periods, and regulating working times. Again, the UK Conservative government was the chief opponent to the proposal. The UK pushed for a six-year derogation, the European Parliament called for tougher standards, but the UK prevailed for procedural reasons.

Conclusion

EU governance in health policy rests on modest treaty provisions concerning occupational health and safety and public health, as well as the growing intrusion of internal market principles into member state health care systems. The positive integration measures in public health and occupational health and safety demonstrate the effects of temporality and institutional gaps on the long-term development of EU health policy competence. The Treaty of Rome established EU competence in worker health and safety because of the importance of the European labour market, allowing the Commission to acquire important policy expertise and establish itself as an important actor in this area. The Commission exploited opportunities associated with the expansion of the internal market in the 1980s and 90s and the inclusion of modest treaty provisions that created an opening for expanded EU action in health. The use of QMV in occupational health and safety also facilitated positive integration. Despite these very real advances, EU regulations only create minimum standards in occupational health and safety, and they coordinate, rather than replace, public health policies in the member states.

In contrast, the activism of the ECJ in health policy demonstrates the ECJ's increasingly important role in determining the legal limits of the internal market. Beginning with the landmark cases in the 1970s concerning patient mobility, the ECJ has created legal openings for different health care actors (patients, service providers) to challenge the borders that kept national health care systems off-limits to the internal market. As the chapter discussed, this market orientation of EU law collides with some of the fundamental principles that have shaped the development of member states' health policies. The challenge is particularly serious for Beveridgean systems. The legal uncertainty produced by the ECJ's legal activism led directly to binding legislation clarifying the limits of EU law on national health care systems. The member states seem to have won a reprieve in terms of the application of competition law to national health services. Recent ECJ rulings confirm that activities, such as health care, that are carried out for social purposes and are based on the principle of solidarity are exempt from competition law. However, there is much uncertainty about the future development of case law in this area. Health care reforms in the member states since the 1980s have often introduced elements of competition into solidarity-based systems, creating internal markets within public systems. And where competition already exists, it is likely that EU competition law will follow.

In sum, the member states have lost control over core aspects of their health policies. Multilevel governance rather than state-centric governance now shapes importance elements of national health systems. Indeed, member state governments now compete with many other actors active in multiple arenas for influence over the direction of EU health regulation.

Chapter 8

Poverty and Social Inclusion

This chapter analyses the remarkable expansion of EU initiatives to combat poverty and social exclusion since the 1970s. The Lisbon Treaty elevated social inclusion to one of the core goals of the EU, and the EU's newest growth strategy – Europe 2020 – emphasizes the goal of inclusive growth. At the level of discourse, then, social inclusion now occupies a prominent place on the EU policy agenda. Concrete results have been disappointing, however, largely because of the difficulty of measuring and comparing social exclusion in different national contexts, variations in the role played by poverty alleviation and social inclusion in the different welfare mixes of EU member states, and the ineffectiveness of the soft law provisions that underpin the EU's social inclusion strategy.

The chapter begins with a brief analysis of how different welfare regimes deal with social exclusion and poverty, followed by a conceptual discussion of poverty and social exclusion. The bulk of the chapter charts the development of the EU's efforts to combat social exclusion and evaluates results achieved thus far.

Conceptual foundations

The literature on welfare regimes does not pay much attention to policies designed to alleviate poverty and social exclusion. This is curious, given that poverty alleviation has been an important social policy for centuries. The literature's focus on social security and social services means that regime typologies largely neglect the role of social assistance, which is the primary means for poverty alleviation in European welfare states. Despite these conceptual difficulties, it is possible to identify the broad outlines of European approaches to fighting poverty and social exclusion.

In contrast to social insurance, social assistance is usually means-tested or income-tested, and is aimed at individuals or families who cannot support themselves from employment or social insurance, such as pensions, unemployment insurance, sickness insurance, or disability insurance. In other words, social assistance is typically a residual part of the welfare state that provides means-tested income support. Social assistance is not the only policy response to poverty and social exclusion; family benefits, child benefits and other sources of income support are usually important parts of the overall package of benefits available to those with low incomes and insufficient access to social services (Saraceno, 2010).

In the Nordic welfare regimes and the Netherlands, poverty rates are generally among the lowest in Europe because of strong employment policies and universal social insurance for those unable to work. Social assistance provides a last resort source of income for a relatively small share of the population. The liberal welfare regimes of the UK and Ireland provide citizenship-based minimum benefits. The conservative welfare states generally rely on dual social assistance systems in which targeted programmes are important, supplemented by a last resort safety net. In the Southern European welfare states, social insurance programmes are often weak or have incomplete coverage, resulting in higher levels of poverty than the rest of Western Europe. Here, targeted measures supplemented by local policies (heating or rent subsidies, for example) provide support to low-income groups. Finally, the new member states (NMS) of Eastern and Central Europe have rudimentary social assistance schemes (Bahle et al., 2010).

As Figure 8.1 shows, there is tremendous variation in the rate of poverty risks after social transfers in the EU, measured as less than 60% of national median equivalized income. This measure of poverty risk is now one of the core indicators used by the EU, but it is important to note that the 60% threshold is calculated using national income data, rather than EU-wide data (Saraceno, 2010). Thus, the very high rates of poverty risk in a country like Bulgaria are calculated using the national median income: as Figure 8.1 shows, nearly 22% of the Bulgarian population had income less than 60% of the Bulgarian median income, after social transfers. Given that the median income in Bulgaria is much lower than that of, say, Germany, those at risk of poverty in Bulgaria have much lower incomes than those at risk of poverty in Germany. Rates of poverty risks are much lower in the Nordic countries, the Netherlands and Germany than in Southern Europe or the NMS.

Figure 8.1 *At risk of poverty after social transfers, in percentage of population, 2005 and 2011*

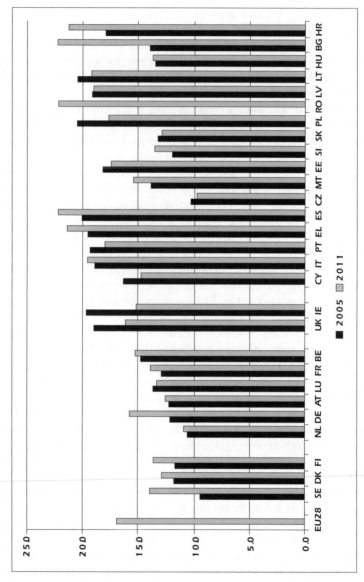

Source: Data compiled from www.epp.eurostat.ec.europa.eu (2005, 2011)

Variations in the institutional structure and performance of poverty and social exclusion policies in the member states shape the development of EU initiatives in two ways:

1. The wide diversity among the EU 28 in terms of their policy strategies for fighting poverty complicates EU-level efforts to formulate a common strategy. The member states typically rely on several kinds of policies to address poverty: housing subsidies, free access to social services, and various kinds of income support. Moreover, the member states differ in the extent to which they prioritize the employment of those with a weak attachment to the labour market. The involvement of different levels of government in poverty and social exclusion policies complicates things further. These very different institutional starting points among the member states shape the bargaining in the Council concerning the content and direction of EU policies.
2. The extreme variation in poverty rates among the member states makes a one-size-fits-all policy approach inappropriate and ineffective simply because the member states face different kinds and levels of problem pressure.

What is social exclusion?

'Social inclusion' is a concept that has only recently entered the vocabulary of social policy analysis. Prior to the 1980s, social policy-makers and analysts focused on material deprivation – poverty – to describe the circumstances of the least privileged members of society. In doing so, they built on a centuries-old tradition in social policy-making and analysis. Long before industrialization and democratization laid the foundations for the welfare state in the early 20th century, local governments, churches and other groups provided assistance to those who were not able to support themselves by working. Before the core elements of the welfare state – pensions, health insurance, unemployment insurance, public education – were established, there was considerable policy activity in the area of poverty reduction (or poor relief as it was called until the mid-20th century).

Despite the centrality of anti-poverty policies in the development of national social policy, the EU has been slow to enter this field, for obvious reasons. The Treaty of Rome, and subsequent revisions until the Treaty of Maastricht, did not foresee EU intervention in social policy unless it was related to the market-building process, especially the construction of a European labour market. This meant that poverty reduction, or what would later be called 'social inclusion', had no place in the social policy portfolio of the EU. Poverty was viewed as something striking individuals and households with a weak attachment to the labour market, so it naturally fell outside the scope of EU policy activity. In other words, until very recently, EU social policy was something that affected workers who wanted to move between the member states, and it did not attempt to address the problem of poverty.

The policy innovation of the Commission in the 1970s changed this. The rapid rise and persistence of unemployment in the 1970s put poverty on the EU social policy agenda because more and more people were excluded from the labour market and experienced drops in income. Prior to the 1970s, poverty was much more likely to strike older people with insufficient retirement income or the disabled than the working age population. Indeed, the experience of full employment – at least for breadwinners – in many member states raised expectations that economic growth would gradually reduce poverty. In the 1970s, however, poverty emerged as a heterogeneous condition and no longer principally an affliction of the elderly. Although the pension systems put in place since the 1930s helped reduce poverty among the elderly, they did not eradicate it, and postwar social and economic changes increased the number of households headed by single parents and those with obsolete or inadequate skills. Thus, by the 1970s, poverty had become a multi-dimensional phenomenon, and policy-makers and analysts began to reframe their understanding of poverty, because existing frameworks ignored the ways in which individuals were excluded from society (Silver, 1994; Abrahamson, 1995). Thus, 'social exclusion' began to replace 'poverty' in policy discourses. In this new perspective, social exclusion is more than the inadequacy of economic resources; it also connoted marginalization, because a person is unable to participate in social and economic activities. Abrahamson (1995, p. 123) observes that the term originates in French social policy discourse and made its way into EU policy-making 'because of French dominance of the sections of Directorate General V responsible for social policy'.

Social exclusion on the EU policy agenda

Despite the weak social policy provisions of the Treaty of Rome, poverty and social exclusion have been objects of EU policy since the 1970s. The 1972 Paris Summit marked the first modest step towards such a policy with the European Council's announcement that it supported the establishment of a Social Action Programme (SAP). The Commission presented its proposed action plan in October 1973, and the Council adopted it in 1974 (Commission, 1974a). The SAP was based on Article 2 (improving living and working conditions) of the treaty and aimed at full employment, the improvement of living and working conditions, and the increased involvement of social partners in EU decision-making and enterprises. The SAP's second goal – improving living and working conditions – was the basis for this initial EU action to fight poverty.

The Commission's first bundle of initiatives later became known as 'Poverty 1' and ran from 1975 to 1980. Poverty 1 included pilot programmes to address poverty and conduct research on different approaches to poverty reduction (Council, 1975). Besides sponsoring 24 pilot programmes, Poverty 1 also aimed to foster the emergence of a network of experts and practitioners (that is, the project leaders for the pilot projects) and promote awareness of the 'European dimension' of poverty and its relationship to social exclusion (Bauer, 2002, p. 386). When it adopted Poverty 1, the Council specifically pointed to the ways that poverty excluded individuals or families 'from the minimum acceptable way of life of the member state in which they live' (Council, 1975). The Commission's final evaluation of Poverty 1 pointed to the persistence of poverty despite 30 years of economic growth in the EU, while emphasizing the multidimensionality of poverty and the difficulty of measuring it. The report estimated that 30 million people were living in poverty in the mid-1970s in the EU 9. This estimate was based on the definition of poverty as less than half the average national incomes (Commission, 1981).

Poverty 1 seemed to demonstrate the added value of EU action to combat poverty. A second poverty programme, Poverty 2, was adopted for the period 1985–89 (Council, 1985), containing more specific actions to stimulate policy innovation, cross-national collaborative projects, and a more comprehensive EU approach to fighting poverty. The EU would co-finance actions in the member states, providing 29 million ecu for the four-year programme.

The Council was sufficiently convinced of the value of Poverty 1 and 2 that it authorized the Commission to undertake a third programme, Poverty 3, in 1989 (Council, 1989a). Poverty 3's title, 'Medium-term Community action programme concerning the economic and social integration of the economically and socially less privileged groups in society', signals the institutionalization of the shift towards a multidimensional view of poverty captured by the concept 'social inclusion'. Poverty 3 ran from 1989 to 1994 and built on the previous two programmes, with expanded financial resources.

The content of Poverty 3 emphasized the difficulty of measuring poverty. The Council had been working with a vague definition since 1984:

> the poor shall be taken to mean persons, families and groups of persons whose resources (material, cultural and social) are so limited as to exclude them from the minimum acceptable way of life in the Member State in which they live. (Council, 1985, Article 1, para. 2)

This definition made quantification impossible, so the Commission began using the definition of less than half the average equivalent per capita national income as an operational definition during Poverty 2. Based on this definition, there were 44 million poor people in the EU in 1985. For Poverty 3, the Commission argued for quantitative indicators that would capture other aspects of poverty and consider differences across the member states. The Commission also pointed to the changing composition of poverty: the elderly remained the largest group requiring income support, but other groups – the unemployed, single-parent families and low wage-earners – were joining the ranks of the impoverished. In other words, new forms of poverty were emerging.

Poverty 3 was a turning point in the EU's poverty strategy because it marked the transition from a policy agenda defined in terms of 'poverty' to one defined in terms of 'social inclusion' (Abrahamson, 1995; Armstrong, 2010). A Council Resolution (Council, 1989b) from September 1989 institutionalized this shift by calling on the member states to take action to enable universal access to a range of activities to promote economic and social integration (education, training, employment, housing, community services and medical care). Indeed, the Council (1989b, para. 6) now defined 'social exclusion' as:

not simply a matter of inadequate resources, and that combating exclusion also involves access by individuals and families to decent living conditions by means of measures for social integration and integration into the labour market.

Thus, the fight against social exclusion would need to promote individual and family access to adequate living conditions by promoting social and economic integration. The three poverty programmes demonstrate the growing importance of social exclusion on the EU's policy agenda. The Council's 1989 Resolution on 'combating social exclusion' illustrates its willingness to elevate social exclusion to a matter of priority for the EU even if it was still absent in the treaties (Council, 1989b). The Resolution stated that fighting social exclusion 'is an important part of the social dimension of the internal market' and emphasized the added value of coordinating efforts by actors at all levels in this area. A Council Recommendation from June 1992 reiterated this perspective, calling on the member states to acknowledge individuals' rights to adequate resources, ensuring existence 'in a manner compatible with human dignity as part of a comprehensive and consistent drive to combat social exclusion' (Council, 1992, para. IA). The Recommendation was important because it recognized the heterogeneity of social exclusion and poverty risks, and it requested the member states to acknowledge that all people have a basic right to adequate resources. The Recommendation authorized the Commission to organize the exchange of information about national social inclusion policies and regularly evaluate national progress in fighting social exclusion. Ferrera et al. (2002) argue that these early soft law initiatives represent the OMC in 'embryonic form'. Indeed, the Commission's 1999 evaluation of the 1992 Recommendation contains a detailed description of minimum income schemes in the member states and an analysis of obstacles to employment for benefit recipients – precisely the kinds of instruments that are central to the OMC (Commission, 1999b).

The first three poverty programmes were important because they not only established EU activity in this area, but they also led to the accumulation of knowledge and expertise concerning poverty and social exclusion (Bauer, 2002; Marlier et al., 2007). Whereas Poverty 1 got actors in the member states talking about poverty at national and EU level and evaluating national efforts to alleviate it, Poverty 2 and 3 helped shift the conceptual focus of EU initiatives from poverty to social exclusion. Moreover, the poverty programmes gave the Commission the opportunity to frame discourses concerning poverty and social exclusion, which meant it could frame not only the policy problem itself, but also potential solutions. The Commission made a plausible case that European integration was at least part of the cause of social exclusion, legitimating a European policy response (Bauer, 2002). The poverty programmes were also instrumental in the establishment of the European Antipoverty Network (EAPN). The Commission helped create the EAPN and financed much of its earlier activities (Bauer, 2002). The Commission has also sponsored other European NGOs involved in anti-poverty work. As Bauer (2002) argued, the Commission created its own constituency, and the network of NGOs helps to keep public attention focused on EU anti-poverty initiatives. Bauer argues that this kind of 'sponsored lobbyism' is important when the Council is divided, because lobbying can help create consensus or a majority in favour of certain policies.

The increasing prominence of social inclusion on the EU's social policy agenda aroused the suspicion of those member states opposed to active social policy at EU level. Germany criticized the Commission's new activism, invoking subsidiarity. The Thatcher government in the UK opposed all EU social policy interventions. This opposition was sufficient to derail a fourth poverty programme. Indeed, the Council rejected the Commission's Poverty 4 proposal (Marlier et al., 2007). The Commission, however, was able to circumvent this veto – it simply repackaged the contents of the Poverty 4 programme under a different name and started to authorize projects. Sceptical member states responded with action of their own. The UK claimed that the Commission's actions were without legal foundation and took the Commission to the ECJ (supported by Denmark and Germany). The ECJ ruled against the Commission in its preliminary ruling. The Commission then joined forces with the anti-poverty NGOs against the Council, drumming up public support for the Commission's initiatives. In addition, the Commission shifted some of the work envisioned by Poverty 4 to a new programme with a secure legal basis in the European Social Fund. The new scheme, the 1997 Employment-Integra programme, repackaged the essence of the Poverty 4 programme into a labour-market reintegration scheme within the Structural Funds (Bauer, 2002).

The stalemate concerning the EU's role in fighting social exclusion was short-lived. The Treaty of Amsterdam, signed in October

1997, was a big boost for the EU's competence concerning social exclusion:

1. The newly elected Labour government in the UK adopted the Agreement on Social Policy, so it was integrated into the Amsterdam Treaty. The agreement is notable for its focus on the goal of integrating people excluded from the labour market, so it strengthened an important dimension of the social inclusion agenda. Indeed, the other 11 member states had committed themselves to the provisions of the agreement in 1993 when the Social Policy Protocol (the predecessor to the Agreement on Social Policy) was added to the Maastricht Treaty.
2. The treaty extended EU powers in the field of social policy. Certainly, Article 136 EC (Article 151 TFEU) reiterates that social policy is a shared competence between the EU and the member states, but the EU acquired competence to undertake initiatives aimed at fighting social exclusion (Article 137(2) EC, Article 153j TFEU). The soft law measures that encourage coop- eration between the member states would be decided by qualified majority under the co-decision procedure, after consulting the Economic and Social Committee and the Committee of the Regions. The fight against social exclusion was now the joint responsibility of the EU and the member states.

The Commission and Council moved quickly to exploit the Amsterdam Treaty's new social policy competences. Ferrera et al. (2002) argue that the Commission's 1999 White Paper on 'modern- ising social protection' (Commission, 1999b) was a 'turning point', because social inclusion was one of the four goals set out in its modernization strategy – the other goals were to make work pay and provide adequate income, ensure the sustainability of pensions, and ensure the quality and sustainability of health care. The White Paper also signalled the Commission's goal of using soft coordina- tion for the social inclusion process. Anti-poverty NGOs also pushed for the use of soft coordination – pointing specifically at the European Employment Strategy (EES) as a model – as an approach for achieving the Amsterdam Treaty's new social inclusion ambi- tions (Armstrong, 2010). The White Paper thus added to the momentum behind the social inclusion agenda, and social inclusion was integrated into the larger strategy of modernizing social protec- tion (Armstrong, 2010).

The Lisbon Strategy and social inclusion

The adoption of the Lisbon Strategy in 2000 also propelled the EU's nascent social inclusion strategy forward. The three central policy goals set out in the Lisbon Strategy were employment growth, competitiveness and social cohesion. Thus, it integrated economic and social goals into a larger modernization and growth agenda. The core social policy elements of the Lisbon Strategy were the financial sustainability of social policies – mainly pensions – and the promotion of social inclusion (Council, 2000a). The key instrument for achieving the goals set out in the Lisbon Strategy was the open method of coordination (OMC). Thus, the Lisbon Strategy provided an integrated analysis of the problems and challenges facing the EU, as well as the policy tools and strategies required to solve these problems. The fight against social exclusion was an important part of the vision of social policy that the Lisbon Strategy represented. Proponents of a more 'Social' Europe saw in the Lisbon Strategy the potential for expanding the social dimension of the market-building process.

The Nice Treaty, signed in February 2001, strengthened the EU social inclusion process even more, moving it beyond the vague terms of the Amsterdam Treaty. Articles 136 and 137 EC (TFEU 151–153) allow the EU to promote cooperation and coordination in social policy, including combating social exclusion. Nice also created a high level group that would later become the Social Protection Committee (SPC), a key actor in the social OMC. Despite these advances, the Nice Treaty ruled out the harmonization of most social policies, including policies promoting social inclusion. Only the reintegration of the jobless could be the basis for binding EU legislation. Nevertheless, the Amsterdam and Nice Treaties created a more favourable constitutional context for EU action concerning social inclusion. As Armstrong (2010, p. 60) puts it, the OMC social inclusion process 'had a clearer legal institutional footing' than the EES.

At the Lisbon Summit, the European Council requested the Council of Ministers to formulate social inclusion targets, and the indicators required to define the targets, by the end of 2000. In October 2000, the Council (Employment and Social Policy) agreed the following common goals for poverty and social exclusion (Council, 2000c, p. 5):

- to facilitate participation in employment and access by all to the resources, rights, goods and services
- to prevent the risks of exclusion
- to help the most vulnerable
- to mobilise all relevant bodies.

The first goal, concerning employment, referred to the role of the EES in promoting access to stable employment for those capable of working. However, employment was now tied to exclusion, in the sense that EU policies would target not only the able-bodied and skilled, but also those at risk of long-term unemployment because of inadequate training. The second aspect of the first goal, promoting access to goods and services, was aimed at improving the material and human conditions (health, for example) of those excluded from the labour market. The second and third goals, concerning the risk of exclusion and vulnerable groups, targeted groups such as the disabled, children, the homeless and the indebted. The final goal concerned governance: the fight against poverty and social exclusion should include all levels of government in the member states, NGOs and the business sector.

These common objectives were adopted at the December 2000 Nice European Council, marking the formal launch of the social inclusion process. Armstrong (2010, p. 74) notes that the Nice objectives were 'relatively broad and exhortative rather than particularly precise about the sorts of reforms that member states might need to undertake'. Despite their vagueness, the targets were clearly in line with the Lisbon Strategy's emphasis on activation as part of the modernization of the European social model.

The social inclusion OMC was flanked by a five-year action programme (2002–06) adopted by the European Parliament and Council in November 2001. The proposal was based on Article 137 (Article 153 TFEU) of the treaty, and provided a budget of €85 million to foster cooperation among the member states to combat social exclusion (Decision No. 50/2002/EC). The programme financed collaborative projects that included not only policy-makers, but also NGOs, the social partners and experts.

One of the challenges of policy-making in relation to social inclusion concerns the measurement of relevant dimensions of social exclusion. The OMC relies on common definitions, measurements and indicators; without them, agreement on common targets is difficult, if not impossible. Moreover, peer pressure and mutual surveillance is difficult without numerical indicators. When the Commission first started becoming active in this area in the 1970s and 80s, many member states did not have reliable statistics concerning poverty and/or social exclusion, and there were no shared indicators that could be used at European level to compare conditions in the member states. By the early 2000s, negotiations were already under way for Eastern enlargement, and these promised to complicate measurement and data issues further because the gap between the richest and poorest member states would increase. The common objectives agreed at Nice did not solve these measurement problems. Indeed, the first round of the social inclusion OMC in 2001–02 proceeded *without* common indicators, because the newly constituted Social Protection Committee (SPC) could not release the first set of indicators until the end of 2001.

In its initial phase, the social inclusion OMC followed a process similar to that of the EES. The Commission formulated objectives (rather than guidelines as in the EES), as discussed above, that were intended to inform the policies of the member states. However, unlike the EES, there were no quantifiable, EU-wide targets. The member states submitted National Action Plans on Social Inclusion (known as 'NAPs/incl') that analysed existing policy and presented a strategy for meeting the common objectives. The Commission and, starting in 2003, the SPC evaluated the NAPs/incl, and on the basis of these evaluations, the Commission and Council issued a joint report, and the cycle would begin again. Like the other OMCs, the process was intended to raise awareness of certain problems, promote the mutual exchange of best practices, foster mutual surveillance, and encourage policy learning.

What were the results of the initial rounds of the OMC for social inclusion? In June 2001, the member states submitted their first NAPs/incl for the period 2001–02, in which they were asked to use the following outline (adapted from Ferrera et al., 2002):

- major challenges: overview of the current situation in the areas identified by the common objectives
- strategic approach and main objectives: overview of strategy for combating poverty and social exclusion, including quantitative targets and financial resources
- policy measures: planned policy measures for 2001–03, including priorities

- indicators: description of indicators used for gauging progress in achieving common objectives
- good practice: examples taken from ongoing programmes.

Given the absence of quantitative goals and common indicators, it is not surprising that the first set of NAPs/incl was diverse. The member states used their own definitions and indicators for measuring progress in this first round, resulting in limited comparability across countries. Despite this, the Commission's first draft of the joint report (Commission, 2001b) included some evaluations of specific NAPs/incl, which generated some controversy among member states whose NAPs/incl were singled out for criticism. After discussions between the Commission and member states, critical references to specific member states' NAPs were dropped (Ferrera et al., 2002; Daly, 2007). Nevertheless, the final version of the joint report (Commission, 2002b) pointed to several weaknesses in many NAPs/incl:

- lack of comprehensive analysis of existing policies
- inattention to gender issues
- absence of specific national targets concerning social exclusion
- too little attention to the future development of policy in the context of the social inclusion OMC.

As Ferrera et al. (2002, p. 236) put it, the first set of NAPs/incl were 'patchy and unsatisfactory'. Despite this, the first OMC cycle provided valuable information about the strengths and weaknesses of existing policies for fighting social exclusion in the member states.

Ferrera et al. (2002) argue that this initial phase of the process was marked by a 'nurturing' approach that emphasized the positive aspects of the NAPs more than their actual content. Other analysts are more critical, pointing to the impossibility of comparison across the member states using different sets of indicators, and the opportunities for the member states to subvert, or at least ignore, the goals of the social inclusion OMC (see Daly, 2007).

The second OMC social inclusion cycle held more promise because of the development of common quantitative indicators by the SPC. The first set of indicators was announced at the Laeken Council in December 2001, well into the first cycle of NAPs/incl. The Laeken indicators included 10 primary indicators and 8 secondary indicators that captured four aspects of social exclusion:

income poverty, lack of access to employment, health and education. The common objectives remained basically the same, with three exceptions; the member states were instructed to:

- set quantitative targets for themselves concerning the reduction of poverty and social exclusion by 2010
- consider gender more in the formulation and implementation of the NAPs/incl
- consider the ways in which immigrants face relatively higher risks of poverty and social exclusion.

Mabbett (2007) analysed the 2003 NAPs for the UK, Germany, Spain and Sweden and found wide variation in the extent to which they had used the indicators and self-set targets. Germany, for example, did not use targets at all and Sweden formulated its own targets. These responses reflected existing institutions for policy-making concerning poverty and social inclusion. In contrast, Spain relied on the indicators more than the UK and Sweden.

These varied approaches to NAP/incl reporting about existing and future policy strategy were reflected in the Council and Commission's joint report, issued in March 2004 (Commission, 2004). The joint report observed that 55 million people, 15% of the EU population, were at risk of poverty (less than 60% of equiv-alized median income) in 2001; Ireland reported the highest proportion at 21%, while Sweden reported the lowest level, at 9% (Commission, 2004). The report also included data on the persis-tence of poverty, defined as the share of the population at risk of poverty in 2001, as well as the previous two years. Again, Sweden was the best performer, with little to no persistent poverty. The highest levels of persistent poverty were reported in Greece and Portugal, at 14% and 15% respectively. The report praised member state efforts to formulate more coherent NAPs, set quantitative targets for the reduction of poverty and social exclusion, and mainstream the reduction of poverty and social inclusion in national policy-making. However, many member state targets remained insufficiently specific and ambitious, and the efficiency and effectiveness of policy measures was not always evaluated. Finally, the report called for expanded participation of civil society in the implementation of the NAPs closer integration of social economic and employment policies.

The third round started in 2004 and included the 10 new member states. The 2004 joint report (Commission, 2004) instructed the member states to prioritize six areas within the common objectives:

1. the promotion of active labour market policies for those who are difficult to employ
2. the maintenance of adequate and accessible social protection that does not reduce work incentives
3. the expansion of access to health care, lifelong learning and housing for the most vulnerable groups
4. measures to prevent early school leaving and promote a smooth transition from school to work
5. measures to eliminate poverty and social exclusion among children
6. measures to reduce poverty and social exclusion among immigrants and ethnic minorities.

The joint report also exhorted the member states to further develop national indicators and other monitoring procedures in order to improve the evaluation process.

The relaunch of the Lisbon Strategy in 2005 brought major changes to the social inclusion OMC process: starting in 2006, the three social OMCs (pensions, social inclusion, and health care/ social care) were combined into a single programme, the OMC for social protection and social inclusion (often referred to as the 'social OMC'). The high level group chaired by Wim Kok evaluated all the components of the Lisbon Strategy, including the social inclusion process, and was highly critical (Kok, 2004). The social inclusion strategy was argued to be too broad and vague. The Commission proposed an overhaul of the implementation architecture, streamlining the social policy OMCs and combining them with other policy areas. Beginning with the period 2006–08, the member states submit National Reform Programmes (NRPs) for strategies on social protection and social inclusion. This is followed by a three-year cycle so that they would run parallel to Europe 2020 (Lisbon II), the revised Lisbon Strategy (Lisbon I), and its new emphasis on jobs and growth (discussed in Chapter 3).

With growth and jobs now the dominant goals of Lisbon II, social inclusion and other areas of social policy were relegated to secondary status. Lisbon I's emphasis on three broad goals – jobs, growth, and inclusion – now gave way to the primacy of economic goals (jobs and growth) over social inclusion in Lisbon II (Daly, 2007). The definition of social inclusion was also recast to emphasize activation.

The social OMC streamlines the soft coordination of pensions, social inclusion, and health care/social care (the OMC for care was established in 2003) and integrates it with the broad economic policy guidelines and the EES. Common objectives were now formulated for all three strands of social protection and inclusion, the member states would formulate NRPs addressing developments in all three fields, and the Commission and Council would publish a joint report on social protection and social inclusion. The revamped social OMC was intended as part of a larger strategy to strengthen the implementation of Lisbon II after the disappointing results of Lisbon I. Policy coordination in all three areas (employment, economic policy and social protection) would now be integrated and synchronized, thereby – it was hoped – producing better results.

During Lisbon II, the soft coordination of social inclusion policies functioned much as it did during Lisbon I. The first joint report under the new regime, released in 2005 (Commission, 2005b), analysed NAPs/incl covering the period 2003–05, as well as the NAPs/incl of the NMS for the period 2004–06. The EU 15 were invited to update their NAPs/incl for the first joint report under Lisbon II, but only 10 did so. The inclusion of the NMS meant that the joint report's survey of social exclusion in the EU revealed much wider disparities in member state conditions. In 2002, 68 million people – 15% of the EU 25 population – were at risk of poverty. This ranged from 10% or less in Sweden, Denmark, the Czech Republic and Slovenia, to 20% or higher in Ireland, Greece, Portugal and the Slovak Republic (Commission, 2005b). The 2007 joint report analysed the first set of integrated NRPs (submitted in September/October 2006) concerning social protection and social inclusion (Commission, 2007). By now, Lisbon II's emphasis on active inclusion was a major theme in the NRPs, as well as the EU's more recent goal (announced at the Barcelona European Council in 2006) of reducing child poverty.

The 2010 joint report (Commission, 2010c) covered the last cycle of policy coordination under Lisbon II. Two events shaped the report: the accession of Bulgaria and Romania in 2007 and the onset of the economic crisis in 2008. In 2008, 17% of the EU 27 population was at risk of poverty. Again, countries like Sweden and the Czech Republic performed well, but Bulgaria and Romania joined the groups of countries with the highest levels of income poverty. Statistics on material deprivation revealed large differences between the new and old member states. 'Material deprivation' is defined as the percentage of the population that cannot afford at least three of nine important items:

- to pay the rent, mortgage or utility bills
- to pay for adequate heating
- face unexpected expenses
- to eat meat or proteins regularly
- go on holiday
- to buy a television, telephone, car or washing machine.

Even if the average level of income poverty in the NMS was similar to those in the EU 15, levels of material deprivation are much higher, on average, than in the EU 15. In 2008, the average proportion of the NMS population experiencing material deprivation was close to 30%, compared to about 13% in the EU 15 (Commission, 2010c).

Lisbon II also marked the shift to a more employment-based conception of inclusion. In 2008, the Commission issued a Recommendation (Commission 2008b) defining and promoting the concept of active inclusion. 'Active inclusion' means the coordination of policy across multiple levels of governments in three areas or 'pillars': adequate income support, inclusive labour markets, and access to quality services. These three goals were intended to be integrated into a larger strategy. The Council approved the strategy in its Conclusions of 17 December 2008 on 'common active inclusion principles to combat poverty more effectively', and the European Parliament endorsed the strategy in May 2009. An assessment by independent national experts published in 2013, however, found that it had had a 'quite limited' impact on the policies in the member states. The report noted that there had been some progress, but that it was 'often uneven and partial' (Commission, 2013d). Specifically, member states focused too much on labour market activation, neglecting other aspects of inclusion. Moreover, labour market activation was often not effectively integrated with policies aimed at other aspects of inclusion. Finally, the goal of participation by 'all relevant actors' in the active inclusion strategy was not achieved in the large majority of the member states.

Despite the limited results of the Lisbon Strategy's focus on promoting social inclusion, the entry into force of the Lisbon Treaty in December 2009 elevated the status of social inclusion among EU policy priorities. Article 3 (TFEU) gives the EU the authority to adopt policies addressing social exclusion. Additionally, Article 9 (TFEU) states that the EU is required to consider the following aspects of social policy when it makes other EU policies: 'a high level of employment, the guarantee of adequate social protection [and], the fight against social exclusion'. As previously, EU competence in social exclusion would be shared with member states (Article 153 TFEU) and rely on soft coordination. Finally, the Lisbon Treaty includes the European Parliament in decision-making concerning social inclusion.

Europe 2020 and social inclusion

Poverty alleviation has a prominent place in the Europe 2020 governance architecture. Indeed, the strategy includes the target of lifting 'at least 20 million people out of the risk of poverty and exclusion' by 2020. Europe 2020 thus marks the return of social policies to a central place on the EU agenda, at least rhetorically, after the downgrading of the social OMCs in the relaunch of the Lisbon Strategy in 2005. The poverty alleviation goal is also notable, because it is the first time that the EU has ever set a numerical goal in the field of social policy (Copeland and Daly, 2012).

Since 2012, the member states also formulate annual National Social Reports (NSRs), in addition to the NRPs, with reference to Europe 2020 objectives concerning pensions, social inclusion and health care/social care. Europe 2020 originally did not include this repackaged social OMC. It was reintroduced in 2011 after the Council adopted an SPC proposal to bring back the social OMCs as a means to strengthen the social dimension of Europe 2020. The SPC argued that the social OMC had made important contributions to the modernization of social protection in many member states, by raising awareness of child poverty, homelessness, the need for pension reform, and active inclusion, and by supporting national reform processes. Moreover, the common indicators developed under the auspices of the social OMCs demonstrated their added value to European policy-making. Above all, the SPC did not want to relinquish the social protection and social inclusion goals included in the Lisbon Strategy. The SPC advocated a leaner form of the social OMC, with lighter reporting requirements. The member states would be invited to submit NSRs at the same time as NRPs (Council, 2011b).

Europe 2020 also includes seven 'flagship initiatives' designed to facilitate achieving the three overarching 2020 targets. One of these initiatives, the European Platform against Poverty and Social Exclusion, is designed as a vehicle for helping to achieve the poverty reduction goal. It is intended to promote and facilitate mutual cooperation between member states, EU institutions and relevant stakeholders.

The adoption of the quantitative target concerning poverty reduction was contentious. The original Commission draft of Europe 2020 adhered to the Lisbon II perspective that growth and employment were prerequisites for social inclusion and poverty reduction, which obviated the need for numerical targets. A coalition of pro-welfare member states, the EAPN and the European Parliament pressured the Commission to change course. Spain supported the numerical target and used its 2010 Council presidency to highlight Social Europe. The European Parliament played an important role because it was often at odds with the Commission concerning Social Europe in the Lisbon II period and could block the re-election of Commission President José Manuel Barroso.

The Commission introduced a numerical target in a revised draft, but the EU's legal authority to act in the social field was a cause for conflict in the Council. Predictably, the UK and Ireland were concerned, but so was Sweden, because of its perspective that employment should take precedence over social exclusion. The UK, Ireland and some of the NMS, on the other hand, were concerned about the viability of the social inclusion target, because it rested on a relative definition of poverty. In the liberal welfare states of the UK and Ireland, and the NMS, the low-wage employment sector generated large numbers of working poor. This meant that many of the employed were at risk of poverty. It was difficult for the European Council to reach a compromise but the efforts of the Spanish presidency and the lobbying efforts of the social NGOs helped to break the deadlock. The compromise included three alternative targets (at risk of poverty, severe material deprivation, and number of people living in households without an employed adult). The member states could choose one of these targets, a combination of two or all three, or they could use their own targets (Copeland and Daly, 2012).

The member states submitted their first NRPs in April 2011. One of the innovations of the Europe 2020 process is that a newly established 'Network of Independent Experts on Social Inclusion' assists the Commission in evaluating the aspects of the NRPs and NSPs related to poverty and social exclusion: Do NRPs/NSPs indicate that the EU is on track to meet its social inclusion objectives? The network publishes reports every year that analyse member state NRPs/NSPs, as well as a synthesis report highlighting the main findings of the country reports. Because these are nongovernmental, expert evaluations, they are not the object of internal negotiation in the Commission or bargaining in the Council, so they offer a reasonable analysis of the contents of the NRPs. The network's synthesis reports for 2011 and 2012 (Frazer and Marlier, 2011, 2012) identify a number of weaknesses in the Europe 2020 process that mirror the problems experienced during the Lisbon Strategy:

- a lack of coherent analysis of the obstacles to reducing social exclusion and poverty
- too much focus on existing policies rather than new or planned policies
- too much focus on economic growth rather than poverty reduction
- inappropriate self-targets – either too ambitious or not ambitious enough.

In addition, the 2011 report found that the integrated nature of Europe 2020 resulted in NRPs that contained too little detail about member states' policy strategies for reducing social exclusion and poverty (Frazier and Marlier, 2011). The 2012 report concerned the NRPs and the NSRs, and it echoed most of the concerns raised in the previous report. The 2012 report (Frazier and Marlier, 2012) found that most NRPs did not sufficiently analyse the main problems related to social exclusion, were too focused on fiscal consolidation rather than social protection, and focused too much on the employment aspects of inclusion. Moreover, the report observed that social exclusion and poverty had increased during the previous year, largely because of the effects of the economic and financial crisis. The report's evaluation of the NSRs was hampered by low compliance: only eight member states had submitted NSRs by May 2012, because of delays in the implementation of the new social OMC. Nevertheless, it argued that the limited focus of the NRPs on social inclusion and social protection demonstrated the urgency of a functioning social OMC to provide more detailed analysis of the social dimension of Europe 2020 (Frazier and Marlier, 2012).

Evaluation the EU's social exclusion policies

More than a decade of EU involvement in the fight against poverty and social exclusion has brought few tangible results, at least in terms of policy outcomes. At risk of poverty rates remain stubbornly high in many member states, and the financial and economic crisis that started in 2008 makes it unlikely that Europe 2020's goal of reducing the number of people at risk of poverty by 20 million by 2020 will be achieved. At the level of discourse and measurement, however, the results are more encouraging:

1. The EU social inclusion policy has led to the emergence – albeit only partially – of a shared understanding of poverty and social exclusion and the kinds of policies that might ameliorate these problems. The emphasis in the Lisbon Strategy and Europe 2020 on the goal of social inclusion within the larger EU growth strategy has no doubt helped to raise awareness in the member states of social exclusion and poverty. The EU now has a common vocabulary for describing and analysing social exclusion and poverty, as well as a set of common objectives, however vaguely defined. In short, social inclusion has become 'Europeanized' (Armstrong, 2010).
2. Daly (2007, p. 5) argues that the original social inclusion goals were 'innovative and in a social policy context potentially radical' because they emphasized access to employment, especially for those with the weakest attachment to the labour market and without resources. Moreover, the social inclusion strategy mobilizes relevant stakeholders; indeed, the poor and those excluded from society are intended to take part in the policy process. This innovation was less emphasized after the mid-term review of the Lisbon Strategy, but it nevertheless contributed to the emergence of a thriving group of NGOs engaged at EU level in favour of poverty reduction.
3. The soft coordination of social inclusion policies in the member states has resulted in the collection of large amounts of data and information about national strategies for combating social exclusion, and common metrics have been developed for measuring

different aspects of social exclusion and income poverty. The OMC in social inclusion is thus supposed to lead to 'learning by numbers', in the sense that policy-makers adhere to the same indicators to measure a particular problem (Mabbett, 2007). This should contribute to a common understanding of the policy problem and the identification of preferred solutions or best practices. In other words, the OMC pushes participants to frame problems in the same way.

Although the results of this framing exercise have been disappointing, the member states are now accountable to the EU in terms of reporting on the poverty and social exclusion situation within their borders and describing what they are doing to address these problems (Armstrong, 2010). Compared to the situation before 1999, this is surely an improvement. The EU now has reliable, publicly available data (Marlier et al., 2007), and the EU bodies and the member states now know much more than they did a decade ago about variations in social exclusion and poverty in the member states (see Daly, 2007 for a contrasting view).

These modest achievements aside, a growing literature on the effectiveness of the EU's social inclusion strategy reveals the limits of EU efforts. There is little evidence that EU policies have made much difference in helping the member states formulate more effective strategies for fighting social exclusion. Even if the OMC social inclusion created a 'nurturing' environment (Ferrera et al., 2002) in terms of policy learning, the OMC remains more of an exercise in reporting existing strategies than experimental, innovative governance. Marlier et al. (2007) find that there is not much evidence that active processes of mutual learning are taking place, simply because of the difficulty of transferring one policy from one country to another.

There are two reasons for this. First, the governance tools embedded in the social OMC are weak. In order for soft coordination to work, there must be common objectives, common indicators and mutual surveillance. In contrast to the EES, the social OMC does not include specific guidelines or targets applicable at the national level. Until 2010, the social OMC included common objectives that were open to wide interpretation. Even after the adoption of a specific EU-level target for poverty reduction as part of Europe 2020, there are no national-level targets (member states' combined efforts are supposed to result in an overall reduction of poverty in the EU). Moreover, the social OMC does not contain country-specific recommendations or sanctions, and the joint reports do not contain much in the way of performance evaluation (Daly, 2007). This means that the naming and shaming function of the OMC does not work very well.

Second, despite the progress on common definitions and indicators, the wide variation of member state policies aimed at the disadvantaged makes a common strategy difficult. Copeland and Daly (2012) point out that poverty is problematic in terms of EU social policy because it differs so greatly across the member states, depending on national models of welfare. Poverty is generally lower in the Nordic and continental welfare regimes and is higher in the liberal and Mediterranean ones. The EU strategy for dealing with this diversity has been to introduce three indicators of social exclusion (at risk of poverty, material deprivation, and living in a jobless household). It is not clear that the establishment of an EU target will address the problem of weak incentives. Copeland and Daly (2012) argue that the new target and the new procedures will continue the pattern established during the Lisbon Strategy, in which the member states choose indicators and targets from an extensive menu. If the joint reports are any indication, however, the quality of the NRPs/NSRs has improved since 2000. The member states now articulate more specific goals, and the reports reflect more strategic thinking concerning the fight against social exclusion.

Conclusion

Three broad conclusions emerge from the analysis presented in this chapter. First, the fight against social exclusion has become a core element of the growth strategies embedded in the Lisbon Strategy and Europe 2020. The elevation of social inclusion to such a central place on the EU policy agenda is remarkable, given that the EU's first policies concerning poverty in the 1970s and 80s were contested and piecemeal. The reluctance of some member states to accept even a small Commission role in fighting poverty highlights the tension between economic and social policy-making that has dominated the EU since the Treaty of Rome. If the member states were willing to transfer some aspects of economic policy to the European level, many of them were wary of such a process concerning social policy. This tension explains much of the contradictory nature of social inclusion policies at EU level: the EU has articulated a numerical objective for social exclusion for the first time, but it is not clear that the EU possesses the resources and tools to achieve it.

Second, the EU's discursive commitment to reducing social exclusion has not been matched by appropriate and effective governance instruments. The growing literature on the EU's social inclusion process provides much evidence of the weakness of the governance instruments that underpin it. In contrast to other soft coordination processes (EES, broad economic coordination), the social inclusion process lacks clear objectives. Moreover, it relies on increasingly sophisticated indicators that, in an effort to accommodate member state diversity, result in competing definitions of social exclusion (Copeland and Daly, 2014). Indeed, one of the central contradictions of the EU's social inclusion strategy is that one of its key indicators – the at risk of poverty rate – is not used by any member state in its own policies (Saraceno, 2010). Thus, one of the most important ways that the EU measures social exclusion has little resonance with the way the member states view their own performance in this area. In addition, the coexistence of three different indicators of social exclusion means that member states can orient themselves to the indicator that best coincides with their own policies and performance. This accommodation to member state diversity, however, leads to policy incoherence (Copeland and Daly, 2014).

Finally, the primacy of economic and financial concerns in the wake of the global financial crisis and the EU sovereign debt crisis reveals the limits of the EU's social inclusion strategy. Both crises have increased the demand for policies aimed at reducing social exclusion, but the thrust of the EU's overall policy response has been one of austerity rather than allowing the member states fiscal room for manoeuvre to respond to social dislocation. In 2011, 17% of the EU population were affected by income poverty (less than 60% of equivalized median income after social transfers). Moreover, the countries most affected by the sovereign debt crisis have seen their income poverty rates increase significantly. In Spain, the share of the population affected by income poverty after social transfers rose from 19.7% in 2007 to 22.2% in 2012. The same figures for Greece are 20.3% and 23.1%. Given that median incomes in both countries have fallen, these figures indicate a substantial increase in income poverty (Eurostat, n.d.).

Chapter 9

Conclusion

The goal of this book has been to analyse the causes and consequences of EU social policy development. The analysis presented here draws on historical institutionalist theory to account for the slow, uneven and often unintended and unexpected process of social policy integration. It would be an exaggeration to say that a fully fledged social policy regime exists at EU level, at least in the form of income maintenance programmes and social services financed by taxation and social contributions. As this book emphasizes, EU social policy is predominantly regulatory – it sets out rules, parameters and prescriptions that constrain and/or guide social policy development in the member states. In other words, the member states share social policy-making competence with EU institutions; national welfare states are nested within the EU's supranational regulatory framework. This final chapter addresses the implications of EU social policy development for the future of national welfare states in the EU, the legitimacy of the EU project, and the future of the European social model.

Historical institutionalism overcomes the limits of the two theoretical approaches that have long dominated the study of European integration – intergovernmentalism and neofunctionalism. As the analysis in this book shows, the development of EU social policy cannot be reduced to the preferences of the most powerful member states, as intergovernmentalism would predict. Certainly, EU social policy remains regulatory and often rudimentary, but it is nevertheless an important constraint on national social policy autonomy. Moreover, it is clear that EU social policy has developed in a manner the member states did not intend. Over time, member state control over the development of EU social policy has diminished. Neofunctionalist theory is likewise unable to account for the development of EU social policy. If anything, the spillovers from European integration should have created powerful incentives for the transfer of more and more social policy competences to the EU level, but this has not

207

happened. Despite the very real impact of social policy integration, EU social policy does not replace national social policies.

A historical institutionalist perspective goes beyond the deficiencies in both intergovernmentalism and neofunctionalism by highlighting the role of temporality, unintended consequences and path dependence in the development of EU social policy. Over time, the member states created EU institutions designed to further economic integration, but the nature of democracy means that short-term goals dominate the strategies of elected governments, so that democratic leaders cannot always anticipate the long-term effects of their decisions. In other words, institutions do not always have the effects intended by their creators. Policy integration is thus not the result of neofunctionalist spillover, but rather the product of democratically elected governments' decision-making in the context of information complexity and short-term time horizons. It is precisely the gaps between the intentions embedded in original institutional designs and the temporal development of those institutions that have shaped the emergence of a multilevel governance system in the EU.

These effects are particularly prominent in the social field. Social policy played little role in the Treaty of Rome, but subsequent treaty revisions expanded EU competence in the social field and extended QMV to more and more aspects of social policy. In addition, the ECJ has emerged as a powerful, independent actor with considerable influence on the interpretation of EU social policies. European integration over time has also encouraged the emergence and growth of civil society and interest groups that mobilize at European level to lobby the Commission's social policy initiatives, influence judicial policy-making by the ECJ, and pressure the European Parliament (Cichowski, 2007; Keleman, 2011). Moreover, the European Parliament is now a powerful competitor to the Council, and has shown its willingness to defend social aspects of European legislation. The European Parliament's influence on the Services Directive (2006) is the clearest illustration of this development.

In sum, by highlighting the gaps that emerge between original institutional design and the long-term development of those institutions, a historical institutionalist account provides a more convincing account of the development of EU social policy than theoretical perspectives that focus on instrumental member state bargaining or autonomous spillover processes. The paradox that emerges from the policy chapters is the slow and uneven accretion of EU social policy competences despite the status quo bias of EU decision-making institutions and member state preferences for national social policy autonomy. Some of the most important advances in social policy integration have resulted from the interdependence of social policies and the construction of the internal market. Even if the member states were not willing to support large-scale EU social policy interventions, they did support modest EU initiatives designed to reconcile specific social policies, such as workplace health and safety and parental leave, with the internal market. In other areas of social policy, independent action by supranational institutions, especially the ECJ and Commission, have driven EU social policy forward.

EU social policy

What are the central contours of EU social policy? As the policy chapters show, EU social policies create regulatory constraints on national social policies. EU legislation does not dictate the detailed content of national social policies. Nor do EU initiatives create European-wide social benefits and services. Instead, EU social policy sets limits on the design of member states' social policies. This is especially true in the field of labour mobility, where the EU's social policy mandate is strongest (as discussed in Chapter 4 on social security and pensions and Chapter 5 on employment). One of the most powerful aspects of negative integration is the requirement that national social policy facilitates labour mobility. This has required the member states to make their social insurance schemes and occupational pension schemes compatible with labour mobility, which has meant the opening up of schemes that were often previously closed to workers from other countries. Today, a highly institutionalized coordination scheme ensures that workers may aggregate benefits earned in all member states and export benefits to any member state.

Negative integration also exerts substantial influence on the development of social services, especially health care, in the member states. Again, the EU does not have a pan-European health care policy, but the ECJ's interpretation of the legal requirements of the internal market has begun to open up national health care institutions to patient mobility and the freedom to provide services (see Chapter 7 on health policy).

Despite pessimistic assessments claiming that European integration undermines the core features of conservative and Nordic welfare regimes, negative integration has also brought tangible and important changes to national social policy regimes. In particular, the ECJ's rulings on equal pay between men and women have prompted the member states to adapt national social insurance schemes and some aspects of labour legislation (especially concerning equal pay and access to employment) to the EU's equality regime. ECJ rulings on equal pay have had a knock-on effect, prompting civil society groups to mobilize in pursuit of more comprehensive equality and antidiscrimination provisions in treaty revisions since the 1990s.

Finally, positive integration was given an important boost by the introduction and expansion of soft modes of governance, particularly the open method of coordination (OMC). This policy-making innovation allowed EU actors, primarily the Council, to enter into policy areas for which the EU had little to no legal mandate to act, particularly employment promotion and combating social exclusion (Chapters 5 and 8). Despite the inherent weakness of soft governance tools, the OMC processes in employment and social inclusion have done much to elevate both policy fields to 'areas of common concern' in the EU and mobilize national and supranational resources in pursuit of effective policy solutions. Soft governance tools are an important innovation in the EU's shared social policy governance structure. EU action does not replace or supersede national policies, rather, it complements and shapes member state responses to common policy challenges.

National welfare states in the EU

The central argument informing the policy chapters of this book is that the distinctive features of national social policies interact with EU governance structures over time to shape patterns of EU social policy integration. National social policies are highly salient in political and social terms, important elements in state-building processes and often the result of decades of political contestation. As such, national social policies are closely linked to processes of democratic legitimacy and national identity. It is thus not surprising that the original six members of the EU were unwilling to subject their social policies to supranational control. Indeed, the Treaty of Rome is based on the (mis)conception that social and economic policy could be kept separate. National social policies not only provide solutions to social risks such as poverty, unemployment, sickness and old age, but are also political resources for national political actors (Lynch, 2006). These attributes of national social policies depend on boundary control, or the ability of national politicians to define which groups qualify for citizenship and access to social provision (Ferrera, 2005). The process of European integration erodes boundary control by opening up national systems of social protection to entrants from other states.

As Meunier and McNamara (2007b) argue, historical institutionalism is particularly suited to analysing the development of EU policy competence over time. Historical institutionalism's focus on historical trajectories and the effect of timing and sequence on long-term policy development helps resolve the central puzzle of EU social policy integration: the expansion of EU competence into nearly all aspects of social policy at the expense of the member states. National social policy is now embedded in a multilevel governance structure.

One of the central arguments informing the policy chapters of this book is that the economic, social and political salience of social policies in the member states constrain the development of a fully fledged, redistributive social policy at EU level. This effect is the result of sequencing: national welfare states emerged decades before the EU was established. Indeed, when the Treaty of Rome was negotiated in the 1950s, the original six EU members were in the midst of consolidating and extending their welfare states as part of the postwar reconstruction process.

National social policies were also closely linked to nation-building and democratization processes. Thus, even if social policies are important aspects of capitalist markets, the Treaty of Rome effectively decoupled social policy from the market-building process. The institutionalization of national social policies, as well as their role in securing democratic legitimacy, meant that there was little support for more than a nominal transfer of social policy competence to the European level.

As the policy chapters show, the artificial decoupling of social policy from the market-building process was short-lived. This is not surprising, given that the development of supranational institutions – the Commission, the ECJ and the European Parliament – has diverged from the intentions of the actors who negotiated the founding treaties. The policy chapters show the entrepreneurial and strategic behaviour of all three actors; each has substantially increased its power beyond what the Treaty of Rome intended. The Council remains a key actor, but its influence has declined dramatically in relative terms.

The development of EU institutions over time – driven by the member states in treaty negotiations and the purposeful action of EU institutions like the Commission, ECJ and European Parliament – has reconfigured the structure of political opportunity in the EU (cf. Marks and McAdam, 1996). The member states now share social policy decision-making authority in important areas with EU institutions, and national political arenas are no longer the central location for political mobilization and decision-making concerning social policy. The emergence of a multilevel governance structure does not mean, however, that the EU has replaced important elements of national social policy with a European alternative. As Scharpf (2002) argues, the loss of member state autonomy in social policy has not been matched by an equivalent expansion of EU social policy competences.

The timing and impact of EU social policy integration vary substantially across policy fields. As the policy chapters show, EU influence on policy was earliest and greatest in policy fields directly linked to labour mobility, a core aspect of the EU's early market-building efforts. EU actors adopted secondary legislation in the 1960s and 70s that introduced and then expanded the conditions under which workers and their families could access host country social security schemes. The emergence of the ECJ as an important actor in the interpretation of EU law in the 1960s added momentum to the integration of social security law to accommodate free movement. The resurrection of Article 119's guarantee of equal pay in the 1970s with the *Defrenne* cases is the clearest example of this (see Chapter 4). More than 55 years after the entry into force of the Treaty of Rome, member state social security regimes are strongly anchored in an EU coordination regime that regulates the aggregation and portability of public social security benefits in the member states. The member states retain control of the rules governing benefit entitlement and financing, but they may not exclude nationals from other member states from their schemes. Moreover, the definition of who is eligible for income support in the host member state has expanded to include the non-economically active – an important break with the worker-based coordination rules established in decades of EU legislation and jurisprudence (Martinsen, 2011).

Similarly, the Treaty of Rome's provisions concerning the training and retraining of workers provided the basis for EU involvement in education and training, even if the member states remained firmly in control of their national education and training systems. Indeed, the early initiatives of the European Social Fund (EES) – virtually the only financial instrument for social policy at EU level – provided co-financing for training programmes organized by the member states. In other words, early EU training initiatives did not disturb the structure and logic of national programmes. In contrast, the member states largely sidelined the EU decision-making process in their efforts to harmonize higher education systems in the 2000s (see Chapter 6).

The introduction of the internal market was the impetus for expansion of the EU social policy remit into new areas. Concern about the neglect of the social dimension of the internal market project was the background to the inclusion of the employment title in the Treaty of Amsterdam in 1997. This innovation drew on recent attempts to use soft coordination to create an EU response to Europe's growing unemployment problem. Here, timing, sequence and context were important drivers of EU policy innovation concerning employment. The issue of employment policy was linked to the internal market's neglect of the social effects of liberalization. As Chapter 5 discusses, the EES has now been in place for more than 15 years, but observers are divided concerning its effectiveness. Indeed, the choice of soft coordination as the central tool of EU employment policy highlights the difficulty of constructing a strong European commitment to employment that would match the EU's commitment to the internal market. There is also a growing asymmetry between soft law initiatives concerning employment policy and the recent activism of the ECJ in labour relations. The ECJ's rulings in *Viking*, *Laval* and *Rüffert* mark a new phase in the judicial interpretation of competition law that affects labour relations. These decisions undermine core elements of industrial relations in several member states and created an opening for firms to use EU competition law to challenge elements of collective bargaining.

The ECJ's judicial activism in the interpretation of internal market legislation has also led to the EU's intrusion into an area long thought to be immune from EU regulation: publicly organized social services. The Treaty of Rome provided very few openings for EU action in health policy. The completion of the internal market led to expanded legal competence in occupational health and safety and in public health in general, but national health services were generally considered to be outside the scope of EU involvement. Again, judicial activism chipped away at member state control over their health care systems. As Chapter 7 shows, a series of important rulings starting in the late 1990s eroded member state control over important aspects of health care, by confirming the right of health care consumers to purchase health care goods and services in other member states.

Finally, the emergence of the OMC in the late 1990s provided the momentum for EU involvement in social inclusion. This development is surprising because social inclusion has no direct connection to the market-building process. Indeed, the founding treaties say nothing about social inclusion, although they referred to the EU's goal of promoting 'harmonious social development'. The Commission has been a key actor in pushing EU competence in social inclusion, despite member state resistance. However, like employment policy, the primary vehicle for EU policy-making in social inclusion is soft coordination. As in employment policy, it is difficult to identify any direct EU impact on social inclusion policies and outcomes in the member states (cf. Heidenreich and Zeitlin, 2009).

How does EU social policy reconfigure national welfare states? The literature on institutional change does not provide a clear answer. For example, Streeck and Thelen's (2005) important typology of institutional change cannot capture the multilevel dimension of the interaction between national and European social policies. The categories of displacement, layering, drift, conversion and exhaustion tell us much about the ways that specific policy fields change as the result of endogenous and exogenous pressures. The emergence of EU social policy competence, instead, is better captured by the multilevel governance perspective (Hooghe and Marks, 2001). European social policies are not layered on top of national ones, nor are national social policies displaced by European ones. It makes more sense to understand the development of EU social policy as a central component of the emergence of multiple levels of governance in the EU. EU social policies add a layer of regulation to national social policies, in the sense that national social policy-making is now nested within a complex, institutionalized set of hard and soft constraints on national social policy-making. Moreover, as noted above, EU social policy-making reconfigures the political opportunity structure for actors seeking to mobilize around specific social policy fields and influence policy development (Marks and McAdam, 1996; Schmidt, 2006). European integration adds an additional level to national social policy-making, providing affected interests with additional opportunities to influence policy-making.

What is the added value of EU social policy? The relevant literature is divided on this topic. One set of arguments emphasizes the
asymmetry between social and economic integration, with social
policy goals clearly subordinate to market integration (Scharpf,
1996; Leibfried, 2010). A second school of thought emphasizes the
progressive elements of EU social policy integration, most prominently efforts to eliminate gender discrimination and encourage the
modernization of national models of social protection (Heidenreich
and Zeitlin, 2009). Other authors highlight the capacity of the
OMC to enhance the problem-solving capabilities of the EU via
innovative deliberative governance tools (Zeitlin, 2008; Hemerijck,
2012). In other words, the added value of EU social policy depends
largely on which aspects of the welfare state are emphasized and the
difficult question of how to measure the impact of the social OMC.

Social policy and the legitimacy of European integration

The economic crisis that began in 2008 threatens to reverse much
of the progress achieved concerning EU social policy. The share of
EU residents in the EU 27 at risk of poverty or social exclusion was
24.2% (119.6 million) in 2011. Unemployment has also increased
sharply in the majority of the member states; in April 2013, 26.6
million EU residents were unemployed, in other words, 11%. Youth
unemployment (15- to 24-year-olds) has risen even more dramatically, to 23.5% in April 2013. These figures are even more alarming
in those member states most affected by the euro crisis: Greece,
Spain, Portugal, Ireland, Italy and Cyprus.

As Scharpf (2013) observes, citizen trust in the EU has declined
sharply in the past decade. Trust in EU institutions has dropped in
seven of eight Eurobarometer polls taken since autumn 2009 (polls
are taken twice yearly, in spring and autumn). In autumn 2013,
39% of respondents trusted the European Parliament, 35% trusted
the Commission, and 34% trusted the ECB (Eurobarometer, 2013).
Trust in the EU as a whole has also hit new lows: 58% of Europeans
state that they do not trust the EU, while 31% trust it (Eurobarometer, 2013). Declining trust in the EU is part of a broader trend.
Only 25% of Europeans trust national parliaments, and 23% trust
national governments (Eurobarometer, 2013).

The EU's institutional response to the financial crisis and the
euro crisis is likely to exacerbate these trends. The new economic

governance structures established in 2010 to deal with the euro crisis lack what Scharpf (1999) calls 'input legitimacy' because they are dominated by centralized expert decision-making, rather than open, democratic procedures. Recent Eurobarometer data suggests that Europeans view these new governance structures ambivalently. In 2013, 63% of respondents thought the EU was responsible for austerity (Eurobarometer, 2013), while 49% disagreed with the statement that 'The EU makes the quality of life better in Europe' (43% agreed with the statement). Finally, only 40% agreed with the statement that 'The EU is creating the conditions for more jobs in Europe' (Eurobarometer, 2013, p. 81).

Public opinion data also indicates that Europeans do not associate the EU with a large role concerning social protection or promoting high living standards. The autumn 2013 Eurobarometer poll asked respondents what the EU stands for, and the most frequent response was 'the freedom to travel, study and work anywhere in the EU' (43% of respondents), followed by the 'euro' (32%), and 'wasting money' (27%). Only 9% mentioned 'social protection', and 12% mentioned 'economic prosperity' (Eurobarometer, 2013, p. 60). These results are alarming from the perspective of 'input' and 'output' legitimacy (Scharpf, 1999) because they suggest that Europeans' perceptions of the EU have less to do with democratic legitimacy and the production of collective goods, and more to do with facilitating individual mobility and economic transactions.

Declining citizen confidence in the performance and legitimacy of European institutions is part of a broader trend. A 'permissive consensus' marked the EU's first three decades; European integration had little salience in national politics, and citizens generally left European decision-making to their elected leaders. With the completion of the internal market, however, European integration has become much more important in national politics. As Hooghe and Marks (1999) argue, the adoption of the Single European Act did not settle the question of how the internal market would be governed or how the EU would shape the relationship between the member states and markets. Thus, the debate about the status of the internal market revealed the tensions inherent in the permissive consensus and exposed the highly political nature of the integration process.

Perhaps the most important source of political conflict in relation to European integration concerns the distinction between neoliberal and regulated capitalism (Hooghe and Marks, 1999). This distinction largely concerns economic inequality and the role of the state, so the successful implementation of the internal market sparked conflict about the relationship between politics and markets. Even if European actors could agree on the benefits of the internal market programme, questions remained about how regulated the internal market should be. Given these two opposing models of market regulation, the internal market was bound to expose conflicting conceptions of the relationship between the member states and markets.

The distinction between regulated and neoliberal capitalism obscures the institutional heterogeneity within both types. The neoliberal group includes the UK and Ireland as well as many of the new member states in Eastern and Central Europe. The regulated capitalism cluster is even more fragmented, encompassing social democratic and conservative welfare regimes, as well as the Southern member states. Given the centrality of market-building to the European integration project, the fragmentation in both groups of countries disadvantages the regulated capitalist member states more than the more liberal member states. Indeed, as Orenstein (2008b) argues, the new member states in Eastern and Central Europe rely on a growth model based on cheap labour, low tax rates and limited regulation. The internal market is ideally suited to accommodate this type of growth model, and the effects are already becoming clear. As Chapter 5 shows, European firms have begun to challenge core elements of regulated capitalism in the EU 15, such as collectively bargained minimum wages and public procurement policies that require firms to pay locally prevailing minimum wages.

The clash between neoliberal and regulated capitalism has sparked intense debate in the scholarly literature about the recent course of European integration. Höpner and Schäfer (2010) argue that the nature of European integration has fundamentally changed in the past two decades. According to this view, supranational actors – the ECJ and the European Commission – are using their resources to push neoliberal capitalism. The ECJ does this by using the doctrines of direct effect and supremacy to extend the four freedoms into new areas, such as labour relations and patient mobility. Similarly, the Commission is argued to use its right of legislative initiative to pursue market-liberalizing goals that undermine key elements of regulated capitalism. The EU's 'liberalization agenda', moreover, decreases the democratic legitimacy of the EU because it provokes protest from the member states. Key examples include the *Viking, Laval* and *Rüffert* rulings, as well as the Services Directive (2006).

These arguments have much in common with Scharpf's (1996) identification of the constitutional asymmetry between negative and positive integration in the EU. In his later work, Scharpf (2010) argues that the EU 'cannot be a "social market economy"' because judicial policy-making strengthens negative integration. Like Höpner and Schäfer (2010), Scharpf advances a profoundly pessimistic view that European integration undermines national welfare states based on regulated capitalism. In particular, the ECJ's interpretation of competition law endangers key elements of regulated welfare capitalism such as public health care and social insurance monopolies. To borrow Ferrera's (2005) terminology, judicial interpretations of EU competition law destabilize national political settlements concerning the welfare state because they open up national systems of social sharing to the demands of the internal market.

An alternative line of theorizing highlights the potential for the EU to enhance its own legitimacy by strengthening individual social rights through European legislation and offering opportunities at the European level for the development of civil society and political mobilization. Caporaso and Tarrow (2009) argue that the EU has shifted towards more market-correcting social policy in the past two decades. The ECJ is portrayed as the agent of this shift towards a more 'Polanyian' integration course in which markets are embedded in civil society. Caporaso and Tarrow (2009, p. 593) argue that the ECJ's recent rulings contribute to the establishment of social rights for EU citizens, thereby 're-embedding the market'.

A growing literature also emphasizes the emergence of civil society at the European level. Keleman (2011) argues that European legal integration has progressed to the point that citizens can mobilize to enforce their own rights according to EU law. In other words, EU legal integration gives individuals the opportunity to pursue rights claims based on EU law. The structure of European institutions facilitates judicial policy-making because of the fragmentation of political authority. Once the ECJ established the doctrines of direct effect and supremacy, it has been difficult for the EU's legislative branch (Commission, Council and European Parliament) to reverse ECJ rulings. Over time, a 'catalogue of EU rights' has emerged that details European citizens' rights as workers, pensioners, consumers, students and dependent family members (Keleman, 2011). European citizens also enjoy the benefits of EU citizenship, which gives them mobility rights beyond those guaranteed to workers and their families.

Other scholars emphasize the ways in which European integration and institution-building have created opportunities for citizen participation in democratic processes. It is now widely accepted that European integration reconfigures political opportunity structures by giving individual and collective actors new channels for influencing democratic decision-making. Simply put, domestic actors can mobilize at the European level in order to influence domestic policy-making. This allows political actors to reopen political decisions that had already been settled in national political decision-making. Although the literature emphasizes examples that illustrate the negative effects of European mobilization, such as the *Viking*, *Laval* and *Rüffert* rulings, recent EU experience also includes progressive examples such as ECJ rulings concerning gender discrimination, the inclusion of the non-economically active in minimum income schemes, and social security rights for same-sex partners. In other words, the effects of judicial policy-making are not unambiguously negative. In addition, arguments about the nondemocratic nature of judicial policy-making do not consider definitions of democratic participation that extend the definition of democracy to include non-electoral democratic arenas.

The future of the European social model

Any discussion of the future of the European social model (ESM) must consider two lines of conflict: the conflict between neoliberal and regulated capitalism and the balance between European and national policy-making competences. Hooghe and Marks (2008) argue that the period since the early 1990s is marked by a 'constraining dissensus', in the sense that the future course of European integration is now politically salient in national politics. In short, domestic electoral considerations constrain the actions of national political leaders in European-level decision-making. An important source of the increased political salience of European integration in national political processes is the relationship between European integration and national models of social protection. Today, national electorates are much more aware of the impact of European integration on important elements of national governance structures, including social policies. As European integration has intruded more and more into national social policy-making, the effects on member state social policies have gained more attention in national political debates and provoked more conflict. The 2005 Eastern enlargement is an important example: only three member states (Sweden, the UK and Ireland) allowed immediate free movement in 2005. The other 12 members of the EU 15 made use of transitional opt-out clauses in order to shield their labour markets and social protection systems from the potentially destabilizing effects of a large influx of migrants from the new member states. Similarly, the rejection of the Constitutional Treaty in 2005 by the French and Dutch electorates was motivated in part by fears that deeper integration would undermine national social protection systems.

It is not surprising that deeper European integration and the accession of 13 member states with less generous social protection systems than those in the EU 15 would lead to conflict concerning the relationship between European and national levels of governance. Much of this conflict is rooted in concerns about the relationship between EU social policy integration and national welfare models. In many, if not most, of the EU 15, national welfare states are important expressions of national identity because they represent institutionalized and politically determined arrangements for social sharing (Ferrera, 2005). As Ferrera (2008, p. 47) puts it:

> postwar social protection systems have built extraordinary bonds between citizens and their national institutions, bringing about a very robust form of allegiance, based on the institutionalized exchange of material benefits for electoral support.

The recent development of primary legislation and ECJ jurisprudence offers some evidence that the future of the ESM may be based on stronger principles of social solidarity. The Lisbon Treaty contains important provisions that allow the member states to shield their systems of social protection from competition rules. It contains important fundamental social rights, a section on solidarity, and a 'horizontal social clause' (Article 9) that requires the EU to consider social protection when it formulates and implements its policies. As discussed in Chapter 3, the Lisbon Treaty also includes stronger provisions concerning the reduction of social exclusion, inequality and discrimination. These treaty provisions build on two decades of jurisprudence concerning the definition of non-economic services of general interest, such as health care systems or pension systems. The Lisbon Treaty also contains procedures that allow a member state to suspend legislative decision-making concerning free movement when national social security interests are at stake (see Ferrera, 2008 for a discussion). In sum, it seems likely that heightened political conflict concerning European integration, exacerbated by enlargement, will mean that the pace of social policy integration will slow.

Appendix

European Court of Justice cases

Albany International BV *v.* Stichting Bedrijfspensioenfonds Textielindustrie, Case C-67/96, 1999.

Barber *v.* Royal Guardian Exchange Assurance Group, case C-262/88, 1990.

Bilka – Kaufhaus GmbH *v.* Karin Weber von Hartz, Case 170/84, 1986.

Nicolas Decker *v.* Caisse de Maladie des Employés Privés, Case C-120/95, 1998.

Flaminio Costa *v.* ENEL, Case C-6/64, 1964.

Defrenne (No. 1) *v.* Belgian State, Case C-80/70, 1971.

Defrenne (No. 2) *v.* SABENA, Case C-43/75, 1976.

Defrenne (No. 3) *v.* SABENA, Case C-149/77, 1978.

Federación Española de Empresas de Tecnología Sanitaria (FENIN) *v.* Commission of the European Communities, Case C-205/03P, 2006.

Fisscher *v.* Voorhuis Hengelo BV and Stiching Bedrijfspensioenfonds voor de Detailhandel, Case C-128/93.

Geraets-Smits *v.* Stichting Ziekenfonds VGZ and Peerbooms *v.* Stichting CZ Groep Zorgverzekeringen, Joined Cases C-157/99, 2001.

Hellen Gerster *v.* Freistaat Bayern, Case C-1/95, 1997.

Françoise Gravier *v.* City of Liège, Case C-293/83, 1985.

Kathleen Hill and Ann Stapleton *v.* The Revenue Commissioners and Department of Finance, Case C-243/95, 1998.

The International Transport Workers' Federation and The Finnish Seamen's Union *v*. Viking Line ABP and OÜ Viking Line Eesti, Case C-438/05, 2007.

Raymond Kohll *v*. Union des Caisses de Maladie, Case C-158/96, 1998.

Landeshauptstadt Kiel *v*. Norbert Jaeger, Case C-151/02, 2003.

Laval un Partneri Ltd *v*. Svenska Byggnadsarbetareförbundet, Svenska Byggnadsarbetareförbundets avd. 1, Byggettan and Svenska Elektrikerförbundet, Case C-341/05, 2007.

V.G. Müller-Fauré *v*. Onderlinge Waarborgmaatschappij OZ Zorgverzekeringen UA and E.E.M. van Riet *v*. Onderlinge Waarborgmaatschappij ZAO Zorgverzekeringen, Case C-385/99, 2003.

The Queen, on the application of Yvonne Watts *v*. Bedford Primary Care Trust and Secretary of State for Health, Case C-372/04, 2006.

Dirk Rüffert *v*. Land Niedersachsen, Case C-346/06, 2008.

Gerardus Cornelis Ten Oever *v*. Stichting Bedrijfspensioenfonds voor het Glazenwassers- en Schoonmaakbedrijf, Case C-109/91, 1993.

Vanbraekel *v*. Alliance Nationale des Mutualites Chretiennes, Case C-368/98, 2001.

Van Gend en Loos *v*. Nederlandse Administratie der Belastingen, Case C-26/62, 1962.

Vroege *v*. NCIV Instituut voor Volkshuisvesting BV and Stichting Pensioenfonds NCIVi, Case 57/93, 1994.

References

Council directives

Council Directive 65/65/EEC of 26 January 1965 on the approximation of provisions laid down by law, Regulation or Administrative Action relating to proprietary medicinal products.

Council Directive 68/360/EEC of 15 October 1968 on the abolition of restrictions on movement and residence within the Community for workers of Member States and their families.

Council Directive 75/117/EEC of 10 February 1975 on the approximation of the laws of the Member States relating to the application principle of equal pay for men and women (Equal Pay Directive).

Council Directive 75/129/EEC of 17 February 1975 on the approximation of the laws of the Member States relating to collective redundancies.

Council Directive 76/207/EEC of 9 February 1976 on the implementation of the principle of equal treatment for men and women as regards access to employment, vocational training and promotion, and working condition (Equal Treatment Directive).

Council Directive 79/7/EEC of 19 December 1978 on the progressive implementation of the principle of equal treatment for men and women in matters of social security.

Council Directive 80/987/EEC of 20 October 1980 on the approximation of the laws of the Member States relating to the protection of employees in the event of the insolvency of their employer.

Council Directive 86/378/EEC of 24 July 1986 on the implementation of the principle of equal treatment for men and women in occupational social security schemes.

Council Directive 89/48/EEC of 21 December 1988 on a general system for the recognition of higher-education diplomas awarded on completion of professional education and training of at least three years' duration (OSH Framework Directive).

Council Directive 89/391/EEC of 12 June 1989 on the introduction of measures to encourage improvements in the safety and health of workers at work.

Council Directive 90/364/EEC of 28 June 1990 on the right of residence.

Council Directive 90/365/EEC of 28 June 1990 on the right of residence for employees and self-employed persons who have ceased their occupational activity.

Council Directive 90/366/EEC of 28 June 1990 on the right of residence for students.

Council Directive 92/51/EEC of 18 June 1992 on a second general system for the recognition of professional education and training to supplement Directive 89/48/EEC.

Council Directive 92/85/EEC of 19 October 1992 on the introduction of measures to encourage improvements in the safety and health at work of pregnant workers and workers who have recently given birth or are breastfeeding (Pregnant Workers Directive).

Council Directive 93/39/EEC of 14 June 1993 amending Directives 65/65/EEC, 75/318/EEC and 75/319/EEC in respect of medicinal products.

Council Directive 93/96/EEC of the Council of 29 October 1993 on the right of residence for students.

Council Directive 93/104/EC of 23 November 1993 concerning certain aspects of the organization of working time (Working Time Directive).

Council Directive 94/33/EC of 22 June 1994 on the protection of young people at work (Young Workers Directive).

Council Directive 94/45/EC of 22 September 1994 on the establishment of a European Works Council or a procedure in Community-scale undertakings and Community-scale groups of undertakings for the purposes of informing and consulting employees.

Council Directive 96/34/EC of 3 June 1996 on the framework agreement on parental leave concluded by UNICE, CEEP and the ETUC.

Council Directive 96/71/EC of 16 December 1996 of the European Parliament and of the Council concerning the posting of workers in the framework of the provision of services (Posted Workers Directive).

Council Directive 97/80/EC of 15 December 1997 on the burden of proof in cases of discrimination based on sex.

Council Directive 97/81/EC of 15 December 1997 concerning the Framework Agreement on part-time work concluded by UNICE, CEEP and the ETUC (Part-time Work Directive).

Council Directive 98/59/EC of 20 July 1998 on the approximation of the laws of the Member States relating to collective redundancies.

Council Directive 99/70/EC of 28 June 1999 concerning the framework agreement on fixed-term work concluded by ETUC, UNICE and CEEP (Fixed-term Work Directive).

Council Directive 2010/18/EU of 8 March 2010 implementing the revised Framework Agreement on parental leave concluded by BUSINESS-EUROPE, UEAPME, CEEP and ETUC and repealing Directive 96/34/EC (Parental Leave Directive).

Council Recommendation 92/24/EEC of 31 March 1992 on child care.

European Parliament and Council Directive 98/43/EC of 6 July 1998 on the approximation of the laws, regulations and administrative provisions of the Member States relating to the advertising and sponsorship of tobacco products.

European Parliament and Council Directive 2001/37/EC of 5 June 2001 on the approximation of the laws, regulations and administrative provisions of the Member States concerning the manufacture, presentation and sale of tobacco products.

European Parliament and Council Directive 2002/98/EC of 27 January 2003 setting standards of quality and safety for the collection, testing, processing, storage and distribution of human blood and blood components amending Directive 2001/83/EC.

European Parliament and Council Directive 2003/33/EC of 26 May 2003 on the approximation of the laws, regulations and administrative provisions of the Member States relating to the advertising and sponsorship of tobacco products.

European Parliament and Council Directive 2003/34/EC of 26 May 2003 amending for the 23rd time Council Directive 76/769/EEC relating to restrictions on the marketing and use of certain dangerous substances and preparations (substances classified as carcinogens, mutagens or substances toxic to reproduction).

European Parliament and Council Directive 2003/41/EC of 3 June 2003 on the activities and supervision of institutions for occupational retirement provision (IORP Directive).

European Parliament and Council Directive 2003/88/EC of 4 November 2003 concerning certain aspects of the organisation of working time (revised Working Time Directive).

European Parliament and Council Directive 2004/23/EC of 31 March 2004 on setting standards of quality and safety for the donation, procurement, testing, processing, preservation, storage and distribution of human tissues and cells.

European Parliament and Council Directive 2004/38/EC of 29 April 2004 on the right of citizens of the Union and their family members to move and reside freely within the territory of the Member States amending Regulation (EEC) 1612/68 and repealing Directives 64/221/EEC, 68/360/EEC, 72/194/EEC, 73/148/EEC, 75/34/EEC, 75/35/EEC, 90/364/EEC, 90/365/EEC and 93/96/EEC.

European Parliament and Council Directive 2005/36/EEC of 7 September 2005 on the recognition of professional qualifications.

European Parliament and Council Directive 2006/54/EC of 5 July 2006 on the implementation of the principle of equal opportunities and equal treatment of men and women in matters of employment and occupation.

European Parliament and Council Directive 2006/123/EC of 12 December 2006 on services in the internal market (Services Directive).

European Parliament and Council Directive 2008/94/EC of 22 October 2008 on the protection of employees in the event of the insolvency of their employer.

European Parliament and Council Directive 2011/24/EU of 9 March 2011 on the application of patients' rights in cross-border healthcare.

European Parliament and Council Directive 2014/40/EU of 3 April 2014 on the approximation of the laws, regulations and administrative provisions of the Member States concerning the manufacture, presentation and sale of tobacco and related products and repealing Directive 2001/37/EC.

European Parliament and Council Directive 2014/50/EU of 16 April 2014 on minimum requirements for enhancing worker mobility between Member States by improving the acquisition and preservation of supplementary pension rights.

Regulations

Regulation No. 3/58 of 25 September 1958.

Regulation No. 4/58 of 3 December 1958.

Regulation No. 15 of 16 August 1961 on initial measures to bring about free movement of workers within the Community.

Regulation (EEC) No. 38/64 of the Council of 25 March 1964 on the free movement of workers within the Community.

Regulation (EEC) No. 1612/68 of the Council of 15 October 1968 on freedom of movement of workers within the Community.

Regulation (EEC) No. 1251/70 of the Commission of 29 June 1970 on the right of workers to remain in the territory of a Member State after having been employed in that State.

Regulation (EEC) No. 1408/71 of the Council of 14 June 1971 on the application of social security schemes to employed persons and their families moving within the Community.

Regulation (EEC) No. 574/72 of the Council of 21 March 1972 on the procedure for implementing Regulation (EEC) No. 1408/71 on the application of social security schemes to employed persons, to self-employed persons and to their families moving within the Community.

Regulation (EEC) No. 2434/92 of the Council of 27 July 1992 on the amendment of Part II of Regulation (EEC) No. 1612/68 on freedom of movement of workers within the Community.

Regulation (EEC) No. 2309/93 of the Council of 22 July 1993 laying down Community procedures for the authorization and supervision of medicinal products for human and veterinary use and establishing a European Agency for the Evaluation of Medicinal Products.

Regulation (EC) No. 883/2004 of the European Parliament and of the Council of 29 April 2004 on the coordination of social security systems.

Regulation (EU) No. 407/2010 Establishing a European Financial Stabilisation Mechanism.

Decisions

Decision No. 50/2002/EC of the European Parliament and of the Council of 7 December 2001 establishing a programme of Community action to encourage cooperation between Member States to combat social exclusion (2002–2006).

Decision No. 1786/2002/EC of the European Parliament and of the Council of 23 September 2002 adopting a programme of Community action in the field of public health (2003–2008).

Decision No. 1350/2007/EC of the European Parliament and of the Council of 23 October 2007 establishing a second programme of Community action in the field of health (2008–13).

Other EU documents

Commission (1958) *First General Report on the Activity of the Community.* 1 January 1958–17 September 1958.

Commission (1961) *Fourth General Report on the Activity of the Community.* 1 April 1960–31 March 1961

Commission (1963) *Sixth General Report on the Activities of the Community.* 1 May 1962–31 March 1963.

Commission (1964) *Seventh General Report on the Activities of the Community.* 1 April 1963–31 March 1964.

Commission (1965) *Eighth General Report on the Activities of the Community.* 1 April 1964–31 March 1965.

Commission (1967) *Tenth General Report on the Activities of the Community.* 1 April 1966–31 March 1967.

Commission (1974a) *Social Action Programme.* Bulletin of the European Communities Supplement 2/74.

Commission (1974b) *Education in the European Community.* Bulletin of the European Communities Supplement 3/74.

Commission (1981) *Report on the First Programme of Pilot Schemes and Studies to Combat Poverty.* COM (81) 769 final.

Commission (1983) *Proposal for a Directive on Parental Leave for Family Reasons.* COM (83) 686 final.

Commission (1985) *Completing the Internal Market.* White Paper, COM (85) 310 final.

Commission (1986) *Europe against cancer programme: proposal for a plan of action 1987-1989 including a draft Council Decision concerning the information of the public and the training of members of the health professions.* COM (86) 717 final.

Commission (1989) *Communication from the Commission concerning its Action Programme relating to the Implementation of the Community Charter of Basic Social Rights for Workers.* COM (89) 568 final.

Commission (1993a) *Growth, Competitiveness, Employment: The Challenges and Ways Forward into the 21st Century.* White Paper, COM (93) 700 final.

Commission (1993b) *Commission Communication on the framework for action in the field of public health.* COM (93) 559 final.

Commission (1994a) *European Social Policy: A Way Forward for the Union.* A White Paper, COM (94) 333 final.

Commission (1994b) *Europe Against Aids Programme 1991-1993. Commission report on the implementation of the Action Plan in 1993.* COM (94) 525 final.

Commission (1995) *Teaching and Learning: Towards the Learning Society.* COM (95) 590 final.

Commission (1998) *The European Social Fund. An Overview of the Programming Period 1994-1999.*

Commission (1999a) *Financial Services Action Plan.* COM (1999) 232.

Commission (1999b) *Communication from the Commission: A concerted strategy for modernising social protection.* COM (1999) 347 final.

Commission (2000) *The future evolution of social protection from a long-term point of view: safe and sustainable pensions.* COM (2000) 622.

Commission (2001a) *Budgetary challenges posed by ageing populations: the impact on public spending on pensions, health and long-term care for the elderly and possible indicators of the long-term sustainability of public finances.* Report from the Economic Policy Committee. EPC/ECFIN/655/01 final.

Commission (2001b) *Draft joint report on social inclusion.* COM (2001) 565 final.

Commission (2002a) *Taking Stock of Five Years of the European Employment Strategy*: Communication from the Commission to the Council, the European Parliament, the Economic and Social Committee, and the Committee of the Regions.

Commission (2002b) *Joint Report on Social Inclusion.*

Commission (2003) *Adequate and sustainable pensions: Joint report by the Commission and the Council.*

Commission (2004) *Joint Report on Social Inclusion 2004.*

Commission (2005a) *Proposal of 20 October 2005 for a Directive on improving the portability of supplementary pension rights.* COM (2005) 507 final.

Commission (2005b) *Joint Report on Social Protection and Social Inclusion.*

Commission (2007) *Joint Report on Social Protection and Social Inclusion.*

Commission (2008a) *Commission communication. A better work-life balance: stronger support for reconciling professional, private and family life.* COM (2008) 635.

Commission (2008b) *Recommendation of 3 October 2008 on the active inclusion of people excluded from the labour market.* COM (2008) 5737.

Commission (2010a) *Progress and key challenges in the delivery of adequate and sustainable pensions in Europe (A Joint Report on Pensions).*

Commission (2010b) Green Paper: *Towards adequate, sustainable and safe European pension systems.* COM (2010) 365/3.

Commission (2010c) *Joint Report on Social Inclusion.*

Commission (2012a) White Paper: *An Agenda for Adequate, Safe and Sustainable Pensions.* COM (2012)55 final.

Commission (2012b) *Proposal for a Council Regulation on the exercise of the right to take collective action within the context of the freedom of establishment and the freedom to provide services.* COM (2012) 30.

Commission (2013a) *Draft Joint Employment Report accompanying the Communication from the Commission on Annual Growth Survey 2014.* COM (2013) 801 final.

Commission (2013b) *Communication from the Commission to the European Parliament, the Council, The European Economic and Social Committee and the Committee of the Regions. Youth Employment Initiative.* COM (2013) 144 final.

Commission (2013c) *Education and Training Monitor.*

Commission (2013d) *Assessment of the implementation of the European commission recommendation on active inclusion: a study of national policies. Synthesis report.*

Commission (2014) *Investment for Jobs and Growth. Promoting Development and Good Governance in EU Regions and Cities. Sixth Report on Economic, Social and Territorial Cohesion.*

Council (1963) *Council Decision of 2 April 1963 laying down general principles for implementing a common vocational training policy.* 63/266/EEC.

Council (1971) *Council Decision of 17 October 1983 on the tasks of the European Social Fund.* 83/516/EEC.

Council (1975) *Council Decision 75/458/EEC of 22 July 1975 concerning a programme of pilot schemes and studies to combat poverty* (Poverty 1).

Council (1976) *Resolution of the Council and of the Ministers of Education, meeting within the Council, of 9 February 1976 comprising an action programme in the field of education.*

Council (1983) *Council Decision of 17 October 1983 on the tasks of the European Social Fund.* 83/516/EEC.

Council (1984) *Conclusions.* European Council Meeting at Fountainebleau, 25–26 June.

Council (1985) *Council Decision 85/8/EEC of 19 December 1984 on specific Community action to combat poverty* (Poverty 2).

Council (1989a) *Council Decision 89/457/EEC of 18 July 1989 establishing a medium-term Community action programme concerning the economic and social integration of the economically and socially less privileged groups in society* (Poverty 3).

Council (1989b) *Resolution of the Council and of the ministers for social affairs meeting within the Council of 29 September 1989 on combating social exclusion.* 89/C 277/01.

Council (1992) *Council Recommendation (92/441/EEC) of 24 June 1992 on common criteria concerning sufficient resources and social assistance in social protection systems.*

Council (1997) *The 1998 Employment Guidelines.* Council Resolution of 15 December 1997.

Council (2000a) *Conclusions of the Lisbon European Council,* March 23–24.

Council (2000b) *Resolution of the Council and the ministers for employment and social policy, on 'the balanced participation of women and men in family and working life'.*

Council (2000c) *Fight against poverty and social exclusion. Definition of appropriate objectives.* 30 November.

Council (2001a) *Presidency Conclusions: Stockholm European Council,* 23 and 24 March.

Council (2001b) *The concrete future objectives of education and training systems.* Doc. 5980/01.

Council (2002) *Presidency Conclusions: Barcelona European Council,* 15 and 16 March.

Council (2003) *Council Decision of 22 July 2003 setting up an Advisory Committee on Safety and Health at Work and repealing Decisions 74/325/EEC and 74/326/EEC.* 2003/C 218/01.

Council (2008) Council Conclusions on common active inclusion principles to combat poverty more effectively. Brussels, 17 December.

Council (2011a) *Conclusions of the Luxembourg European Council.*

Council (2011b) *The Future of the Open Method of Coordination (OMC): Endorsement of the Opinion of the Social Protection Committee,* 23 May.

Council (2013) *Council Recommendation of 22 April 2013 on establishing a Youth Guarantee* (2013/C 120/01).

ECOFIN (1998) *Declaration of 1 May 1998. Economic and Monetary Union, Legal and political texts,* General Secretariat of the Council of the European Union and European Commission.

Books, articles and other sources

Abrahamson, P. (1995) 'Social Exclusion in Europe: Old Wine in New Bottles?', *Družboslove razprave,* 11(19/20): 119–36.

Allen, D. (2010) 'The Structural Funds and Cohesion Policy: Extending the Bargain to Meet New Challenges', in H. Wallace, M. Pollack and A.

Young (eds) *Policy-making in the European Union*, 6th edn (Oxford: Oxford University Press): 229–52.

Alter, K. (1998) 'The European Court's Political Power: The Emergence of an Authoritative International Court in the European Union', *West European Politics*, 19(3): 458–87.

Alter, K. (2000) 'The European Union's Legal System and Domestic Policy: Spillover or Backlash?', *International Organization*, 54(3): 489–518.

Anderson, K.M. (2010) 'Promoting the Multi-Pillar Model? The EU and the Shift toward Multi-Pillar Pension Systems', in Y. Borgmann-Prebil and M. Ross (eds) *Developing Solidarity in the EU: Citizenship, Governance and New Constitutional Paradigms* (Oxford: Oxford University Press): 216–34.

Annesley, C. (2007) 'Lisbon and Social Europe: Towards a European "Adult Worker Model" Welfare System', *Journal of European Social Policy*, 17(4): 195–205.

Armingeon, K. and Baccaro, L. (2011) The Sorrows of the Young Euro, unpublished paper.

Armstrong, K. (2010) *Governing Social Inclusion* (Oxford: Oxford University Press).

Armstrong, K., Begg, I. and Zeitlin, J. (2008) 'The Open Method of Coordination and the Governance of the Lisbon Strategy', *Journal of Common Market Studies*, 46(2): 436–50.

Bachtler, J. and Mendez, C. (2007) 'Who Governs EU Cohesion Policy? Deconstructing the Reforms of the Structural Funds', *Journal of Common Market Studies*, 45(3): 535–64.

Bahle, T., Pfeifer, M. and Wendt, C. (2010) 'Social Assistance', in J. Lewis, H. Obinger and S. Leibfried (eds) *The Oxford Handbook of the Welfare State* (Oxford: Oxford University Press): 448–61.

Baldoni, E. (2003) 'The Free Movement of Persons in the European Union: A Legal-historical Overview', PIONEUR Working Paper No. 2.

Barnard, C. (2006) *EC Employment Law*, 3rd edn (Oxford: Oxford University Press).

Barnard, C. (2012) *EU Employment Law*, 4th edn (Oxford: Oxford University Press).

Barnard, C. (2013) *Substantive Law of the EU* (Oxford: Oxford University Press).

Bauer, M.B. (2002) 'Limitations to Agency Control in European Union Policy-Making: The Commission and the Poverty Programmes', *Journal of Common Market Studies*, 40(3): 381–400.

Bercusson, B. (2007) 'The Trade Union Movement and the European Union: Judgement Day', *European Law Journal*, 13(3): 269–308.

Berkhout, J. and Lowery, D. (2010) 'The Changing Demography of the EU Interest System since 1990', *European Union Politics*, 11(3): 447–61.

Beyers, J. and Kerremans, B. (2004) 'Bureaucrats, Politicians, and Societal

Interests: How is European Policy-making Politicized?', *Comparative Political Studies*, 37(10): 1–31.

Blomqvist, P. and Larsson, J. (2009) Towards Common European Health Policies: What are the Implications for the Nordic Countries? Working Report, Institute for Futures Studies.

Borrás, S. and Jacobsson, K. (2004) 'The Open Method of Coordination and the New Governance Patterns in the EU', *Journal of European Public Policy*, 11(2): 185–208.

Börzel, T. (2002) 'Pace-setting, Foot-dragging, and Fence-sitting: Member State Responses to Europeanization', *Journal of Common Market Studies*, 40(2): 193–214.

Bridgen, P. and Meyer, T. (2011) 'Britain: Exhausted Voluntarism – The Evolution of a Hybrid Pension Regime', in B. Ebbinghaus (ed.) *The Varieties of Pension Governance: Pension Privatization in Europe* (Oxford: Oxford University Press): 265–92.

Brine, J. (2004) 'The European Social Fund: The Commission, the Member State and Levels of Governance', *European Educational Research Journal*, 3(4): 777–89.

Brockmann, M., Clarke, L. and Winch, C. (2008) 'Knowledge, Skills, Competence: European Divergences in Vocational Education and Training (VET) – The English, German and Dutch Cases', *Oxford Review of Education*, 34(5): 547–67.

Buch-Hansen, H. and Wigger, A. (2011) *The Politics of European Competition Regulation* (London: Routledge).

Büchs, M. (2007) *New Governance in European Social Policy* (Basingstoke: Palgrave Macmillan).

Buonanno, L. and Nugent, N. (2013) *Policies and Policy Processes of the European Union* (Basingstoke: Palgrave Macmillan).

Burley, A.-M. and Mattli, W. (1993) 'Europe before the Court: A Political Theory of Legal Integration', *International Organization*, 47(1): 41–76.

Busemeyer, M. and Trampusch, C. (eds) (2012) *The Political Economy of Collective Skill Formation* (Oxford: Oxford University Press).

Caporaso, J. and Jupille, J. (2001) 'The Europeanization of Gender Equality Policy and Domestic Structural Change', in M. Green Cowles, J. Caporaso, and T. Risse (eds) *Transforming Europe: Europeanization and Domestic Change* (Ithaca, NY: Cornell University Press): 21–44.

Caporaso, J. and Tarrow, S. (2009) 'Polanyi in Brussels: Supranational Institutions and the Transnational Embedding of Markets', *International Organization*, 63(4): 593–620.

Caracciolo di Torella, E. and Masselot, A. (2010) *Reconciling Work and Family Life in EU Law and Policy* (Basingstoke: Palgrave Macmillan).

Casey, B. (2009) 'Employment Promotion', in M. Gold (ed.) *Employment Policy in the European Union* (Basingstoke: Palgrave Macmillan): 27–45.

Cedefop (2013) *Analysis and Overview of NQF Developments in European Countries. Annual Report 2012.* Working Paper No 17. (Luxembourg: Publications Office of the European Union).

Cerami, A. (2006) *Social Policy in Central and Eastern Europe: The Emergence of a New European Welfare Regime* (Münster: LIT).

Chalmers, A.W. (2011) 'Interests, Information and Influence: Comparing the Influence of Interest Groups in the European Union', *Journal of European Integration*, 33(4): 471–86.

Chuliá, E. and Asensio, M. (2007) 'Portugal: In Search of a Stable Framework', in E.M. Immergut, K.M. Anderson and I. Schulze (eds) *The Handbook of Western European Pension Politics* (Oxford: Oxford University Press): 605–59.

Cichowski, R. (2007) *The European Court and Civil Society* (Cambridge: Cambridge University Press).

Coen, D. and Richardson, J. (eds) (2009) *Lobbying the European Union* (Oxford: Oxford University Press).

Collins, D. (1975) *Social Policy of the European Economic Community* (New York: John Wiley & Sons).

Collins, D. (1983) *The European Social Fund* (London: Croom Helm).

Conant, L. (2002) *Contained Justice* (Ithaca, NY: Cornell University Press).

Copeland, P. and Daly, M. (2012) 'Varieties of Poverty Reduction: Inserting the Poverty and Social Exclusion Target into Europe 2020', *Journal of European Social Policy*, 22(3): 273–87.

Copeland, P. and Daly, M. (2014) 'Poverty and Social Policy in Europe 2020: Ungovernable and Ungoverned', *Policy and Politics*, 42(3): 351–65.

Copeland, P. and ter Haar, B. (2013) 'A Toothless Bite? The Effectiveness of the European Employment Strategy as a Governance Tool', *Journal of European Social Policy,* 23(1): 21–36.

Copenhagen Declaration (2002) Declaration of the European Ministers of VET and the EC Convened in Copenhagen on November 29–30.

Cowles, M., Caporaso, J. and Risse, T. (eds) (2001) *Transforming Europe: Europeanization and Domestic Change* (Ithaca, NY: Cornell University Press).

Craig, P. (2010) *The Lisbon Treaty: Law, Politics and Treaty Reform* (Oxford: Oxford University Press).

Cram, L. (1993) 'Calling the Tune Without Paying the Piper? Social Policy Regulation: The Role of the Commission in European Community Social Policy', *Policy and Politics*, 21(2): 135–46.

Cram, L. (2009) 'From "Integration by Stealth" to "Good Governance" in EU Social Policy', in A. Verdun and I. Tömmel (eds) *Innovative Governance in the European Union* (Boulder, CO: Lynne Rienner): 87–99.

Daly, M. (2007) 'Whither EU Social Policy? An Account and Assessment of Developments in the Lisbon Social Inclusion Process', *Journal of Social Policy*, 37(1): 1–19.

De la Porte, C. and Pochet, P. (eds) (2002a) *Building Social Europe through the Open Method of Co-ordination* (Brussels: PIE/Peter Lang).

De la Porte, C. and Pochet, P. (2002b) 'Public Pension Reform: European Actors, Discourses and Outcomes', in C. de la Porte and P. Pochet (eds) *Building Social Europe through the Open Method of Co-ordination* (Brussels: PIE/Peter Lang): 223–50.

Duina, F. and Kurzer P. (2004) 'Smoke in Your Eyes: The Struggle over Tobacco Control in the European Union', *Journal of European Public Policy*, 11(1): 57–77.

Ebbinghaus, B. (ed.) (2011) *The Varieties of Pension Governance: Pension Privatization in Europe* (Oxford: Oxford University Press).

Eckardt, M. (2005) 'The Open Method of Coordination on Pensions: An Economic Analysis of its Effects on Pension Reforms', *Journal of European Social Policy*, 15(3): 247–67.

EIOPA (European Insurance and Occupational Pensions Authority) (2012) *Report on Market Developments*, available at https://eiopa.europa.eu/en/publications/reports/index.html, accessed 23/10/2014.

Esping-Andersen, G. (1990) *The Three Worlds of Welfare Capitalism* (Cambridge: Polity Press).

Eurobarometer (2010) *Eurobarometer 71. Future of Europe.* (Brussels: European Commission).

Eurobarometer (2013) *Standard Eurobarometer 80. Public Opinion in the European Union*, Autumn (Brussels: European Commission).

Eurostat (2013) *European Social Statistics* (Brussels: European Commission).

Eurostat (2014a) *Statistics in focus*. General government expenditure by economic function. Issue 8/2014. (Brussels: European Commission).

Eurostat (2014b) 'Euro area unemployment rate at 11.5%,' eurostat news-release, 146/2014, 30 September.

Eurostat (n.d.) *European Statistics of Income and Living Conditions* (EU- SILC), available at http://appsso.eurostat.ec.europa.eu/nui/show.do?dataset=ilc_li02&lang=en, accessed 23/10/2014.

Falkner, G. (1996) 'European Works Councils and the Maastricht Social Agreement: Towards a New Policy Style?', *Journal of European Public Policy*, 3(2): 192–208.

Falkner, G. (1998) *EU Social Policy in the 1990s: Towards a Corporatist Policy Community* (London: Routledge).

Falkner, G., Treib, O., Hartlapp, M. and Leiber, S. (2005) *Complying with Europe: EU Harmonization and Soft Law in the Member States* (Cambridge: Cambridge University Press).

Ferrera, M. (1996) 'The "Southern Model" of Welfare in Social Europe', *Journal of European Social Policy*, 6(1): 17–37.

Ferrera, M. (2005) *The Boundaries of Welfare* (Oxford: Oxford University Press).

Ferrera, M. (2008) 'Mapping the Components of Social EU: A Critical Analysis of the Current Institutional Patchwork', in E. Marlier and D.

Natali (eds) *Europe 2020: Towards a More Social EU?* (Brussels: PIE/ Peter Lang): 45–68.

Ferrera, M., Matsaganis, M. and Sacchi, S. (2002) 'Open Coordination Against Poverty: The New EU "Social Inclusion Process"', *Journal of European Social Policy*, 12(3): 227–39.

Frazer, H. and Marlier, E. (2011) *Assessment of Progress Towards the Europe 2020 Social Inclusion Objectives. September 2011. Main Findings and Suggestions on the Way Forward.* European Union Network of Independent Experts on Social Inclusion.

Frazer, H. and Marlier, E. (2012) *Assessment of Progress Towards the Europe 2020 Social Inclusion Objectives. July 2012. Main Findings and Suggestions on the Way Forward.* European Union Network of Independent Experts on Social Inclusion.

Geyer, R. (2000) *Exploring European Social Policy* (Oxford: Polity Press).

Goetschy, J. (1999) 'The European Employment Strategy: Genesis and Development', *European Journal of Industrial Relations*, 5(2): 117–37.

Goetschy, J. (2003) 'The European Employment Strategy, Multi-level Governance, and Policy Coordination: Past, Present and Future', in J. Zeitlin and D. Trubek (eds) *Governing Work and Welfare* (Oxford: Oxford University Press): 59–87.

Goetschy, J. and Pochet, P. (1997) 'The Treaty of Amsterdam: A New Approach to Employment and Social Affairs?', *Transfer*, 3(3): 607–20.

Gomez, R. (2014) 'The Economy Strikes Back: Support for the EU during the Great Recession', *Journal of Common Market Studies*, 1–16.

Graziano, P. and Vink, M. (eds) (2007) *Europeanization: New Research Agendas.* (Basingstoke: Palgrave Macmillan).

Greer, S.L. (2006) 'Uninvited Europeanization: Neofunctionalism and the EU in Health Policy', *Journal of European Public Policy*, 13(1): 134–52.

Greer, S.L. (2009) *The Politics of European Union Health Policies* (Maidenhead: Open University Press).

Greer, S.L. (2013) 'Avoiding Another Directive: The Unstable Politics of European Union Cross-border Health Care Law', *Health Economics, Policy and Law,* 8(4): 415–21.

Greer, S.L. and Kurzer, P. (eds) (2013) *European Public Health Policy* (London: Routledge).

Hacker, J. (2002) *The Divided Welfare State* (New York: Oxford University Press).

Hall, P. and Soskice, D. (2001) *Varieties of Capitalism: The Institutional Foundations of Comparative Advantage* (Oxford: Oxford University Press).

Hantrais, L. (2007) *Social Policy in the European Union*, 3rd edn (New York: St. Martin's Press).

Hatzopoulos, V. (2010) 'Casual but Smart: The Court's New Clothes in the Area of Freedom, Security and Justice (AFSJ) after the Treaty of Lisbon', in J. Monar (ed.) *The Institutional Dimension of the European Union's*

Area of Freedom, Security and Justice (Brussels: PIE/Peter Lang): 145–68.

Haverland, M. (2000) 'National Adaptation to European Integration: The Importance of Institutional Veto Points', *Journal of Public Policy*, 20(1): 83–103.

Haverland, M. (2007) 'When the Welfare State Meets the Regulatory State: EU Occupational Pension Policy', *Journal of European Public Policy*, 14(6): 886–904.

Heidenreich, M. and Zeitlin, J. (eds) (2009) *Changing European Employment and Welfare Regimes: The Influence of the Open Method of Coordination on National Reforms* (London: Routledge).

Hemerijck, A. (2013) *Changing Welfare States* (Oxford: Oxford University Press).

Hennessy, A. (2008) 'Economic Interests and the Construction of a European Single Pension Market', *British Journal of Politics and International Relations*, 10(1): 105–28.

Hennessy, A. (2014) *The Europeanization of Workplace Pensions* (Cambridge: Cambridge University Press).

Hervey, T. (1998) *European Social Law and Policy* (New York: Longman).

Hervey, T. (2007) 'EU Law and National Health Policies: Problem or Opportunity?', *Health Economics, Policy and Law*, 2(1): 1–6.

Hervey, T. (2011) 'If Only It Were So Simple: Public Health Services and EU Law', in M. Cremona (ed.) *Market Integration and Public Services in the European Union* (Oxford: Oxford University Press): 179–250.

Hervey, T. and Vanhercke, B. (2010) 'Health Care and the EU: The Law and Policy Patchwork', in E. Mossialo, G. Permanand, R. Baeten and T. Hervey (eds) *Health Systems Governance in Europe* (Oxford: Oxford University Press): 84–133.

Heyes, J. and Rainbird, H. (2009) 'Vocational Education and Training', in M. Gold (ed.) *Employment Policy in the European Union: Origins, Themes and Prospects* (Basingstoke: Palgrave Macmillan): pp. 188–209.

Hinrichs, K. and Brosig, M. (2013) 'Die Staatsschuldenkrise und die Reform von Alterssicherungssytemen in europäischen Ländern', *ZeS-Arbeitspapier*, February.

Hoareau, C. (2012) 'Deliberative Governance in the European Higher Education Area: The Bologna Process as a Case of Alternative Governance Architecture in Europe', *Journal of European Public Policy*, 19(4): 530–48.

Hooghe, L. (ed.) (1996) *Cohesion Policy and European Integration* (Oxford: Oxford University Press).

Hooghe, L. and Marks, G. (1999) *The Making of a Polity: The Struggle over European Integration. Continuity and Change in Contemporary Capitalism* (Cambridge: Cambridge University Press).

Hooghe, L. and Marks, G. (2001) *Multi-level Governance and European Integration* (Lanham, MD: Rowman & Littlefield).

Hooghe, L. and Marks, G. (2008) 'A Postfunctionalist Theory of European Integration: From Permissive Consensus to Constraining Dissensus', *British Journal of Political Science*, 39(1): 1–23.

Höpner, M. and Schäfer, A. (2010) 'A New Phase of European Integration: Organised Capitalisms in Post-Ricardian Europe', *West European Politics*, 33(2): 344–68.

Hoskyns, C. (1996) *Integrating Gender: Women, Law and Politics in the European Union* (London: Verso).

Huber, E. and Stephens, J.D. (2001) *Development and Crisis of the Welfare State: Parties and Policies in Global Markets* (Chicago: University of Chicago Press).

ILO (International Labour Organization) (1956) 'Social Aspects of European Economic Co-operation: Report by a Group of Experts (summary)', *International Labour Review*, 74: 99–123.

Immergut, E.M. and Anderson, K.M. (2008) 'Approaches: Historical Institutionalism and West European Politics', *West European Politics*, 31(1–2): 346–69.

Immergut, E.M., Anderson, K.M. and Schulze, I. (2007) *The Handbook of West European Pension Politics* (Oxford: Oxford University Press).

Jachtenfuchs, M. (2001) 'The Governance Approach to European Integration', *Journal of Common Market Studies*, 39(2): 221–40.

Jacobsson, K. and Vifell, Å. (2005) 'Soft Governance, Employment Policy and Committee Deliberation', in E.O. Eriksen (ed.) *Making the European Polity: Reflexive Integration in the EU* (London: Routledge): 214–36.

Johansson, K.M. (1999) 'Tracing the Employment Title in the Amsterdam Treaty: Uncovering Transnational Coalitions', *Journal of European Public Policy*, 6(1): 85–101.

Keleman, D. (2003) 'The EU Rights Revolution: Adversarial Legalism and European Integration', in T. Börzel and R. Cichowski (eds) *The State of the European Union* (Oxford: Oxford University Press): 221–34.

Keleman, D. (2011) *Eurolegalism: The Transformation of Law and Regulation in the European Union* (Cambridge, MA: Harvard University Press).

Kok, W. (ed.) (2004) 'Facing the Challenge: The Lisbon Strategy for Growth and Employment', Report for the High-Level Working Group chaired by Wim Kok, November.

Lamping, W. (2013) 'European Union Health Care Policy', in S.L. Greer and P. Kurzer (eds) *European Union Public Health Policy* (New York: Routledge): 19–35.

Lange, P. (1992) 'The Politics of the Social Dimension', in A. Sbragia (ed.) *Euro-politics: Institutions and Policymaking in the New European Community* (Washington, DC: Brookings Institution): 225–56.

Lange, P. (1993) 'Maastricht and the Social Protocol: Why Did They Do It?', *Politics and Society*, 21(1): 5–36.

Lehmann, W. (2009) 'The European Parliament', in D. Coen and I. Richardson (eds) *Lobbying the European Union: Institutions, Actors, and Issues* (Oxford: Oxford University Press): 39–69.

Leibfried, S. (2010) 'Social Policy: Left to the Judges and the Markets?', in H. Wallace, M. Pollack and A. Young (eds) *Policy-making in the European Union*, 6th edn (Oxford: Oxford University): 253–81.

Leibfried, S. and Pierson, P. (1995) *European Social Policy: Between Fragmentation and Integration* (Washington, DC: Brookings Institution).

Lewis, J. (2006) 'Work/Family Reconciliation, Equal Opportunities and Social Policies: the Interpretation of Policy Trajectories at the EU Level and the Meaning of Gender Equality', *Journal of European Public Policy*, 13(3): 420–37.

Lynch, J. (2006) *Age and the Welfare State* (Cambridge: Cambridge University Press).

Mabbett, D. (2007) 'Learning by Numbers? The Use of Indicators in the Coordination of Social Inclusion Policies in Europe', *Journal of European Public Policy*, 14(1): 78–95.

Mabbett, D. (2009) 'Supplementary Pensions between Social Policy and Social Regulation', *West European Politics*, 32(4): 774–91.

McKee, H., Hervey, T. and Gilmore, A. (2010) 'Public Health Policies', in E. Mossialos, G. Permanand, R. Baeten and T. Hervey (eds) *Health Systems Governance in Europe: The Role of EU Law and Policy* (Cambridge: Cambridge University Press): 231–81.

Majone, G. (1996) *Regulating Europe* (London: Routledge).

Malmberg, J. and Sigeman, T. (2008) 'Industrial Actions and EU Economic Freedoms: The Autonomous Collective Bargaining Model Curtailed by the European Court of Justice', *Common Market Law Review*, 45(4): 1115–46.

Manow, P. and van Kersbergen, K. (eds) (2009) *Religion and the Welfare State* (Cambridge: Cambridge University Press).

Mares, I. (2003) *The Politics of Social Risk: Business and Welfare State Development* (New York: Cambridge University Press).

Marks, G. (1996) 'Exploring and Explaining Variation in EU Cohesion Policy', in L. Hooghe (ed.) *Cohesion Policy and European Integration* (Oxford: Oxford University Press): 388–422.

Marks, G. and McAdam, D. (1996) 'Social Movements and the Changing Structure of Political Opportunity in the European Union', *West European Politics* 19(2): 249–78.

Marlier, E. and Natali, D. (eds) (2008) *Europe 2020: Towards a More Social EU?* (Brussels: PIE/Peter Lang).

Marlier, E., Atkinson, A.B., Cantillon, B. and Nolan, B. (2007) *The EU and Social Inclusion: Facing the Challenges* (Bristol: Policy Press).

Marshall, T.H. ([1950] 1992) Citizenship and Social Class, in T.H. Marshall, and T. Bottomore (eds) *Citizenship and Social Class* (London: Pluto Press).

Martin, C.J. and Swank, D. (2001) 'Employers and the Welfare State: The Political Economic Organization of Firms and Social Policy in Contemporary Capitalist Democracies', *Comparative Political Studies*, 34(8): 889–923.

Martinsen, D.S. (2007) 'The Europeanisation of Gender Equality: Who Controls the Scope of Non-discrimination?', *Journal of European Public Policy*, 14(4): 544–62.

Martinsen, D.S. (2011) 'Judicial Policy-making and Europeanization: The Proportionality of National Control and Administrative Discretion', *Journal of European Public Policy*, 18(7): 944–61.

Matsaganis, M. (2011) 'The Welfare State and the Crisis: The Case of Greece', *Journal of European Social Policy*, 21(5): 501–12.

Meunier, S. and McNamara, K. (eds) (2007a) *Making History: European Integration and Institutional Change at Fifty* (Oxford: Oxford University Press).

Meunier, S. and McNamara, K. (2007b) 'Making History: European Integration and Institutional Change at Fifty', in K. McNamara and S. Meunier (eds) *Making History: European Integration and Institutional Change at Fifty* (Oxford: Oxford University Press): 23–50.

Minderhoud, P. (2013) 'Directive 2004/38 and Access to Social Assistance Benefits', in E. Guild, C. Gortázar Rotaeche and D. Kostakopoulou (eds) *The Reconceptualization of European Union Citizenship* (Leiden: Brill): 209–26.

Moravcsik, A. (1998) *The Choice for Europe: Social Purpose and State Power from Messina to Maastricht* (Ithaca, NY: Cornell University Press).

Mossialos, E., Permanand, G., Baeten, R. and Hervey, T. (eds) (2010) *Health Systems Governance in Europe: The Role of EU Law and Policy* (Cambridge: Cambridge University Press).

Mudde, C. (2014) 'The far right in the 2014 European elections: Of earthquakes, cartels and designer fascists' *The Monkey Cage*, 30 May, available at www.washingtonpost.com/blogs/monkey-cage/wp/2014/05/30/the-far-right-in-the-2014-european-elections-of-earthquakes-cartels-and-designer-fascists, accessed 23/10/2014.

Natali, D. (2009) 'The Open Method of Co-ordination on Pensions: Does it De-politicize Pensions Policy?', *West European Politics*, 32(4): 810–28.

Nickless, J. (2001) 'A Guarantee of Similar Standards of Medical Treatment Across the EU: Were the European Court of Justice Decisions in Kohll and Decker Right?', *Eurohealth*, 7(1): 16–18.

Obermeier, A. (2009) *The End of Territoriality? The Impact of ECJ Rulings on British, German and French Social Policy* (Aldershot: Ashgate).

OECD (Organisation for Economic Co-operation and Development) (2011) *Government at a Glance* (Paris: OECD).

OECD (2013) *Government at a Glance* (Paris: OECD).

OECD (2014) *Social Expenditure Database*. (Paris: OECD).

O'Grada, C. (1969) 'The Vocational Training Policy of the EEC and the Free Movement of Skilled Labour', *Journal of Common Market Studies*, 8(2): 79–109.

Olsen, J.P. (2002) 'The Many Faces of Europeanization', *Journal of Common Market Studies*, 40(5): 921–52.

Orenstein, M. (2008a) 'Post-Communist Welfare States', *Journal of Democracy*, 19 (4): 80–94.

Orenstein, M. (2008b) 'Out-liberalizing the EU: Pension Privatization in Central and Eastern Europe', *Journal of European Public Policy*, 15(6): 899–917.

Orloff, A.S. (1993) 'Gender and the Social Rights of Citizenship: The Comparative Analysis of Gender Relations and Welfare States', *American Sociological Review*, 58(3): 303–28.

Ottawa, B. (2013) 'Mercer Germany blasts Portability Directive's stance on vesting periods', *Investments and Pensions Europe*, 1 August, available at www.ipe.com/mercer-germany-blasts-portability-directives-stance-on-vesting-periods/55123.fullarticle, accessed 23/10/2014.

Palier, B. and Pochet, P. (2005) 'Toward a European Social Policy – At Last?', in N. Jabko and C. Parsons (eds) *The State of the European Union* (Oxford: Oxford University Press): 253–74.

Palier, B. and Thelen, K. (2010) 'Institutionalizing Dualism: Complementarities and Change in France and Germany', *Politics and Society*, 38(1): 119–48.

Pépin, L. (2006) *The History of European Cooperation in Education and Training. Europe in the Making: An Example* (Brussels: European Commission).

PES (Party of European Socialists) (1994) *The European Employment Initiative: Put Europe to Work* (the Larsson Report).

Pierson, P. (1994) *Dismantling the Welfare State?* (Cambridge: Cambridge University Press).

Pierson, P. (1996) 'The Path to European Integration: A Historical Institutionalist Analysis', *Comparative Political Studies*, 29(2): 123–63.

Pierson, P. (2000) 'Increasing Returns, Path Dependence, and the Study of Politics', *American Political Science Review*, 94(2): 251–67.

Pierson, P. (ed.) (2001) *The New Politics of the Welfare State* (Oxford: Oxford University Press).

Pierson, P. (2007) 'Public Policies as Institutions', in S. Skowronek, D. Galvin and I. Shapiro (eds) *Rethinking Political Institutions: The Art of the State* (New York: New York University Press): 114–34.

Pochet, P. (2003) 'Pensions: The European Debate', in G.L. Clark and N. Whiteside (eds) *Pension Security in the 21st Century: Redrawing the Public-Private Debate* (Oxford: Oxford University Press): 44–63.

Pochet, P. (2011) 'Social Europe. Why Hard Law Remains Important', in R. Dehousse (ed.) *The Community Method: Obstinate or Obsolete?* (Basingstoke: Palgrave Macmillan): 166–85.

Powell, J.J. and Trampusch, C. (2012) 'Europeanization and the Varying Responses in Collective Skill Systems', in M.R. Busemeyer and C. Trampusch (eds) *The Political Economy of Collective Skill Formation* (Oxford: Oxford University Press): 284–316.

Raedelli, C. (2003) 'The Europeanization of Public Policy', in K. Featherstone and C. Radaelli (eds) *The Politics of Europeanization* (Oxford: Oxford University Press): 27–56.

Ravinet, P. (2008) 'From Voluntary Participation to Monitored Coordination: Why European Countries Feel Increasingly Bound by their Commitment to the Bologna Process', *European Journal of Education*, 43(3): 353–67.

Rhodes, M. (2005) 'Employment Policy: Between Efficacy and Experimentation', in H. Wallace, W. Wallace and M.A. Pollack (eds) *Policy-making in the European Union* (Oxford: Oxford University Press): 280–304.

Sainsbury, D. (1996) *Gender, Equality and Welfare States* (Cambridge: Cambridge University Press).

Saraceno, C. (2010) 'Concepts and Practices of Social Citizenship in Europe: The Case of Poverty and Income Support for the Poor', in J. Alber and N. Gilbert (eds) *United in Diversity?* (Oxford: Oxford University Press): 151–75.

Sbragia, A. (2002) 'The Treaty of Nice, Institutional Balance, and Uncertainty', Conclusion to Special Issue of *Governance*, 15(3): 393–412.

Scharpf, F. (1994) 'Community and Autonomy: Multi-level Policy Making in the European Union', *Journal of European Public Policy*, 1(2): 219–42.

Scharpf, F. (1996) 'Negative and Positive Integration in the Political Economy of European Welfare States', in G. Marks, F. Scharpf, P.C. Schmitter and W. Streeck (eds) *Governance in the European Union* (London: Sage): 15–39.

Scharpf, F. (1997) 'Economic Integration, Democracy and the Welfare State', *Journal of European Public Policy*, 4(1): 18–36.

Scharpf, F. (1999) *Governing in Europe: Effective and Democratic?* (Oxford: Oxford University Press).

Scharpf, F. (2002) 'The European Social Model: Coping with the Challenges of Diversity', *Journal of Common Market Studies*, 40(4): 645–70.

Scharpf, F. (2010) 'The Asymmetry of European Integration, or Why the EU Cannot be a "Social Market Economy"', *Socio-Economic Review*, 8(2): 211–50.

Scharpf, F. (2013) 'Monetary Union, Fiscal Crisis and the Disabling of Democratic Accountability', in A. Schäfer and W. Streeck (eds) *Politics in the Age of Austerity* (Cambridge: Polity Press): 108–42.

Scharpf, F. and Schmidt, V. (2000a) *Welfare and Work in the Open Economy. Diverse Responses to Common Challenges*, vol. 1 (Oxford: Oxford University Press).

Scharpf, F. and Schmidt, V. (2000b) *Welfare and Work in the Open*

Economy. From Vulnerability to Competitiveness, vol. 2 (Oxford: Oxford University Press).

Schmidt, V. (2006) *Democracy in Europe: The EU and National Politics* (Oxford: Oxford University Press).

Schulze, I. and Moran, M. (2007) 'Ireland: Pensioning the Celtic Tiger', in E.M. Immergut, K.M. Anderson and I. Schulze (eds) *The Handbook of Western European Pension Politics* (Oxford: Oxford University Press): 758–803.

Sedelmeier, U. (2012) 'Europeanization', in E. Jones, A. Menon and S. Weatherill (eds) *Oxford Handbook of the European Union* (Oxford: Oxford University Press): 825–39.

Shanks, M. (1977) *European Social Policy, Today and Tomorrow* (Oxford: Pergamon Press).

Silver, H. (1994) 'Social Exclusion and Social Solidarity: Three Paradigms', *International Labour Review*, 133(5/6): 531–78.

Silvia, S. (1991) 'The Social Charter of the European Community: A Defeat for European Labor', *Industrial and Labor Relations Review*, 44(4): 626–43.

Sohrab, J.A. (1994) 'An Overview of the Equality Directive on Social Security and its Implementation in Four Social Security Systems', *Journal of European Social Policy*, 4(4): 263–76.

Sorbonne Declaration (1998) *Joint Declaration on Harmonisation of the Architecture of the European Higher Education System by the four Ministers in charge for France, Germany, Italy and the United Kingdom. Paris, the Sorbonne, 25 May.*

Springer, B. (1992) *The Social Dimension of 1992: Europe Faces a New EC* (New York: Praeger).

Stepan, M. and Anderson, K.M. (2014) 'Pension Reform in the European Periphery: The Role of EU Reform Advocacy', *Public Administration and Development*, 34(4): 320–31.

Streeck, W. (1995) 'From Market-making to State-building? Reflections on the Political Economy of European Social Policy', in S. Leibfried and P. Pierson (eds) *European Social Policy: Between Fragmentation and Integration* (Washington, DC: Brookings Institution): 389–431.

Streeck, W. and Thelen, K. (2005) 'Introduction: Institutional Change in Advanced Political Economies', in W. Streeck and K. Thelen (eds) *Beyond Continuity: Institutional Change in Advanced Political Economies* (Oxford: Oxford University Press): 1–39.

Swenson, P. (2002) *Capitalists against Markets* (Oxford: Oxford University Press).

Taggart, P. (2006) 'Questions of Europe: The Domestic Politics of the 2005 French and Dutch Referendums and their Challenge for the Study of European Integration', *Journal of Common Market Studies*, 44(1): 7–25.

Teague, P. and Grahl, J. (1991) 'The European Community Social Charter and Labour Market Regulation', *Journal of Public Policy*, 11(2): 207–32.

Thelen, K. (1999) 'Historical Institutionalism in Comparative Politics', *Annual Review of Political Science*, 2(1): 369–404.

Titmuss, R. (1974) *Social Policy* (London: Allen & Unwin).

Tomkin, J. (2009) 'The Worker, the Citizen, their Families and the Court of Justice: Tales of Free Movement from Luxemburg', in P.E. Minderhoud and N. Trimikliniotis (eds) *Rethinking the Free Movement of Workers: The European Challenge Ahead* (Nijmegen: Wolf Legal): 39–59.

Trampusch, C. (2009) 'Europeanization and Institutional Change in Vocational Education and Training in Austria and Germany', *Governance*, 22(3): 369–95.

Triantafillou, P. (2007) "Greece: Political Competition in a Majoritarian System', in E.M. Immergut, K.M. Anderson, and I. Schulze (eds) *The Handbook of West European Pension Politics* (Oxford: Oxford University Press): 97–149.

Van der Vleuten, A. (2007) *The Price of Gender Equality* (Aldershot: Ashgate).

Verschraegen, G., Vanhercke, B. and Verpoorten, R. (2011) 'The European Social Fund and Domestic Activation Policies: Europeanization Mechanisms', *Journal of European Social Policy*, 21(1): 1–18.

Visser, J. (2009) 'Neither Convergence nor Frozen Paths: Bounded Learning, International Diffusion of Reforms, and the Open Method of Coordination', in M. Heidenreich and J. Zeitlin (eds) *Changing European Employment and Welfare Regimes: The Influence of the Open Method of Coordination on National Reforms* (London: Routledge): 37–60.

Von Wahl, A. (2006) 'Liberal, Conservative, Social Democratic, or ... European? The European Union as Equal Employment Regime', *Social Politics*, 12(1): 67–95.

Watson, P. (1991) 'The Community Social Charter', *Common Market Law Review*, 28(2): 37–68.

Welbers, G. (2011) 'The European Social Fund: Changing Approaches to VET', *European Journal of Education*, 46(1): 54–69, Part I.

Wise, M. and Gibb, R. (1993) *Single Market to Social Europe: The European Community in the 1990s* (Harlow: Longman).

World Bank (1994) *Averting the Old Age Crisis* (Washington, DC: World Bank).

Zeitlin, J. (2008) 'The Open Method of Co-ordination and the Governance of the Lisbon Strategy', *Journal of Common Market Studies*, 46(2): 436–50.

Index